Cambridge Studies in the History and Theory of Politics

EDITORS

MAURICE COWLING
G. R. ELTON
E. KEDOURIE
J. R. POLE
WALTER ULLMANN

TWO ENGLISH REPUBLICAN TRACTS

WALTER MOYLE of Bake in Cornval Esq.
obijt 9. Jun. 1721. æt. 49.

TWO
ENGLISH REPUBLICAN
TRACTS

PLATO REDIVIVUS
or, A DIALOGUE CONCERNING
GOVERNMENT
(*c.* 1681)
by HENRY NEVILLE

AN ESSAY
UPON THE CONSTITUTION OF
THE ROMAN GOVERNMENT
(*c.* 1699)
by WALTER MOYLE

Edited by
CAROLINE ROBBINS

CAMBRIDGE
AT THE UNIVERSITY PRESS
1969

Published by the Syndics of the Cambridge University Press
Bentley House, 200 Euston Road, London N.W.1
American Branch: 32 East 57th Street, New York, N.Y.10022

Library of Congress Catalogue Card Number: 68-24483

Standard Book Number: 521 07252 2

Printed in Great Britain
at the University Printing House, Cambridge
(Brooke Crutchley, University Printer)

Contents

Preface   *page* vii

List of Abbreviated Works   ix

INTRODUCTION

  I   Neville and Moyle Compared   3

  II   Henry Neville, 1620–94   5
     The Works of Henry Neville   19

  III   Walter Moyle, 1672–1721   21
     The Works of Walter Moyle   38

  IV   The English Republicans   40
     Republican Proposals   43
     Sources of Republican Thought   50
     Interpretation of History   54
     Influence and Significance   56

PLATO REDIVIVUS: or, A Dialogue concerning Government   61

AN ESSAY UPON THE CONSTITUTION OF THE ROMAN   201
GOVERNMENT

Appendixes
  I   English Chronology   260
  II   Roman Chronology   261
  III   Authors Cited by Moyle   262
  IV   Works on Roman History   264

Index   265

The portrait of Walter Moyle (preceding title-page) is reproduced from the frontispiece in volume I of *The Works* (1726)—an engraving by G. Vertue. H. Walpole in *A Calendar of Engravers* (2nd ed. 5 vols. 1786, p. 289) lists Vertue's Moyle, but he does not say who was responsible for the original drawing. Although a portrait of Henry Neville is mentioned in late eighteenth-century sources, it cannot now be traced

Preface

Much of the work on Neville and Moyle was done a long time ago. When Cambridge University Press asked me to prepare an edition of the two tracts here reprinted, I was able to obtain very considerable assistance from Miss Dorothy M. Broome in checking references in English collections and in getting reproductions of material not available to me here. The officials of the Berkshire Record Office at Reading have been very kind. At the Houghton Library of Harvard University Miss Carolyn Jakeman has once more generously assisted me. At Bryn Mawr both the library and the departments of Latin and Greek have been helpful and patient. Dr Myra Uhlfelder has saved me from many an error, though she is in no way responsible for those I may still have made. My debt to Professor Lily Ross Taylor is enormous; she read Moyle's *Essay*, and her comments have been invaluable, as well as the information afforded by her *Roman Voting Assemblies* (Ann Arbor, 1966). Caroline Burlingham has helped to catch many a textual slip and inconsistency. Dr Mary Maples Dunn, Dr Douglass Adair, Dr Alain Silvera and Dr Felix Gilbert have given me valuable advice on a variety of matters. Gail Lippman has helped greatly with the index.

The text of Neville's *Plato Redivivus* was enlarged in the second edition of 1681, the last he can have had any part in revising. Additions there included are between asterisks in the text of this edition and are referred to in footnotes. A list of editions of the tract has been given, but in none but the second are any substantial changes to be found; so-called editors did little even to correct obvious mistakes. The last or fourth edition published through the efforts of Thomas Hollis has been used here, but in effect this is the same as that of 1681, the second. Spelling has been modernized for the most part, though a few seventeenth-century versions of proper names, notably Machiavel for Machiavelli, have been retained. The punctuation remains Neville's with the insertion only of an occasional period or paragraph; the rhythm of the prose of Neville and his contemporaries is so different from our own that it seems best to follow his guides to continuity and pause. Foreign words and phrases, save where Neville himself explains

vii

them, have been translated or provided with an equivalent in English. Proper names of persons and places are identified in the index; references to contemporary or historical events and persons, when necessary and possible, in the footnotes. A few, notably the persons pardoned by Charles II, have proved elusive; perhaps some more learned reader will supply them.

The first printed version of Moyle's *Essay* appeared in *The Works* in 1726, though it had probably circulated in manuscript since its composition in 1699. Copious quotations in Latin and innumerable citations attest Moyle's erudition. In 1796 when the last English edition of *An Essay* appeared, John Thelwall translated the quotations and omitted the footnotes. The authorities cited by Moyle are listed in an appendix here, but in general Thelwall's text has been followed with two exceptions: Moyle's paragraphs have been restored, and only a few of Thelwall's own notes have been reproduced.

I have already acknowledged Professor Taylor's help with Moyle. I am also greatly indebted to the kindness and advice of two good Cornishmen, Donald Carter, Esq., of Fowey and Dr A. L. Rowse, who sent photographs, reports on buildings, and gave much bibliographical information. I cannot hope that they will feel I have done justice to one of Cornwall's most brilliant sons, but only that they will appreciate my interest in their versatile countryman.

C. R.

Rosemont, Pennsylvania
1968

List of Abbreviated Works

CJ	*Commons Journals.*
Crino (1)	A. M. Crino, *Fatti e Figure del Seicento Anglo-Toscano* (Florence, 1957).
Crino (2)	*Il Popish Plot* (Rome, 1954).
CSPD	*Calendar of State Papers, Domestic.*
DNB	*Dictionary of National Biography.*
GM	*Gentleman's Magazine.*
HLQ	*Huntington Library Quarterly.*
HMC	*Historical Manuscripts Commission.*
OPH	*Old Parliamentary History.*
PMLA	*Publications of the Modern Language Association of America.*

INTRODUCTION

I. *Neville and Moyle Compared*

The lives of Neville and Moyle span the century in which republicanism of the kind proposed by English Commonwealthmen ran its course. Neville was born in 1620 when James I and his parliaments were very much at odds. Abroad at the beginning of the Civil Wars, he came back to gain not a little political experience when his associates were, intermittently to be sure, in the ascendant. After the Restoration in 1660, every republican was suspected of conspiracy, and he found it convenient to spend nearly four more years abroad. Returning, he played no further active role in politics. Moyle as a young man was a member of William's first Triennial Parliament (1695-8), and later carried out some local administrative duties in his native Cornwall. He never held important office, nor did he manage to travel in any of those areas whose history interested him so much. Neville was obliged to leave London during Oliver Cromwell's Protectorate, and suffered incarceration for more than fourteen months during the reign of Charles II. Moyle ruined chances of government preferment by outspoken opposition to the ruling Williamite Whigs in parliament, and by his share in the writing of important polemical tracts, but he experienced neither exile nor imprisonment.

Both men achieved a considerable reputation outside the political arena; Neville by his *novella*, *The Isle of Pines*, and by his edition of the works of Machiavelli in English; Moyle, as a youth, for his knowledge and translation of classical authors and, posthumously, for learned epistolatory commentaries on biblical, classical and Christian myth and legend. Both were gentlemen, deeply versed in ancient, renaissance and contemporary literature, history and politics.

Widely separated in age, the two probably had at least a brief encounter in the early 'nineties when Moyle was studying at Middle Temple and enjoying the life of neighbouring coffee houses also frequented by Neville. Neither man was a martyr to 'the good old cause', nor did either leave direct descendants. Both showed a capacity and willingness to adapt to what they felt were the current needs of an England obviously not as yet ripe for that 'new modelling' they admired in *Oceana*. Their recognition of contemporary problems and sympathy with many of their countrymen's prejudices and the brilliance of the presentation of their theories long maintained the circulation of the tracts. With the coming of the American and French revolutions, and the development not only of more radical programmes but also of the philosophies of Jeremy Bentham in England and John Taylor and Thomas Jefferson among others in the United States, a new age of political speculation and experiment began, and brought about the eclipse of all but the greatest of republican reputations. Yet the careers, associations and work of two gifted but less familiar Commonwealthmen help to make comprehensible the role in English history of a number of talented individuals, and may suggest some conclusions about the origins of seventeenth-century republicanism and some factors in the failure to achieve practical implementation of the policies proposed.

II. Henry Neville, 1620-94

Henry Neville was the namesake of his grandfather, an Elizabethan ambassador (1564–1615), and his father (d. 1629), of Billingbear Park, not far from Windsor in Berkshire. His mother was Elizabeth (1595–1669), daughter of Sir John Smith (1558–1608), of Ostenhanger in Kent, and sister to Thomas, first Viscount Strangford (1599–1635). At a very early age, long before he went to university, Henry's marriage to Elizabeth, daughter and heiress of Richard Staverton (d. 1636), of Heathley Hall in Warfield, was arranged.

By the settlement then made, Henry became possessed of Staverton lands, and, since he died childless, these eventually passed to his nephew Richard. Nothing else is known of this marriage save that Henry was buried in the Staverton aisle of the Warfield church, where a stone memorializes the family into which he married.

After matriculating in 1635, Henry attended Merton and University Colleges in Oxford. On 11 May 1641, probably on the occasion of his coming of age, he took the oath of allegiance, and was then listed as 'of Heathley Hall'.[1] Soon afterwards, Henry left England on the grand tour. Travelling through France, he arrived in Italy and visited Florence. In Rome, shortly before he died, Henry met the renowned Cardinal Guido Bentivoglio, author of *The Wars in Flanders* (1632, tr. 1654). In Venice he studied that Republic's famous institutions. As he travelled he made friends and acquaintances, among them a

[1] The *DNB* account of Neville by J. M. Rigg derives chiefly from Anthony à Wood (1632–95), *Athenae Oxonienses* (2nd ed. Oxford, 1721), II, 591, 713, 918–19; and from the introduction by Thomas Hollis (1720–74) to his edition of *Plato Redivivus* (London, 1763 for 1765), also dependent on Wood. Daniel Rowland, *Historical and Genealogical Account of the Nevilles* (London, 1830), table v, 'The Nevilles of Billingbear', provides indispensable information about the family. Volume I, *Berkshire*, of Daniel Lysons's *Magna Britannia* (6 vols. London, 1806–22), is useful for Nevilles and Stavertons. On Henry's marriage there is almost nothing but a tombstone at Warfield, the evidence of Henry's will (PCC, box Irby, 174) about his property, and a couple of early references to his marriage and residence at Heathley Hall—see *CSPD*, 1633–4, ed. J. Bruce (1863), p. 388. Henry, then about thirteen but married, wants permission to fell trees to repair Heathley. Takes the oath of allegiance—see *CSPD*, 1640–1, ed. W. D. Hamilton (1882), p. 574. Presumably Elizabeth died very young; her parents also being dead, some of the Staverton property went to other Stavertons at Wokingham in 1636, but it seems likely that the entire family was dead before the Civil War began.

5

Florentine lawyer, Ferrante Capponi, in whose house he stayed in Rome. It was probably at this time that he began what was to be a lifelong intimacy with Bernard Gascoigne (1614–87), another Florentine who, as early as 1644, was serving in the royalist regiment of Henry's elder brother Richard (1615–76). Sometime in 1645 as the first Civil War was reaching a climax, Henry returned to England.[1]

About his doings for the next three or four years, there is little evidence, except the appearance in two parts, in the summer of 1647, of a very bawdy piece reputedly his, *The Parliament of Ladies*, making free with the reputations of prominent women on the roundhead side. Neville was already a republican, but he had little affection for the sectaries. An answer, *Match me These Two* (1647), associated the author with the Levellers, though this was certainly unjustified, and suggested that, when found, he should be thrown to the ladies he had so much abused. In the same vein, *Newes from the New Exchange* appeared in 1650. If these indeed be Neville's, they anticipate the kind of rough and boisterous humour which marked *The Isle of Pines* in 1668.[2]

Neville's public career seems to have started after the execution of the King, when he stood at Abingdon in Berkshire in April 1649 as a recruiter for the Rump of the Long Parliament. The election was allowed, after discussions in which Algernon Sidney (1622–83) and Sir Henry Vane (1613–62) took part, in the following autumn after parliament reconvened. About the same time, Edward Neville, possibly a distant relative, was elected for East Retford. Only when the *Journals* use a Christian name is precise differentiation of the two Nevilles' activities possible. Henry may be presumed to be the member defeated over a motion to introduce the use of the ballot; he was already well enough known to be appointed to the Goldsmiths' Hall committee for

---

[1] Crino (1), pp. 173–208, 'Lettere inedite italiane e inglesi di Sir Henry Neville', contains valuable new material from the Berkshire Record Office at Reading, and from Florentine archives. Crino (2), *passim*, also contains new Neville material. The knighthood bestowed upon Neville probably stems from a similar error in *CSPD*, 1667, ed. M. A. E. Green (1866), p. 218—a mis-translation of *signore* in a letter from Richard to Henry Neville. In Crino (1), 173–5, two letters from Capponi, 1643–4, throw light on his tour. In the same article, letters from both Nevilles to Gascoigne from the state archives of Florence are printed. See below. On Gascoigne, see *DNB*; the notice prefaced by G. T. Gargani to *Relazione delle Storie d'Inghilterra scritto l'anno 1647* (Florence, 1886); and C. H. and Thompson Cooper, *GM*, vol. 218 (1865), 616–20, a most useful and well-documented article.

[2] *Relazione*, noted above, displays prejudices about presbyterians probably very similar to Neville's. Joining the names of Lilburne and Neville rests on no better evidence than that of common opposition to the ruling clique.

raising money out of confiscated estates.[1] Long after, when *Plato Redivivus* was being criticized for anti-clericalism, the allegation was made that Neville's bitterness sprang from the forced return of the bishops' lands he was said to have acquired at this time.[2] In November 1651, Neville was chosen to serve on the Council of State, obtaining half the number of votes cast for Colonel Herbert Morley (1616–67), but four more than those for Harry Marten (1602–80), a well-known republican politician. During his year of office, Neville was occupied with diplomatic and legal matters. His term was not renewed, and in April 1653, with the rest of his fellow members, he was ejected from St Stephen's by Oliver Cromwell (1599–1658) and his troopers.[3]

With Vane, Sidney and Edmund Ludlow (1617–92), Neville opposed the Protectorate. He lived under it in semi-forced retirement. He emerged in August 1655 by special licence, to settle some private affairs in London, and again, over a year later, to sue the sheriff of Berkshire in Common Pleas. One letter writer ascribed to him the authorship of a tract against Cromwell, possibly an earlier version of *Shufling, Cutting, and Dealing in a Game of Pickquet* (1659), a short, vigorous skit at the expense of Protector and army grandees. Neville has also been credited with a hand in *A Letter to his Highness from an Officer in Ireland* (1656), mentioned in the publisher's foreword to *Plato Redivivus*. Thomas Hobbes is said to have declared he had a finger in the writing of *Oceana* (1656), by James Harrington (1611–77). There is nothing else to prove his share in either, but by this time Neville was certainly among Harrington's friends.[4]

In the summer of 1656 Neville decided to try his luck in the coming elections. The poll at Reading on 20 August was taken amid considerable confusion. Neville had many friends, and was reported to have enough votes to win one of the five seats. He refused an offered bargain by which he would be paired with a 'Mr Trumbull'. The

[1] D. Brunton and D. H. Pennington, *Members of the Long Parliament* (London, 1954), p. 33; *CJ*, VI, 305–6, etc.; *CSPD*, 1649–50, ed. Mary Green (1875), p. 373, 2 Nov. 1649.
[2] W.W., *Antidotum Britannicum* (London, 1681), pp. 137–8. There is no firm evidence about Neville's acquisition of episcopal lands, though very likely he took over nearby property if available.
[3] Council of State, *CJ*, VII, 41–2 (24–5 Nov. 1651), and 220–1 (Nov. 1652); Neville's activities may be traced *passim* in *CSPD*, 1651–2, ed. M. A. E. Green (1877).
[4] *CSPD*, 1655 (1881), 3 Aug. 1655. *HMC*, V (1876), 148, Newport to Langlye, enclosing pamphlet. Hobbes's remark in Wood, II, 591. On the authorship of *A Letter from an Officer*, see P. Zagorin, *A History of Political Thought in the English Revolution* (London, 1954), p. 150; below, p. 68.

sheriff, William Strode, or Stroode, with the assistance of 'corrupt and flattering ministers', soldiers and major-generals, to the accompaniment of fisticuffs and threats of decimation for opponents, returned all five members of the Cromwellian persuasion. Neville took his wrongs to court, and sued the sheriff under the statute of 23 Hen. 6. c. 15 for damages. These the jury awarded, but the presiding judge, uneasy about the verdict, decided that parliament, after fifty years of exercising the right to determine the validity of returns, must be consulted in the matter. Sheriffs were liable to penalties for misconduct, but, even in the later and similar case of Barnardiston versus Soames, sheriff of Suffolk in 1674, so learned a judge as John Vaughan (1603-74) professed himself unclear on the law. What is obvious is, first, that the election, described, possibly by Neville himself, in *A True and Perfect Relation of the Manner and Proceeding held by the Sheriff for the County of Berks at Reading upon the 20th August* (1656), was highly irregular, and involved John Boult of Warfield and other Neville supporters in all sorts of trouble. Secondly, it is also plain that, though juries might sympathize with Neville and Sir Samuel Barnardiston (1620-1707), the sheriffs, discriminating against known opponents of the government in power, evaded the penalties which the Henrician statute seemed to allow. Neville's case was discussed in the Parliaments of 1659-60, eventually sent to Exchequer Chamber, and never determined. The Suffolk case ran a similar course.[1]

For Richard Cromwell's Parliament, Neville and the republican Daniel Blagrave (1603-68) were 'unanimously' elected, and formed part of that lively and eloquent Commonwealth group about whom John Thurlow (1616-68) wrote bitterly to Henry Cromwell (1628-74) in Ireland, and Andrew Marvell (1620-78) in similar vein to George Downing (1623-84) at the Hague. *The Diary of Thomas Burton* more than confirms the tributes wrung from the Cromwellian sectaries. Sir Arthur Haselrigg (d. 1661), Vane, Neville, the regicide Thomas Scot (d. 1660), and John Weaver (d. 1685) had indeed 'much the odds' in speaking. Neville's friends were prominent, but his enemies were

---

[1] *A True Relation* (B.M. press mark 513.l.5 (3)) describes the election in detail. For the case see *CJ*, VII, 597, 3 Feb. 1658-9; *Diary of Thomas Burton*, ed. J. T. Rutt (4 vols. London, 1828), III, 51-4 and *passim*: thereafter Neville's case was referred to in the contest 'Barnardiston v. Soames', A. Grey, *Debates of the House of Commons* (10 vols. London, 1763), IV, 145; W. Cobbett, *State Trials* (34 vols. London, 1809-20), VI, 1069 and *passim*.

numerous enough to make trouble. On 16 February, these debated for five hours the matter of his religion or lack of it. If it were established that he was an atheist and blasphemer, then he ought to be ejected. Neville had, perhaps in too public a place, declared a preference for reading Cicero to the Bible, and the fanatics pounced upon the heresy. *England's Confusion*, a leaflet of this year, referred satirically to 'levelling Ludlow', 'preaching' Vane, and, surely with this debate in mind, 'religious' Neville. Enthusiasm was certainly distasteful to Neville; he often expressed sympathy for catholics, asserting that penal laws should be unnecessary in a well-ordered government; but he remained to the end of his life a protestant, free to worship 'only in spirit and in truth'.[1]

In the House in this spring of 1659, Neville's objectives were threefold: the rescuing of some old associates, like Colonel Robert Overton (*fl.* 1640–68), once parliamentary governor of Hull, but imprisoned by Oliver; the thwarting of protectorial foreign policy on Sweden's behalf, England's true interest running counter, Neville thought, not to Denmark, but to Spain; and, last and chiefly, the preventing of recognition of Richard Cromwell as anything but the *de facto* head of state, while Parliament reconsidered the whole constitutional problem. Neville thought both Protector and 'other house' improperly established; the union of the three kingdoms merely a device to strengthen the executive through the virtual appointment of their representatives in parliament; the control of the armed forces dangerously concentrated in the Protector's hands.

He was, Neville said, for a single person and for two houses, but not for the arrangements made for the Cromwells. If there were to be a king, he was said to have told Oliver, Charles Stuart had the better title. Much later, during the Exclusion crisis (1679–81), Neville was to write to a friend that he was not interested in the substitution of one monarch by another—that was, of course, of a Monmouth for a James. Only a republic was worth the risks of conspiracy. Neville disliked Cromwell, the enemy of the Commonwealth, and he disapproved wholly of a small military junto deciding the form of government. A

[1] *HMC*, xi, app. vii, Reading MSS. (1888), 193, 30 Dec. 1658; *CJ*, vii, 596, 1 Feb. 1659. *Thurloe Papers*, ed. Thomas Birch (7 vols. London, 1742), vii, 588 and 616; Marvell's *Letters*, ed. H. M. Margoliouth (Oxford, 1952), 294, 11 Feb. 1659. Marvell had earlier listed, as having for a motto 'all power is in the people', Haselrigg, Vane, Weaver, Scott, St Nicholas, Reynolds, A. A. Cooper, Packer, Lambert and Neville. On Neville's religion his will is illuminating and see below. On this debate, see *Burton's Diary*, iii, 296–305; F. P. G. Guizot, *The History of Richard Cromwell* (2 vols. tr. London, 1856), i, 308.

single person, he said in 1659, as he was to write later in *Plato Redivivus*, should not have a veto, nor should he control the army and militia. Nations had lost prized liberties through their ruler's unrestricted command of an armed guard; the army could intimidate, the veto could restrict the legislature. As for the 'new lords', they neither deserved the respect commanded by the old Lords' independence and property, nor did they properly balance the Commons. Privileged persons should never, he vowed, have the power to obstruct the passage of laws desired by the popular or lower house. Neville did not wish to restore the old constitution, Stuart or Oliverian; he wanted to force a reconsideration of government, evolving and implementing, if not an *Oceana*, at least an arrangement reflecting changed social conditions. In this Parliament efforts were futile. Richard could, to be sure, command a slight majority in the House, but in April 1659 an uneasy alliance of Commonwealthmen with the army brought about his fall.[1]

So in May the Rump returned. Neville was allowed to sit in spite of his service in Richard's House, and he was once more elected to the Council of State. During the next months, until a *coup d'état* in October again evicted the Rump, the Harringtonians tried to put and keep their views before Parliament and people. *The Armie's Dutie: or, Faithful Advice to the Souldiers* appeared on 2 May. Its address 'to the Reader' was signed by six initials, of which one may indicate Neville. Written before Richard's Parliament met in January, it opposed the support apparently being given him at that time, and proposed a popular assembly to set up a government determined by the 'immutable laws of nature', recognizing shifts in property and power. All that Neville had spoken for in Parliament was also here, but with no trace of his wit or style. Appeals to Christ, and more than a touch of unctuousness, make it unlikely to have been penned by him, even if he shared its fundamental principles.[2]

In the House on 6 July, Neville brought in 'The Humble Petition' of his associates. This may have been his own composition, or that of Harrington himself, in whose works it may be found. The government,

---

[1] *Burton's Diary*, III, 45, 48; *ibid.* IV, 150, 154, 162, 213; *ibid.* III, 314, 387, 451; *ibid.* III, 34, 72, 132–5, 330–1, 368, 461; *ibid.* IV, 23, 76, 105, 188, 219, 278, 347, 349. Cromwell story, *GM*, vol. 83 (1813), II, 123, letter signed 'E.J.'.
[2] *OPH*, XXI (1760), 407–8, 14 May 1659. Tellers, Haselrigg and Sidney. Discussion about Richard's members, p. 376. For collaborators in *The Armie's Dutie*, see Zagorin, *History of Political Thought*, p. 155, n. 2: Marten, Lawson, Wildman, Jones, Moyer.

the petition declared, was dissolved, and the time therefore at hand to quell distractions by the institution of a new and stable regime. The interests of ruler and ruled would be identical; all would in turn be subject and officer. No single assembly would be permanent, but a system of rotation would be devised. Executive and legislature would be separate. All would enjoy Christian liberty. A constitutional convention would be called, properly representative in character, and it would determine the government. A small body, to last for a stated period only, would be created to guard the infant system against enemies and infringers of its rules. This was the most succinct proposal of the Harringtonians. The Commons seemed to have received it kindly, but, beyond the appointment of a committee on government some time later, did no more. Only more futile than this restored Rump was the government by the army from 13 October until 26 December, when the Rump returned for what was to be its last session.[1]

Parliament and printer were not the only means by which the Harringtonians worked. During an autumn of anarchy, the Rota Club met. From around Michaelmas until 21 February 1660, they discussed politics at Miles' coffee house by the parliament stairs. Often the butt of town wits, the club was none the less sufficiently the mode to attract many, not members, to its sessions. Round the oddly shaped table, Harrington, Neville—by now his recognized lieutenant—and their friends, articulate and gifted, staged the best debates of the century, but they talked in a vacuum. They never seem to have attracted any considerable support, and, without it, their suggestions were unlikely to have any perceptible result.[2]

With the return of the Rump in December, Neville was once more on the Council of State, but George Monck (1608-70) was already a public figure, the writing was on the wall, and the country awaited a decision unlikely to favour the Commonwealth. In defiance of signs and portents, Neville brought in a motion in the House for an oath renouncing Charles Stuart, even as fellow republicans were under attack. Ludlow was suspended from his duties as Monck marched south,

---

[1] *CJ*, VII, 706; and see James Harrington, *Works* (London, 1747), pp. 541-6. Toland (*ibid.* p. xxviii) says Neville presented the document.

[2] John Aubrey, *Brief Lives*, ed. A. Clark (2 vols. Oxford, 1898), I, 288-95; Neville a true friend to Harrington, 293. Ludlow pays a similar tribute to Neville's friendship for him—*Memoirs*, ed. C. H. Firth (2 vols. Oxford, 1898), II, 210, and pays him many other tributes *passim*.

Neville almost alone attempting his defence. With the re-entry into the House of the survivors of Pride's Purge, led by William Prynne (1600–69), thirty-two of the Rumpers, Neville among them, retired from the Commons and took no further part in the activities of the Long Parliament.[1]

The Commonwealthmen scattered, Ludlow to Vevey in Switzerland; Sidney, abroad in 1660, to Italy; Neville probably to Warfield or nearby Billingbear. Statements that he was imprisoned at the Restoration seem to be incorrect. His brother Richard wrote cheerfully to a mutual Italian friend late in 1660, and no hint of Harry's trouble, if it existed, was given. In the following year Neville's letters were being opened, but nothing actionable was found in them. Harrington, however, was arrested and examined. Asked if he knew Neville, he replied, 'very well', but neither then nor in any other source at present known was any hint given of when this intimacy began. When Neville was in town, he would stop by of an evening. Once, 'in venison time', the autumn, they had eaten an excellent pasty with Colonel William Legge (1609–70) and Sir Bernard Gascoigne, two reputable cavaliers, as the interrogators commented. But Harrington was imprisoned and Neville remained faithful to him throughout subsequent troubles. Sharp and censorious at times, he was a true friend, obviously inspiring in Italians and English alike a well-deserved confidence and affection.[2]

Widespread, but probably exaggerated, conspiracy in 1663 brought Neville under suspicion, and with Richard Salway (1615–85), ambassador and councillor during the Interregnum, and Colonel John Hutchinson (1615–64) he was brought before official examiners and imprisoned in the Tower. The Colonel was to die there during the coming year, but Neville's efforts for release were successful, and in May 1664 he obtained a pass to go abroad.[3] On the eve of imprisonment he had entrusted properties in Warfield to John Boult, no doubt

[1] *CJ*, VII, 800, 30 Dec. 1659, Neville to number the House—62; 31 Dec., one of Council of State; *ibid.* 803, 3 Jan., teller for the renunciation of Charles Stuart; *ibid.* 815, 19 Jan., the suspension of Ludlow; and see *Memoirs*, II, 210, Neville said to have spoken for his friend. See David Masson, *Life of Milton*, V (1877), 544, on the exodus of the Rumpers.
[2] Crino (1), p. 177, Richard Neville writing to Gascoigne 18–28 Nov. 1660; *CSPD*, 1661–2 (1861), p. 119, 21 Oct. 1661; for the examination of Harrington, see *Works*, pp. xxxi–xxxiv. Aubrey lists Marvell (I, 293) as another faithful friend.
[3] The rising of 1663: *CSPD*, 1663–4 (1862), 317–18, 29 Oct. 1663, and *passim*. *HMC*, XI, Leeds (1888), 6, on imprisonment of Neville, Overton and Salway; no evidence against Neville except some alleged remarks reporting a new parliament; *CSPD*, 20 May 1664, p. 591, pass to go to France, and *passim* for investigations of previous winter.

the same friend who, at some inconvenience to himself, had supported his election at Reading in 1656. By then, if not long before, presumably Elizabeth Neville was dead.

Neville made his way to the court of Ferdinand II of Tuscany, and there obtained some kind of court employment. He enjoyed hunting at Pisa and other diversions of what he regarded as the 'happiest land' in the world. For the first time he met Cosmo (1643-1723), then heir to the duchy. Returning also to Rome, at the age of forty-four, he fell deeply in love with a married woman and wrote of the affair to Gascoigne. Italian customs, it seems, made the way of illicit lovers less easy than in Restoration London. In Frascati in 1666, he was distressed by news of the great fire of London, and worried about the fate of documents there entrusted to his care. Even at the risk of hanging, he wrote, he wanted to return, but 1667 found him in Rome and in touch with his brother Richard. Sometime between August 1667, when his brother wrote, and the publication of *The Isle of Pines* in 1668, he returned to England, apparently with no personal embarrassment.[1] His *novella* was to achieve an enormous success for much the same reasons that later made *Robinson Crusoe* so popular. The survivors of a shipwreck on a fruitful and healthy island established under George Pine, sole male of the company, a well-regulated menage. In the course of years, the little paradise was populated with Pine's progeny. Some have found in the story a social moral, but more probably it sprang simply from Neville's high spirits and Rabelaisian humour, writing to amuse himself.[2]

Young Cosmo came to England in the spring of 1669, and, with the exception of the state dinner given by Charles II for his distant cousin, Neville accompanied the Italian prince everywhere, to amusements like cock-fighting, on sightseeing expeditions, and to an evening spent with his brother at Billingbear. Correspondence between them continued after Cosmo's departure. Neville wrote condolences on the death of Ferdinand in 1670, and was rebuked by the Grand Duke for

---

[1] Crino (1) has new material on Neville's Italian sojourn and prints, pp. 182-7, letters to Gascoigne, Aug. 1665-Jan. 1667. Marvell, *Letters*, p. 91, Neville in London 1669.

[2] *The Isle of Pines* appeared in two parts. Modern reprints from Hollis (1768) to the Everyman *Shorter Novels* have not used all, or even the most interesting half, of the little book. Worthington Chauncey Ford, for the Club of Odd Volumes (Boston, 1920), wrote a splendid study of the book, its variants and translations, and reprinted the best text. For a suggestion that Neville was interested in polygamy, see A. Owen Aldridge, 'Polygamy in early fiction: Henry Neville and Denis Veiras', *PMLA*, 65 (1950), 464-72.

the obsequiousness of his new manner of address. Reports about English representatives in Italy and London were sent. Neville watched the activities of Sir John Finch (1626–82) very closely. He sent books for the royal library. John Starkey, the publisher, sent *The Works of Machiavelli* in 1675, which Neville had edited, and this was to be followed by both editions of *Plato Redivivus*, in 1681, on which Neville eagerly demanded an opinion. Communications were sent through Francesco Tierrisi, the Tuscan resident in London, who also reported on Neville's welfare to his royal master. Cosmo sent Italian wine to Neville, and some red damask especially woven to adorn his bedroom. He also gave advice and sent prescriptions for family illness, commentary and invitations. During the crises of Exclusion and the Rye House conspiracies, the Duke worried about the safety of the Englishman he so obviously loved and admired.

Neville was republican and protestant, Cosmo reigning prince and proselytizing catholic, yet these facts seem in no way to have hindered frank exchange of opinion between them. The Grand Duke thought that Neville could find comfort in the catholic faith, but he did not press him. He also sought information about the situation of catholics in England. Neville made it clear that he personally would always oppose persecution; he knew the virtues of catholics in Italy, he remembered that, in other times, English catholics had fought for liberty. But, he pointed out, prejudices were widespread, and sprang mainly from two causes. When Queen Elizabeth's birth and position had been questioned, catholics spoke against her, and, though this was now in the past, Englishmen loved freedom, national and personal, and feared that popery and tyranny were associated. They looked at France; they listened to the often foolish declarations made by cavaliers and courtiers against parliament; catholicism and arbitrary government seemed to go together. If catholics, he suggested, would support the popular cause, and make it clear that they were not necessarily proponents of absolutism, their troubles would diminish. In *Plato Redivivus*, Neville reiterated the desirability of allowing the full privileges of citizenship to loyal papists, instead of making them, by the severity of penal laws, real or potential conspirators against parliament.[1]

[1] Crino (1) gives much about Neville, the travels of Cosmo and some of the other personalities concerned. For the account kept at the time see Lorenzo, Count Magalotti, *Travels of Cosmo III, Grand Duke of Tuscany, through England in 1669*, tr. from the

Neville's *Machiavelli*, the first collected English edition, was probably in the main his own work, though he seems to have used an earlier translation of 'The Marriage of Belphegor' and may well have utilized others. The 'Preface to the Reader' was followed by 'Nicholas Machiavel's Letter to Zanobius Buondelmontius in Vindication of himself and his Writings'. This denied common charges: Machiavelli's 'insinuation' of democratical government, his vilifying the church, and teaching monarchs 'execrable' villainies. This 'Letter' was followed by table of contents and text. Though the 'Preface' suggested the missive had been brought to England from Italy by Neville himself, everything about it, including the date—1 April 1537, that is, April Fool's Day ten years after Machiavelli's death—points to its being an invention, to please Cosmo perhaps, and to make Machiavelli, whom Neville so vastly admired, more acceptable to the English public. The letter has provoked much speculation. Soon after its appearance it was used, in typically seventeenth-century fashion, as party propaganda. In 1689 and 1691 it was issued separately in much enlarged form and with what amounts to a different emphasis. The evils of popery were stressed, and the argument thus obviously supported the Revolution of 1688 and exclusion of James II. In this form the letter was reprinted in both editions of the *Harleian Miscellany*. Did Neville also write this revised version? More probably it was the handiwork of Thomas Wharton (1648-1715), the first Marquis. The republican Neville had declared over and over again that he was not interested in succession disputes. The Revolution, though it was to limit the power of future English kings, by no means carried the recommendations put forward in *Plato Redivivus*.[1]

Anthony à Wood stated that for twenty years before he died Neville resided in Silver Street, near Covent Garden, and not far from the Grecian coffee house. The landlord may have been that same Ewen with whom his brother Richard lodged in 1667, and the husband of the

Italian and illustrated (London, 1821). A picture of Billingbear faces p. 208, Crino (1). See *ibid.* p. 200 (24 Nov. 1676); and Neville's long letter on English catholicism, 15-25 July 1672, from the Berkshire Record Office, on pp. 196-7 (cf. *Plato Redivivus*, pp. 153-4, below).

[1] On Neville's *Machiavelli*, *inter alia*, see Giuliano Procacci, *Studi sulla Fortuna del Machiavelli* (Rome, 1965), pp. 255-9, where the authorship of the 'Letter' is discussed; F. Raab, *The English Face of Machiavelli* (London, 1964), chapter VII and appendix, pp. 267-72. Neither refers to the differences between the separate reprints of the Letter, in 1689, 1691 and in the *Harleian Miscellany* (1808), I, 78-90. For the story about Wharton's authorship, see J. Nichols, *Illustrations*, II (1817), 88; Crino (1), pp. 199-200.

Mrs Susan Ewen to whom Neville bequeathed the 'Venice Point' in 1694. In spite of hospitable offers by Cosmo, Neville does not seem to have returned to Italy after 1668, though ten years later, according to the earl of Danby's informant, he and John Wildman (1621–93) accompanied George Villiers (1628–88), second duke of Buckingham, to France, and were 'completely French' in their attitude. During the Popish Plot, Miles Prance the informer (d. 1689) tried to implicate Neville in supposed conspiracies against Anthony Ashley Cooper (1621–83), first earl of Shaftesbury, but the Privy Council record reveals that Prance had confused Neville of Berkshire with Henry Neville of Holt in Leicestershire. By the summer of 1679, the 'Politic Statesman', as one writer dubbed him, must have been writing *Plato Redivivus*. References in this tract suggest its composition as between the dissolution of the Habeas Corpus Parliament, and the meeting of the next, the Westminster or second Exclusion Parliament, on 21 October 1680.[1]

At that time England was disturbed, controversy was rife, men talked of '41, and rumours multiplied. Neville thought affairs were critical, and wrote to suggest remedies for national disorders. The trouble went back two hundred years, and would require drastic action to prevent civil war. This, the Interregnum had shown, provided no solution. Neville preferred to hope that King and Parliament could between them work out a means of restoring peace, stability, and the adaptation of the constitution to a new social order. Exclusion of James of York, already seriously mooted in parliament, was to Neville no remedy at all. The first edition of *Plato Redivivus* dismissed this subject briefly, but the second, perhaps because of the obvious determination of some important people to pursue the matter, contained, among other shorter additions, a long examination of Monmouth's candidature. A middle way, between 'two infamous factions, the courtiers and the madmen of the people' according to Neville, was a remodelling and limitation of the executive by arranging for the parliamentary appointment of four councils controlling war and peace, armed forces, appointment of ministers, and revenue. Of the two parties, he wrote in a letter, 'the first would like to introduce tyranny, the other anarchy and

[1] M. Ashley, *John Wildman* (London, 1947), p. 217. A. Browning, *Danby* (3 vols. Glasgow, 1951), I, 264 n. Miles Prance, *A True Narrative* (London, 1679), p. 28, but this is a confusion which Crino (1) has kept, pp. 200–1; also Crino (2), pp. 229, 252–5. London PRO, P.C. 2/68 f. 78, f. 79, 31 May 1679, case of Henry Neville of Holt, Leicestershire.

confusion, threatening utter ruin to all those who are not of their way of thinking, and who do not support certain of their expedients and caprices'.[1]

The many answers provoked by *Plato Redivivus* started in the autumn of 1681, and continued until the end of the reign. Their authors did not regard Neville as moderate, and repudiation of rebellion seemed valueless since it sprang solely from a realization of failure during earlier struggles to achieve a republic. A common dislike of Monmouth failed to commend Neville even to the author of *A Seasonable Address*, since *Plato Redivivus* advocated limitations which would have made the King merely a 'doge of Venice'. The anti-clericalism of Neville's treatise was equally distasteful to catholic, anglican or dissenting believer and anathema to many. Neville was accused of evil associations with such varied persons as the jesuits, Machiavelli, Richard Baxter, Thomas Hobbes, Thomas Hunt, Shaftesbury and Sidney. The more effective rebuttals concentrated on errors in historical and constitutional interpretation and of course on the proposed changes. Thomas Goddard examined the admired republics of Rome and Venice with some acumen. Neville seems to have replied to none. Opponents of Neville's book had much to commend their interpretation. Yet his attempt to adapt Harringtonian republicanism to the needs of a disturbed country commands respect as the last thoroughgoing presentation of the ideas of the Commonwealthmen as they could be applied to the current circumstance of the English polity.[2]

[1] Crino (1), pp. 205-6 (27 Sept. 1680).
[2] Answers to *Plato Redivivus*: Besides *A Seasonable Address*, attributed in *The Somers Tracts* to George Savile (1633-95), marquis of Halifax, at least two others appeared in 1681. *The Head of Nile, or the Turnings and Winding of the Facteous since Sixty in a Dialogue between Whigg and Barnaby*, probably by Thomas Baker, soon mentioned *Plato Redivivus* and then later recurred to its 'New Modell'd Government'; H.N. should suffer as much as Coleman, convicted during the Popish Plot trials, since he treasonably designed 'the subversion of Monarchy and the introduction of another form of Worship' (p. 34); nowhere is any distinction drawn between the Exclusion of James and the limitations, which might render a catholic prince powerless to harm protestantism of the sort Neville proposed. W.W., in *Antidotum Britannicum*, attacked Neville's suggestions and his interpretations; throughout, W.W. emphasized the anti-monarchical tendencies of *Plato Redivivus*. In 1684 Edward Pettit, in *Visions of Government*, dwelt on the bad company Neville was supposed to keep. In 1685 *The Tryumph of our Monarchy*, by John Northleigh (1657-1705), attacked in its 765 pages Hunt, John Somers, Sidney, the Rev. Samuel Johnson and Neville (pp. 145-348), all rebels and 'drudges of sedition'. In the same year *Plato's Demon*, by Thomas Goddard, presented discourses between a traveller and a merchant in which Neville's book was discussed. The contrary argument eventually prevailed over the rather slight defence of *Plato Redivivus* by the merchant. Goddard, the

During the period of the Rye House Plot, Roger L'Estrange (1616–1704) and his minions closely watched well-known republicans. Neville emerged unscathed and it seems probable that he kept himself entirely aloof from the conspirators, realizing the futility of republican aspirations. What he thought, as events moved towards the accession of William and Mary in 1689, is unknown. His friend Ludlow, in London soon afterwards, found republicanism no more popular then than earlier. Neville may well have been absorbed by personal and family concerns. His brother Richard was dead, his beloved nieces married, helped by his not inconsiderable wealth to useful dowries. In 1690 he was severely ill and this may have prompted the drawing up of the will dated in that year. In 1692 he and Wildman were asked to attend meetings of 'The Dry Club', founded by John Locke to discuss religious liberty. Whether either accepted and took part is not known, nor what prompted the invitation. Locke and Neville had a mutual friend in James Tyrrell (1642–1718) but of this association, as with others, little can be discovered. A reference in *Plato Redivivus* suggests familiarity with William Petyt (1636–1707) and William Atwood (d. 1705), two learned lawyers who probably lived near by. But of course some intimates like Harrington were dead, others like Ludlow, save for his brief disappointing visit after the Revolution, living abroad. There is not a word in the *Secret History of the Rye House Plot*, the work of a connexion by marriage, Ford Grey (1655–1701), earl of Tankerville, to suggest that Neville was seeing much of the malcontents of the 'eighties. The London circle in which he moved, save for Wildman, remains a mystery. When Narcissus Luttrell reported his death in September 1694, he referred only to the much earlier association with the Long Parliament.[1]

Neville bequeathed the bulk of his property to his nephew Richard,

traveller, was sensible and moderate, though he discovered greater danger from dissenters than papists. He cited Grotius; he explained the advantages of the true English hereditary monarchy, where advancement was open to men of merit, in contrast to the vice and rigidity of Venice and the confusions of Rome. Goddard stressed the recent statute of Habeas Corpus and the advantages of parliamentary liberties; and dismissed attacks upon 'pensioners' with the statement that he could see no wrong in holding office of the Crown.

[1] *CSPD*, 1683–4, ed. F. H. Blackburn Daniel (1937), p. 136; Crino (1), pp. 206–8; Bodleian Library, the Lovelace Collection of the Papers of John Locke, MS. Locke, c. 17. f. 205 (2 March 1692/3, Popple to Locke); Thomas Hearne, *Reliquiae Hearnianae*, ed. Philip Bliss (3 vols. London, 1869), II, 7; Narcissus Luttrell, *A Brief Relation* (6 vols. Oxford, 1857), III, 374.

who with John Fawkener, husband of one of his nieces, acted as executor. The nieces were affectionately remembered with money and with pieces of the red damask woven in Florence by Cosmo's command for his republican friend. Gifts, for the poor of Warfield, personal servants and helpers, were provided. Neville wished burial to be without 'Jewish ceremonies', eating and drinking, and that 'unprofitable form of words' in the prayer-book. Christ's coming had, he wrote, purged all excrescences of this kind from the spirit and truth of the Christian religion.[1] In the rational piety thus displayed and in the moderate republicanism shown in *Plato Redivivus*, Neville was typical of a small, intellectual and talented fraction of his contemporaries. England's limited monarchy and parliamentary system, and the civil and religious rights enjoyed by Englishmen, were to be greatly admired in the eighteenth century. But the contribution of Neville to this is to the development of a political theory of liberty and not to implementation of it in day-to-day constitutional practice.

THE WORKS OF HENRY NEVILLE

Plato Redivivus

1   *Plato Redivivus: or, A Dialogue concerning Government, Wherein, by Observation drawn from other Kingdoms and States both Ancient and Modern, an Endeavour is used to discover the present Politick Distemper of our Own, with the Causes, and Remedies.* London, Printed for S.I. in the Year MDCLXXXI. The Publisher to the Reader; Errata; The Argument, pp. 1–3; The First Day, pp. 3–15; The Second Day, pp. 15–173; The Third Day, pp. 174–271.

2   The same, but the Second Edition with additions [indicated in the text of the edition below by **...*]. London, Printed for S.I. and Sold by R. Dew, 1681. The Publisher to the Reader, A 2.3.4; Errata; Political Discourses and Histories worth reading; The Argument, pp. 1–3; The First Day, pp. 3–15; The Second Day, pp. 15–180; The Third Day, pp. 181–292.

3   *Discourses Concerning Government in way of Dialogues* by Henry Neville, Esq. London, A. Baldwin, 1698. The Publisher to the Reader—'These Discourses were printed privately and handed about...but when truth is better entertained ...thought well to print...' A.B. The Argument, p. 1; in all, 293 pages.

4 and 6   Printed at the end of *The Works of James Harrington*. Dublin, Printed by R. Reilly for J. Smith, W. Bruce, on the Blind Key, MDCXXXVII. *Plato Redivivus* has a separate title-page and is called 'The Third Edition, with Additions'. The Publisher to the Reader, pp. 549–52; The Argument and The First Day;

[1] Will as before Somerset House, PCC, box Irby, 174.

The Introduction, pp. 553–7; The Second Day, pp. 557–608; The Third Day, pp. 608–42. No. 6 is exactly the same except that the title-page reads Printed for W. Williamson, Dublin, 1758.

5 *Plato Redivivus, or Dialogues Concerning Government* by the Honourable Henry Neville, The Third Edition, London, Printed for R. Dodsley, Pall Mall, 1742. Advertisement [the success of *Oceana* encourages this edition of the work of a friend, and, according to Hobbes, collaborator of Harrington]; The Argument, pp. 2–4; 283 pages. Print and pagination are exactly those of no. 7. Thomas Hollis purchased the plates from Joseph Spence (1699–1768).

7 *Plato Redivivus, or a Dialogue Concerning Government*...The Fourth Edition, London, Printed for A. Millar, MXCLXIII [although it did not appear, apparently, until 1765]. Some Account of H. Neville, pp. 1–8 [by Hollis, but derived from Wood]; The Publisher to the Reader, pp. iii–ix; Title and Argument, pp. 1–4; The First Dialogue, pp. 5–17; The Second Dialogue, pp. 18–176; The Third Dialogue, pp. 177–283.

Other works

[A dagger indicates only that these are commonly attributed to him.]

† *The Parliament of Ladies, or Divers Remarkable Passages of Ladies in Spring-Garden, in Parliament Assembled, Vespere Veneris Martis*, 26 (1647). *The Ladies a second time assembled in Parliament*... (2 Aug. 1647). Reprinted by Thomas Hollis, *The Parliament of Ladys* (1768).

† *Newes from the New Exchange, or the Commonwealth of Ladies* (London, 1650). Reprinted 1731.

† *A Letter from an Officer in Ireland* (1656).

† *Neville v. Stroode, A True and Perfect Relation*... Published by 'an eye witness' (London, 1656).

Shufling, Cutting, and Dealing in a Game of Pickquet (London, 1659). Possibly an earlier version was published in 1656. Reprinted in the *Harleian Miscellany* (1810), VII, 46–50.

† *The Armie's Dutie* (1659). H.M., *H.N.*, I.L., L.W., I.I., S.M.

† *The Isle of Pines*, both parts, 1668. For reprints and translations, see Worthington Chauncey Ford for the Club of Odd Volumes (1920).

The Works of the famous Nicholas Machiavel, John Starkey (London, 1675). Reprinted 1680, 1695, 1721. This included N.M.'s Letter. Reprints of the letter may be found in Richard Baron, *Pillars of Priestcraft Shaken* (4 vols. London, 1768), IV, 245–77; and with a different title and altered text as *Machiavel's Vindication of himself* (London, 1689, 1691). On this see Raab, *The English Face of Machiavelli*, p. 268 n. *Machiavel's Vindication* appeared in volume I of both editions of the *Harleian Miscellany* (8 vols. 1744–6; 10 vols. 1808–13). Professor Crino's research has demonstrated that, as commonly thought, Neville was the editor chiefly responsible for this publication.

III. *Walter Moyle, 1672-1721*[1]

His tombstone described Walter Moyle as 'A gentleman well known by his learned, tho' posthumous Works. Better known by the great Deference paid to him by his learned Cotemporaries. Best known by his Life. For he was as eminent by his good Temper and great integrity, as he was for his Wit, Learning, and Judgement.'[2] During the forty-nine years of his life, many of them marred by ill health, Moyle's unusual erudition and versatility was recognized early, and admiration for his accomplishments continued for at least three-quarters of a century after his death. Today he is seldom read and almost forgotten. A brief account of his family, life and work, in succeeding and varied phases, may explain the immediate fame, if not the eventual neglect. In the first of the two volumes of *The Works* (London, 1726) the frontispiece shows a slight, bewigged, plump-faced gentleman, benign, with only a hint round the mouth of the humour and vigour revealed in the personal letters, in the learned correspondence, in the tracts, and so fully attested by his popularity and eighteenth-century reputation.[3]

The Moyles were a well-known Cornish family, and in the seventeenth century a branch resided at Bake in the parish of St Germans. John (1589–1661), at Oxford at the same time as John Eliot (1592–1632), reported home about his neighbour's shortcomings as a student, with the result that the future parliamentary hero and martyr attacked him sword in hand, only to apologize afterwards for what might well be thought a deserved, if over violent, resentment of tale-bearing. Both John and his son Walter (1627–1701) served in parliament on the

---

[1] The life in the *DNB* by William Prideaux Courtney provides much the best account of Moyle, and facts about his life and work, except where otherwise noted, are taken from it.
[2] [Polsme], *The Parochial History of Cornwall* (4 vols. Truro, 1867–72), IV, 42, gives this quotation from the funerary monument; among other local histories see J. L. Vivian, *Visitation of Cornwall* (Exeter, 1887), pp. 334–5, for genealogical tables; Richard Polwhele, *History of Cornwall* (Falmouth and London, 1803–16), for much other Cornish material.
[3] See footnote below on *The Works* for details, but throughout the footnotes the two-volume collection of 1726 will be referred to as *The Works*, and the one volume published in 1727 as *The Whole Works*. See frontispiece above: I have not traced the original portrait, but perhaps it, like the house and books, disappeared in the great fire at Bake, 1813.

popular side. The younger Walter was the third but first surviving son of this Walter and his wife Thomasine (d. 1682), daughter of the author and diplomat Sir William Morice (1602–82).

Like his father and grandfather, the author of *An Essay upon the Roman Government* attended Exeter College, Oxford, matriculating 18 March 1689, and leaving without a degree sometime before January 1691, when he entered Middle Temple. Early schooling, probably at the Liskeard Grammar School, and study in Oxford and London resulted in an extraordinary familiarity with classical authors, impressing all who met him, and still remarkable to his modern readers. To this erudition was added a knowledge of the English constitution acquired in the Inns of Court, though 'there was a drudgery', so his friend and memorialist Anthony Hammond (1668–1738) reported, in what he called '*Law-Lucrative* which he could never submit to'.[1]

The Temple not only afforded opportunity for acquiring learning, but through its membership at this time, and close proximity to the coffee houses of Covent Garden and the Strand, offered easy entry into London's literary and political society. Maynwaring's, but more especially Will's, off Covent Garden, and the Grecian in Devereux Court, off Essex Street, provided centres for entertainment and conversation. Middle Temple could claim among Restoration dramatists George Etherege (1635–91), whose *Comical Revenge* had amused the court of Charles II, and Thomas Shadwell (1642–92), whose *Sullen Lovers* had introduced something of French verve to the English stage. William Wycherley (1640–1716) produced *The Country Wife* in 1672, and Moyle was to make his acquaintance before 1695. Scarcely two months after the young Cornishman took up residence, William Congreve (1670–1729) entered the Inns of Court and became a friend and correspondent. Like Moyle, Congreve was to write his major work within the next ten years. *The Old Bachelor* was staged in 1693, the most delicious but last play, *The Way of the World*, in 1700. The two men shared a love of classical literature and common political prejudices and philosophy. Moyle was interested in the progress of *The Mourning Bride* in 1695, and Congreve eagerly anticipated Moyle's parliamentary career. At Will's they both sat at the feet of John Dryden (1631–1700).[2]

---

[1] Anthony Hammond, 'Some account of Mr Moyle and his writings' (hereafter 'Some Account'), prefaced to *The Whole Works*, p. 3.
[2] See G. C. Boase and W. Prideaux Courtney, *Bibliotheca Cornubiensis* (3 vols. London, 1874–82), I, 375–7, for the various collections in which letters to and from Moyle appeared,

Dryden had lost the office and pension enjoyed under James II: he was catholic and Tory. His genius towered over that of contemporaries. A truly great man, he recognized and generously praised talent in his younger friends, Congreve and Moyle. Moyle's early translations of Lucian, written at this time, were published in 1711 with Dryden's commentary, and other translations. While the older man worked at the English verson of *The Art of Painting* (Fr. 1668) by Charles de Fresnoy (1611–65), Moyle provided appropriate passages from Aristotle and Horace, and his own explanation of why imitation in art pleases. 'As truth', wrote Moyle, 'is the end of all our speculations, so the discovery of it is the pleasure of them; and since a true knowledge of nature gives us pleasure, a lively imitation of it, either in poetry or painting, must of necessity produce a much greater'...both arts being wrought to a nobler pitch, they unite, by 'a happy chemistry', all the scattered beauties of nature. Dryden incorporated not only warm acknowledgement of help received but this explanatory passage. He could, he said, never sufficiently commend Moyle's learning, judgement and familiarity with 'all the studies of humanity'.[1]

Others in the literary coterie at Will's included John Dennis (1657–1734), editor of two collections of letters by Congreve, Wycherley, Moyle and others, indifferent playwright, but a critic stimulating enough—it was said—to have extracted from Dryden his rationale of comedy. Minor poets celebrated Moyle: Charles Hopkins (1664–1724) in his youth and John Glanvill (1664–1735) after his death. Others of the circle were Charles Gildon (1665–1724), deistical author and editor of *Original Letters and Miscellaneous Essays* (1694) by his friends; 'silver tongued' Anthony Hammond (1668–1738), introduced to Moyle by Robert, son of the famous antiquarian Sir John Masham (1602–85); and the economic journalist Charles Davenant (1656–1714), son of the dramatist Sir William, and at this time cherishing theatrical ambitions of his own. The young men exchanged compliments and letters. They shared a common taste in literature and in women. Most of them despised Sir Richard Blackmore (d. 1729), author of *Prince Arthur* (1695),

and in which poems to him were printed. Hammond reprints some poems and letters; other letters 'upon Various Subjects' are in *The Works*, I, 365–430. John C. Hodges, *William Congreve, Letters and Documents* (New York, 1964), provides much about the literary life of London when Moyle and Congreve were young, and prints the letters between them.

[1] W. Scott and G. Saintsbury, *The Works of John Dryden* (18 vols. Edinburgh, 1882–92), XVII, 314–15.

rejected the criticism of Thomas Rymer (1641–1715) and resented the diatribes of Jeremy Collier (1650–1726), foe of the theatre they all loved.[1]

The 'Wits' were lively and talented. Whether they were, as Moyle's cousin Dean Humphrey Prideaux (1648–1724) wrote to his sister Anne Coffin, given over to libertinism may or may not be true, but reading their productions, private and public, makes it difficult wholly to endorse Prideaux's gloomy opinion.[2] Moyle and Congreve were still under thirty in 1700; they chased the ladies of the stage, but in spite of all diversions, they managed to write more, and that of higher quality, than those less high-spirited contemporaries who escaped clerical censure. Thus by 1695 Moyle had already endeared himself to Dryden, made a host of friends, and had even found time to be of use in the matter of the ornithology and botany of Cornwall to the great John Ray (1627–1705), whose second edition of *Synopsis Methodica Stirpium Britannicarum* (1696) reported some of his contributions.[3]

His coffee house acquaintance expected 'oracles' from Moyle when he should return victorious from the election of Saltash which in the summer of 1695 he went to Cornwall to secure. Successful, he served in the Parliament which met from the following November until July 1698. These three years and the two which followed, absorbed in politics, mark a new phase of Moyle's career. Even when he failed to seek—or to obtain—re-election in 1698, his studies were coloured by political reflexions. The member, student and writer merged. Moyle had gained experience in two arenas, the floor of the Commons, and that afforded by the printing presses flooded by himself and his friends with polemics against public policies they feared. There is no reason

[1] On the coterie, see Hodges, *William Congreve*; Curt Zimansky, *Thos. Rymer* (Yale, 1956), *passim*.

[2] Humphrey Prideaux, eventually dean of Norwich, was the son of Moyle's aunt, a daughter of Joseph Moyle (1592–1661); and, like his cousin, he went to school in Liskeard and to college at Oxford. In *HMC*, v (1876), MSS. J. R. Coffin, esq., 370–86: Prideaux's letters to his sister, Anne Coffin, refer three times—in March 1695, in February and August 1699—to 'Wat', 376–7.

[3] F. A. Turk, 'Natural History Studies in Cornwall, 1700–1900', *Journal of the Royal Institution of Cornwall*, n.s. III, part 3 (Truro, 1959), 229–79, an excellent account of Moyle's interest in natural history, with many useful references, including that to his correction of Ray's 'gross error' about the Cornish gannet. For references to the work of Moyle and his friend Lewis Stephens on marine plants, see John Ray, *Synopsis Methodica Stirpium Britannicarum* (2nd ed. London, 1696). Preface, p. 4, 'an ingenious young gentleman'; pp. 7, 8, 34, 295, etc.

to think that Moyle dropped his acquaintance at Will's, but the focus of interest had now shifted for him to coffee houses like the Tun, the Rose, the Grecian, where, it will be recalled, 'Old Plato Neville' used to talk. Here John Trenchard (1662–1723) and Moyle were said to have written *An Argument* against the retention of troops. At the Grecian, Hammond was later to recall, Moyle picked up 'some disgust' against the clergy. There Moyle probably became friendly with the Scots republican Andrew Fletcher (1656–1715), described by him as 'a surly patriot, who all his life long talked, writ and rebelled for liberty', and there he probably consorted with Davenant, with whom he joined in production of tracts for the times.[1]

In the Commons, in spite of his youth, Moyle evidently made his mark, though there are few recorded speeches. Interests are chiefly indicated by activities noticed in the *Journals*, and by Hammond's 'Account', written many years later by way of introduction to *The Whole Works* (1727). By this time Hammond had confused the dates of Moyle's parliamentary service. Yet his vivid summary of his friend's pronouncements may still be regarded as reasonably authentic from one who served in the House from 1695 to 1707, first for Huntingdon County, then for Cambridge University, and who declared that he shared with Moyle the same opinions about most matters, until their association was interrupted by Hammond's departure for Spain in 1711.[2]

Moyle was selected to confer with the Lords on five occasions; about the shipwrights' petition, about a matter concerning re-coinage, about the Greenland trade, about the King's speech in February 1696, and about the affairs of Charles Mordaunt (1658–1735), earl of Monmouth (and later of Peterborough), a peer for whose role in the upper House in 1699 he expressed admiration.[3] On 10 February 1697 he took the chair of the whole House, and two days afterwards reported findings in the matter of public accounts, surely a signal honour for so young and recent a member. As befitted a student of Middle Temple, Moyle's name appears on committee lists for bills about the relief of debtors,

---

[1] *The Whole Works*, p. 227, Congreve to Moyle on 'oracles'; p. 243, on Fletcher; pp. 75–6, 22–7, on Neville, the last in 'Some Account' by Hammond.

[2] 'Some Account', *The Whole Works*, pp. 27–33; Hammond writes as if Moyle had been in the Parliament of 1701–4, but *The Returns of Members of Parliament* lists no member of the family in the House, even on the occasion of the by-election at Saltash in 1703: Hammond remarks on their identity of views in 'Some Account', p. 4.

[3] *CJ*, XI (1803), conferences, 369, 377, 380, 465, 561, 661; on Peterborough, see 'Some Account', letter 7 Feb. 1698–9, p. 17.

oaths, the disinheritance of protestant heirs by papists, outlawries and, among others, ecclesiastical courts, institutions of which he disapproved. With the usual quota of private bills committees, he seems, since he was appointed to carry it when passed to the Lords, to have originated a bill for the naturalization of Henry de Nassau.[1]

Both Davenant and Hammond remarked on their friend's concern with the regulation and improvement of trade. Without trade, Moyle thought, great numbers of people could not live together, and, like so many of his contemporaries, believed a large population essential to national welfare. Sound money and profitable industry were also necessary to general prosperity. In 1698 a translation of *A Discourse upon improving the Revenue of the State of Athens*, by Xenophon, appeared with Davenant's *Discourses upon the Public Revenues and on the Trade of England*, Moyle's work following the first part of the *Discourses*. In a note to this Davenant expressed the hope that Moyle's example would encourage others of similar age, rank and fortune 'to study the *Business* of *trade* and the *Revenues* of their *Country*'.[2] In the Commons, Moyle served on a committee about a bill concerning the manufacture of lustre. He was active in the matter of re-coinage, opposing a proposal to call in plate to be coined, and twice acting as teller in divisions, with Sir Thomas Pope Blount (1649–97, Hereford County) on a motion to consider the price of guineas; with Sir Walter Yonge (1653–1731, Honiton), one of Locke's circle, on a motion to force receivers of clipped money to turn it in.[3]

Closely connected with 'the augmenting our domestick trade' was the employment of the poor. Yet, Moyle was reported to have told the House, England neither relieved all that were truly impotent, nor employed all capable of employment. The government was, he thought, responsible for all those reduced to the hard and criminal necessity of begging or stealing. In October 1696 Moyle was named to a committee about the Poor Laws, and had served in the previous December on another about hawkers and pedlars. In *An Essay upon the Roman Government*, at which he was at work three years later, he discussed the 'excellent use of colonies' to that Commonwealth: to defend it, to multiply its people, to transport poor citizens, to prevent seditions by

[1] *CJ*, XI, 701, in the chair; 703, reports. Committees on legal matters: 388, 440, 469, 487, 517, 524, 526, 533, 556; XII, 129. Nassau bill, XI, 432, 428.
[2] 'Some Account', pp. 6–7, 28–30, quoting Davenant.
[3] *CJ*, XI, 738, lustre; 400, 562, teller; 377, coinage.

the removal of dissidents, and to reward veterans. A keen sense of the advantages and the responsibilities of empire may be detected in the analysis. Moyle indeed reportedly regretted that Spain rather than England ruled Chile and Peru. Like Davenant in the *Discourses*, he not only stressed the usefulness of plantations but thought of them as a trust for the spreading of Roman or English liberty and civilization.[1]

A large and well-employed population was beneficial and only by numbers could liberty be properly guarded. Colonies, by providing new opportunities, aided this beneficial increase. Another device successfully used by the Roman Republic, he wrote, was 'the promiscuous naturalization of all foreigners'. Moyle himself on 22 February 1697 acted with Sir Henry Colt, member for Newport, as teller for the winning ayes for a bill for a general naturalization. On the subject of population in general, Moyle sent to Hammond 'excerpta' from a book by Sir Matthew Hale (1608–76), *On the Origination of Mankind* (1677), fully endorsing the judge's opinion that England at least had been more sparsely populated in Roman times. The argument, as Hale developed it and Moyle summarized it, rested in large part upon evidence for England only, but often seems on the point of reaching, by a different route, David Hume's conclusions half a century later about the populousness of ancient nations.[2]

Under the later Stuarts, corruption in public life was a recurring complaint. Moyle was named to a committee about regulating elections and a few weeks later acted as teller for the losing side. He was also on a committee, with Robert Harley (1661–1724, Radnor), Rowland Gwynn (Beeralston) and others, dealing with the sale of offices.[3] In 1747 a tract of some thirty pages, 'written by those two ever memorable Patriots, Anthony Hammond and Walter Moyle', was published as *The Honest Elector: or unerring Reasons for the Prevention of Chusing Corrupt Members to serve in Parliament, with Instructions for the Choice of a Speaker*. The last part of this, originally issued in 1698, had already been reprinted in *The State Tracts of the reign of William III* (3 v. 1705-7). In collecting *The Whole Works* Hammond, if his friend indeed had a share in these, appears to have overlooked them, though the sentiments

[1] *Ibid.* 573, 366; 'Some Account', pp. 29–30; for Chile and Peru, p. 52; see *An Essay*, below, p. 251–2, and Caroline Robbins, 'The Excellent use of Colonies', *William and Mary Quarterly*, 3rd ser. XXIII, no. 4, 620–6.
[2] *An Essay*, below, p. 229, 251; *CJ*, XI, 706; 'Some Account', pp. 37–49.
[3] *CJ*, XI, 440, 742.

expressed therein about corruption and the dangers presented by it to the continued existence and usefulness of parliaments were those of their circle. Corruption might well thwart the intentions of the Triennial Act of 1694. Nearly twenty years later Moyle, writing to Horace Walpole, supported the proposed Septennial Bill. The Triennial, he thought, had proved the occasion for even greater bribery, and he expressly dissociated himself from the disgruntled politicians at his old resort, the Grecian, who loudly condemned the new measure. Neville had praised annual parliaments, but, even when praising the Triennial, Moyle and Hammond had feared the frequent tumults these would bring, by which 'like a baker's oven, the nation would never be cool'.[1]

The necessity for a strong navy and the dangers of a standing army were important considerations with Moyle. Among the committees on which he served are to be found those concerning prizes and the embezzlement of naval stores. He was anxious to promote the recruitment of good seamen and, according to Hammond, believed that, if sailors were secured against personal arrest and detention in prison, exempted from the machinations of parish officers and from certain parish duties, provided with proper 'habitations', and paid with money or bills 'current in all branches of the revenue', the royal fleet would never lack men.[2]

The second half of 1697 was concerned with the army. The Peace of Ryswick was signed in the summer. On 10 December Robert Harley brought in a bill for the disbandment of troops. On 14 December Moyle and Hammond were ordered by the House to bring in a bill to enable soldiers that should be disbanded 'to exercise their trades', free, that was, of the old laws about apprenticeship. This bill, if they drafted one, did not pass in this Parliament. In April 1699, early in the next, a similar bill became law (10 William III c. 17).[3] Outside the House there was frantic activity in the campaign to reduce William's troops. At the Grecian, Fletcher, Trenchard, and numerous friends and followers, were writing works some of which were long to be famous.

[1] *The Honest Elector* is in the British Museum; *Instructions* (1698) in the Folger Library, and reprinted in *State Tracts*, II, 651–3; for the letter to Horace Walpole, see William Coxe, *Memoirs of Sir Robert Walpole* (3 vols. London, 1798), II, 62–3; 'Some Account', p. 26, elections.
[2] *CJ*, XI, 632, 749; XII, 262. 'Some Account', pp. 30–1.
[3] *CJ*, XII, 9.

Moyle's exact share in *An Argument shewing that a Standing Army is inconsistent with a Free Government, and absolutely destructive to the Constitution of the English Monarchy* is not determined. Hammond and Curle reprinted it as his in *The Whole Works.*[1] Shortly after it appeared, Prideaux wrote of his cousin's reputed part in writing 'a dangerous libel'—undoubtedly this tract.[2] As with the collaboration of Thomas Gordon in the composition of *The Independent Whig* (1720–1) and *Cato's Letters* (1720–3), precise allocation of responsibility to the eloquent Trenchard and partners or amanuenses is impossible. Like Dryden in another connexion, Trenchard may well have been grateful for Moyle's fund of classical information and for his ready wit.

There can be no doubt that *An Argument* reflected the beliefs of both men and the teaching of their political prophets. Machiavelli, Francis Bacon, James Harrington and Neville were cited; the lessons of antiquity rehearsed to bring home the threat posed by a standing army in any age, as well as their own, to liberty. Innumerable examples were used not only from Greek and Roman history but also from the sad story of developing French, Spanish and Danish absolutism, the last recently and vividly described in a famous *Account* published by Robert Molesworth. Freedom could only be maintained where a citizen army defended the nation. Fletcher, whose *Discourse* was perhaps the ablest of the tracts of these months, greatly admired Harrington's emphasis upon the connexion of property and power. This, he thought, was best provided by what seems like an idealized feudal system, tenants-in-chief leading their vassals against foreign foe and domestic tyrant. The arguments against the Grecian coterie, put forward by John, Lord Somers (1651–1716), in *A Letter, Ballancing the Necessity of keeping a Land-Force in Times of Peace* (1697), seem devastatingly effective, but at the time failed to wrest victory from the opposition. Moyle praised Somers's detractors, and rejoiced at his discomfiture not many months later. *An Argument*, appearing in the works of both Trenchard and Moyle, continued to be the widest circulated and most often reprinted tract of the coming century.

About a year after *An Argument* appeared, Moyle sent to Hammond

---

[1] *An Argument* reprinted, *The Whole Works*, pp. 155–208. Useful in this connexion: Lois G. Schwoerer, 'The Literature of the Standing Army Controversy, 1697–1699', *HLQ*, v, xxviii, no. 3 (May 1965), 187–212; *A Bibliography of John Trenchard, 1662–1723*, compiled by J. A. R. Sequin and privately printed (Jersey City, 1965).
[2] Prideaux in *HMC*, v, 377.

'An Essay on the Lacedaemonian Government', which was probably not published until 1727. In this Moyle discussed the wise provisions made by Lycurgus for Sparta. Ancient prudence, Moyle declared, echoing the admired Harrington, provided an empire of laws and a balance of power within the administration. Envy, fraud, violence, indolence, luxury, and oppression were banished. Inequality, except that deriving from virtue, was made impossible, and the gap between richer and poorer narrowed. An agrarian or equal distribution of lands, a rotation of magistrates, a legislature kept within bounds with executive power, an austere and disciplined way of life which made even war seem natural to Spartan youths, secured stability for hundreds of years. The people selected the lawgivers who formed the legislature. Ephors or tribunes protected the people. Sparta was well governed. No government, wrote Moyle, quoting a saying favoured by both Neville and Harley, can last for long under an ill administration.[1]

Along with this rather idealized description of the Greek republic, Moyle offered almost the only direct commentary he seems to have left upon the English constitution. In it, as in so many contemporary tracts, may be found reflexions of John Fortescue's encomium of an empire of laws and of the protection afforded Englishmen by the courts at Westminster. In it, also, Moyle paid a warm tribute to Algernon Sidney, whom he defended from those critics who found his view on obedience 'too precarious and loose' and whom he praised for his use of history. The author of 'The A.B.C. of Politicks', John Locke, as well as Neville and Harrington, was recommended.[2] Moyle condemned the clergy, though not without a tribute to their conduct at the Revolution, because they had for a number of years perplexed the notions and muddled the brains of a great many people about the English constitution. The principle of divine right caused the Civil War, brought England to the brink of ruin before the Revolution, and could again bring about tumults. Monarchy by divine right cannot be bounded by laws. All rights and liberties, all jurisdictions and properties could be yielded up if required at will and pleasure if this clerical theory be accepted. 'My principle is', Moyle stated, 'that the King is King by the fundamental law of the land, and by the same law and no other, the meanest subject enjoys the liberty of his person and property in his

[1] *The Whole Works*, pp. 47–77; reference to Harley, p. 60.
[2] *Ibid.* p. 58.

estate, and it is everyman's concern to defend this to the uttermost.' The House of Lords and Commons were an essential part of the government established by 'laws of equal force and validity' with those by which regal power is settled. Every honest man must defend all branches, not give up one to the other. The ephors guarded liberty in Sparta. In England, parliament provided security against the encroachments of regal power. The lack of such protectors in Mycenae, Moyle quoted Neville as pointing out, caused 'perpetual broils among themselves' and ultimately defeat at the hands of their enemies.[1]

This essay belongs to the year 1698, and in the following year Moyle wrote to Hammond that he was hard at work at nothing but Roman history.[2] In this way he was finding some solace for his exile from London and from parliament. Retirement from politics was at first very hard for Moyle, and letters amply attest a longing for news from the capital and delight in the exploits of his friends. Why he did not return may be due to a preference by Saltash for a Morice or a Buller. Or Moyle's father, already arranging a marriage for his son, may have insisted on attention to that 'dull scene of business' to which a letter cryptically referred. Health may well have had something to do with retreat from the pleasures of metropolitan life for what Dennis was to call 'twenty tedious years'. Whatever the reason, Moyle continued at first to write eagerly for political news and, in writing *An Essay upon the Roman Government* fresh from the excitements of Westminster, expressed a considered opinion on the elements of greatness and the factors in decline in ancient Rome and in modern England. Like Jonathan Swift in *A Discourse of the Contests and Dissensions Between the Nobles and the Commons in Athens and Rome* (October 1701), provoked by the polemics of his friend Charles Davenant, Moyle was writing a tract for the times.[3]

Before those last two decades in Cornwall are examined Moyle's political alignment must be assessed. His political affiliation, Prideaux wrote in 1699, was with 'the King's bitter enemies', and had kept him from that court employment which he needed, or which, more prob-

---

[1] *Ibid.* pp. 62–6; on Spartan virtue, p. 76; Neville correctly cites Messene below, p.190.
[2] 'Some Account', p. 17.
[3] John Dennis, *Original Letters* (2 vols. London, 1721), I, 159–62, 211–13, January and May 1720. 'Twenty tedious years' is quoted from this in *DNB*. A new edition of Swift's tract by Frank H. Ellis (Oxford, 1967) provides much information about the controversies of the turn of the century in elaborate critical accompaniment to the text.

ably, the family had hoped he would obtain. Yet Moyle had come into the world 'with a zeal for the Protestant succession', and had, unlike his friend and fellow Cornishman Jack Tredenham (1668–1710, Mawes), signed the Association of 1696. Again, according to Hammond, 'he was apt to distinguish between the *King* and some of his *Ministers*, between the *legally established Government*, and the *Interest* of a *Party*'.[1] The letters betray a spirit of vigorous opposition to the government in power, of distrust for the 'junto', of admiration for Peterborough when he attacked them, of sympathy with the financier Charles Duncombe when he was in disgrace. Moyle delighted in 'ministry hunting', and loved to hear of what his friend Walter Wymondsolde (c. 1670–1710) called 'a great fight' in the House.[2]

In parliament Moyle was associated with the Tory Hammond and the near jacobite Tredenham. He seems to have been one of the new 'country' amalgam of which Harley was the leader. Moyle collaborated in writing with Davenant, with the 'Independent Whig' Trenchard and with the republican Fletcher. The range of political designation is great; Davenant, Hammond and Tredenham were accused of 'closeting' with Poussin, the French agent, in 1701 and appearing treacherously opposed to the war then developing with Louis XIV.[3] Harley, like Moyle, had Whig traditions; his religious connexion was presbyterian whereas Moyle was anglican with a decided anti-clerical bias, shared by such republicans as Neville and Sidney and continually manifested in his writing. Harley had assisted the cause of the pamphleteers against a standing army by moving the reduction of the number of troops in 1697; he promoted the cause of the 'Protestant Succession' by helping the passage of the Act of Settlement in 1701.[4]

In some divisions Moyle along with Harley was listed as Tory, but at this time, the last six years of the reign of William III, both certainly thought of themselves as 'old Whigs' or 'country'. In Davenant's tract *A True Picture of a Modern Whig* (1701), probably inspired by

[1] Prideaux, *HMC*, v, 376–7; 'Some Account', p. 4; *CJ*, XI, 471.
[2] 'Some Account', pp. 14–21; *The Whole Works*, pp. 240–3, letter dated 26 Jan. 1698–9.
[3] For the Poussin affair, see Ellis, cited p. 31, n. 3, above and, *inter alia, A Vindication of Dr Charles Davenant, Anthony Hammond, Esq., and John Tredenham, Esq.* (London, 1702); and *A Full and True Relation of a Horrid and detestable Conspiracy* (London, 1701).
[4] Harley has been the subject of reconsideration recently: Angus McInnes, 'The political ideas of Robert Harley', *History*, L, no. 170 (October 1965), 309–22; Henry Horwitz, 'Parties, Connections and Parliamentary Politics, 1689–1714, Review and Revision', *The Journal of British Studies*, VI, no. 1 (November 1966), and authorities there cited.

Harley, these 'old Whigs' were contrasted with the 'new Whigs' of the 'junto'. The old had supported triennial parliaments, fair treason laws, frugality in public expenditure, the report of the Irish Commissioners (of whom Trenchard was one) criticizing grants to courtiers from forfeited estates; and had steadily opposed arbitrary government, the partition treaties and a standing army in time of peace. From 1701 until 1708 Harley was to work closely for Godolphin in support of the war with France and the Union with Scotland.[1] Later he sought to fulfil his ambitions in the leadership of the Tories and of course then became the ally, willingly or perforce, of the High Church party. Moyle served too short a time in parliament to become an important member of the country faction in spite of Thomas Hearne's remark that he was the Coryphaeus of the Whigs. Hearne, like Edward Gibbon later (when warning Moyle's readers against his 'Whig' bias), was uninterested in the lights and shades of party politics at the beginning of the eighteenth century.[2] In parliament, country-oppositionist, at the Grecian, Commonwealthman and classical republican, Moyle was, as he said, 'on the side of liberty'. He believed in a balance of the three estates, the virtues of general naturalization, of impeachment or accusation, in a rotation in office, and the use of the ballot; he wished for the detachment of the 'diviners' or clergy from the exercise of political power. The Revolution of 1688 had done much to secure England from tyranny but Moyle believed that 'the Boundaries and Limits of Prerogative' were not yet 'so well stated' as desirable. The writings were intended to show the advantages of Commonwealth expedients, and to warn against possible dangers to English liberties yet remaining, in spite of the exile of the Stuarts.[3]

On 6 May 1700 Moyle married Henrietta Maria Davis (1677–1762) of Bideford in Devonshire, just across the county line. A year later the

---

[1] *The Works of Charles Davenant*, collected by Sir Charles Whitworth (7 vols. London, 1771), IV, 125–266; in a letter printed in *The Whole Works*, p. 241, Moyle describes himself (26 Jan. 1698–9) as an 'Old Whig'.

[2] Henry L. Snyder, 'Godolphin and Harley, a study of their Partnership in Politics', *HLQ*, XXX, no. 3 (May 1967), 241–71; Moyle and Harley shared not only the acquaintance of Hammond and Davenant, but of Fletcher, who was an 'old friend' of Harley's. *HMC*, Portland Papers, VIII (1907), 142.

[3] *The Whole Works* (Sparta), p. 63, on side of liberty; p. 62, 'boundaries'. Hearne, *Reliquiae Hearnianae*, ed. Bliss, II, 265, 'Coryphaeus'; 290, on publication of *The Works* by 'Sergeant of the Tower' against the consent of Moyle's son, then travelling abroad; but Sergeant obviously had the help of Moyle's brother, Joseph. Edward Gibbon, *The Decline and Fall*, ed. J. B. Bury (7 vols. London, 1925), III, 189, n. 4.

elder Walter died, and Moyle settled down to married life at Bake. Two sons and a daughter grew up, but all died without surviving issue. Their mother long outlived husband and children. In 1710 Moyle, in accordance with the terms of the marriage settlement, made a will, and in it suggested that, if it seemed advisable (though he obviously hoped it would not be), his library could be mortgaged to raise money for portions. Evidently the widow did not find this necessary, and the library, for which a building was completed in 1713, remained until destroyed by fire early in the nineteenth century. The books, which Moyle was reported to have annotated copiously, might have yielded valuable material on a variety of subjects, but scholars apparently did not, as suggested at times, make use of them, and much erudition perished in the flames. The house now standing on the old foundations bears no trace above ground of the charming dwelling in which Moyle lived. He was, it seems, bedevilled by poor health which obliged him to drop botanical expeditions and hampered his investigations of Cornish birds, though near the end, in 1721, he wrote that only a 'hard winter' lay between him and the completion of this continuing work. Two neighbours, George Jago, vicar of Looe, illustrator of Ray's work on fishes, and Lewis Stephens, vicar of Menheniot, companion in botanical walks, shared Moyle's enthusiasm for natural history, and with them he compared notes on progress. He also corresponded with William Sherard (1659–1728), long consul at Smyrna and afterwards professor of Botany at Oxford, and Dr Tancred Robinson (d. 1746). Only the letters and a few references by contemporaries preserve any part of Moyle's research.[1]

With another friend, Dr William Musgrave (1655–1721), an Exeter physician and like himself the possessor of a considerable collection of books, Moyle exchanged visits, gossip on current events and notes on antiquities. Some engraved stones Moyle had remarked were transcribed. The questions whether the Romans conquered Cornwall, the meaning of *aurum*, usually translated as 'gold', and a number of similar matters engaged the attention of the men and the letters reveal yet another aspect of Moyle's versatility. He was not, of course, always right, and misread entirely the first word of a cunomorus pillar at

[1] *The Works*, I, 414, 'hard winter'; much about his study of natural history in 'Various Letters', *ibid*. 365–430, *passim*. Moyle's will is at Somerset House, PCC, Buckingham, 206; John Ray, *Synopsis Methodica Avium* (1713), refers to Tancred Robinson and incorporates George Jago's pictures of Cornish fishes opposite pp. 162, 164.

Fowey as *cerusius* instead of *drustard*, so missing a great Arthurian story unravelled by later investigators.[1]

Though there seems to be no record of Moyle's serving as justice of the peace as his earlier legal studies and standing in the county might suggest, an address of 1706 by him to the Grand Jury at Liskeard is included in *The Works*. He admonished the jurors about the corruption of manners, criticizing those who felt that 'a fiery zeal' for one particular church atoned for 'lewdness and debauchery'. He condemned popery, commended the civil rights enjoyed by Englishmen, and referred to the just war against France in which they were engaged. In 1708 he was sub-warden of the Stanneries, a court for the regulation of the ancient tin mines of the Duchy. He deplored 'the Sacheverell madness' towards the end of Anne's reign, when most Whigs became alarmed by an anglican sermon seemingly belittling the Glorious Revolution. During the 'unnatural rebellion' of the Fifteen, he was active in defence measures. Early in the century Joseph Moyle represented Saltash, but after that the Moyles seem, during the lifetime of the brothers, to have taken no part in the politics of St Stephen's.[2]

The pursuit of natural history and the study of antiquities, as well as the local duties and interests mentioned, by no means occupied all Moyle's days. In his study he wrote two famous series of letters and 'A Dissertation', printed posthumously in *The Works* and, as noticed below, achieving renown in scholarly circles. While Moyle was sowing his wild oats, his cousin Prideaux was busy writing what became a very popular *Life of Mahomet* and *A Letter to the Deists* (1697), attempting to vindicate Christianity from charges of being an imposture or cheat upon mankind, and in so doing displaying considerable erudition put to pious uses. Even more readers were to study what was called 'Prideaux's Connection', that is *The Old and New Testaments connected in the History of the Jews and Neighbouring Nations* (1714–18). Moyle's careful commentaries on this subject were gratefully received by his cousin, who often admitted correction. This correspondence attained wide currency. It was reprinted from *The Works* with *An Argument* and the essays on Rome and the Lacedaemonian Government in *A Select*

[1] *The Works*, I, 167–282, letters to Musgrave; and see C. A. Radford, 'Report on the Excavation at Castle Dore', *Journal of the Royal Institution of Cornwall*, n.s. I, app. I (Truro, 1951), 1–119, for the Arthurian story Moyle might have uncovered.
[2] *The Works*, I, 149–66, 'A Charge'. Remarks on events: 205, Sacheverell; 234, death of Anne; 253, rebellion.

Collection of Tracts (Dublin, 1728; Glasgow, 1750), translated into French, and, generally speaking, wherever 'Prideaux's Connection' was read Moyle's remarks were also carefully considered.[1]

Another series of letters with some rather acrimonious rejoinders, published in *The Works*, provoked controversy and obtained even wider repute than that with Prideaux. This was the exchange between Moyle and a 'Mr K.' about the alleged miracle of the Thundering Legion. 'Mr K.' has been identified as a minister, Richard King, but J. L. Mosheim, the ecclesiastical historian who translated the letters into Latin and published them at Leipzig in 1733, declared that Moyle's correspondent was Locke's young cousin, Peter King, later Lord Chancellor. Peter was born in Exeter, and qualified for the bar at Middle Temple in 1698. He had already, in 1691, published a book on the primitive church, and in 1702 was to produce another on the history of the Apostles' Creed. King and Moyle are known to have exchanged views on other antiquarian subjects and Mosheim's statement seems both possible and probable.

Somewhat later, Joseph Priestley (1733–1804), interested in this work, obtained through the good offices of Samuel Merivale (1713–71) of the Exeter Academy, and the generosity of Francis Gregory, Moyle's nephew, an unpublished manuscript. This, 'A Discourse to prove Marcus Antoninus a Persecutor of the Christians', was printed in Priestley's *Theological Repository*. In both the communication to 'Mr K.' and 'A Discourse', Moyle set out to disprove what he thought long-standing misconceptions of history. According to legend, a legion, entirely Christian, in the army of Marcus Aurelius was sent with others of his forces to fight the Marcomanni. During the campaign the Christians observed the thirst of their fellow soldiers and began to pray for relief. A storm ensued, disrupting the enemy with hail and thunderbolts, and quenching the thirst of the Romans, Christian and pagan, with rain-water. Moyle did not believe the story, nor approve attempts to demonstrate that the much admired philosopher-emperor was tolerant. Miracles, though they did not lack defenders, were not fashionable among the eighteenth-century philosophers. On the other hand the story of the legion was picturesque, and some theologians were loath to see it discredited. Moyle's commentary attracted many readers;

[1] *The Works*, II, 1–78, and see Boase and Courtney, *Bibliotheca Cornubiensis*, I, bibliography of the discussions roused by this and succeeding commentaries by Moyle.

'A Discourse' was accorded a respectful reception; the matters in them continued to be discussed.[1] In a shorter essay, 'A Dissertation upon the Age of the Philopatris', a dialogue commonly atttibuted to Lucian (*fl.* A.D. 120–64), Moyle threw doubts upon the supposed authorship, and, in spite of the fury with which his remarks were studied by Thomas Hearne, seems to put forward views in accordance with modern scholarship.[2]

According to John Dennis, Moyle's health would have benefited and his friends been cheered if he had ridden to London in 1720. His advice and invitation came too late, and Moyle died in the following year. With death of children and widow and the destruction of house and library, only the tombstone in the Moyle aisle at St Germans, and a couple of small glass windows bearing the arms, still remain to recall a brilliant Cornishman.[3] The publication of his works and subsequent reprinting of them, and occasional appearance of a letter or letters in press or collection, kept his memory green for the rest of the eighteenth century, but in the last 150 years his reputation, like Neville's, suffered a decline.

Moyle, like some others of the classical republicans, deserves to be studied as a late seventeenth-century wit and scholar. That brilliance which so impressed contemporaries and made him briefly a personage in the London literary world also makes the reading of his letters and essays worth the effort of any serious student of his times.

Of all these, perhaps *An Essay upon the Roman Government* deserves now the closest scrutiny by students of eighteenth-century political theory, and of an important phase of a continuing classical tradition. Analogy between their contemporary world and that of the ancients was no novelty, but no one before Moyle examined in such detail the causes of the rise and fall of republican Rome and related these

---

[1] *The Works*, II, 79–390, the 'Thundering Legion'; *Theological Repository*, edited by Joseph Priestley (London, 1767), I, 77–9, 147–73, 'A Discourse'. About 1713, Moyle and King were in contact on the same subject as that of the letters to Musgrave (*The Works*, I, 213), as a surviving note from Moyle to King shows. (Bodleian Library, The Lovelace Collection of the Papers of John Locke, c. 38, f. 14.) In 'A Vindication' [*The Works of Gibbon*, ed. J. Walker McSpadden (New York, 1907), pp. 183–277], Gibbon warmly praised Moyle's refutation of this 'silly story' of the Legion, pp. 255–6.

[2] *The Works*, I, 283–364, 'A Dissertation'; Hearne, *Reliquiae*, II, 265.

[3] Dennis as p. 31, n. 3, above; in spite of the twenty tedious years, Moyle had been in London at least twice during the period; in 1708 about a matter of family property (*Calendar of Treasury Books* (1708), ed. W. A. Shaw (1950), pp. 144, 292), and in 1716 when he wrote to Walpole about the Septennial.

pronouncements so precisely to current political controversy. He was followed, as Barère remarked, by a whole series of essays and treatises by Englishmen and quite probably stimulated the greatest of eighteenth-century analysts to write *The Grandeur and Declension* (1734). Rome and England, as even Noah Webster, the American, declared, were widely believed to have enjoyed the best constitutions ever known. The ways in which these two resembled each other were examined and the mistakes of the one, it was hoped, would be corrected by the other. These political theorists dwelt at length, and in a manner now unfamiliar, on the good laws and austere virtues of Rome during that period described by Moyle. In this study the republican found encouragement, the imperialist support, the moralist a lesson. *An Essay* significantly illustrates this phase in historical interpretation and political thought.[1]

THE WORKS OF WALTER MOYLE

G. C. Boase and W. Prideaux Courtney, *Bibliotheca Cornubiensis*, I, 375–7, and III, 1,289–90, give a very full listing of Moyle's works in print and in manuscript, with valuable references to other relevant material. An abbreviated note by Courtney follows the excellent life in the *DNB*. On Moyle's theories, see H. F. Russell Smith, *Harrington and his Oceana* (Cambridge, 1914), pp. 199–200, 217–18. Smith discussed and confirmed evidence for Moyle's authorship of *An Essay upon the Constitution of the Roman Government*, confused by H. R. Fox Bourne's attribution to Locke (*Life*, 2 vols. 1876), an assumption based on the evidence of a MS. copy among the Shaftesbury papers in Locke's hand, and made without search for early printed editions. Zera S. Fink, *The Classical Republicans* (Evanston, 1945), pp. 170–4, dubbed Moyle the very model of a Whig historian of the Roman Republic. Caroline Robbins, *The Eighteenth Century Commonwealthman* (Harvard, 1959), chapter IV, pp. 88–133, 'Molesworth and his friends in England', places Moyle among his contemporaries.

An Essay upon the Constitution of the Roman Government

1 *An Essay upon the Constitution of the Roman Government. The Works*, I (1726), 1–148.

2 *A Select Collection of Tracts*, by W. Moyle, Esq., containing I. 'An Essay upon the Roman Government'. II. 'Remarks upon Dr Prideaux's Connection...' III. 'An Essay upon the Lacedaemonian Government'. IV. 'An Argument against

See below for a partial list of works on ancient republics and for the introduction to Barère's translation of Moyle's *Essay*. Noah Webster, *An Examination into the leading Principles of the Federal Constitution* (Philadelphia, 1787); for this, I have used Paul L. Ford, *Pamphlets on the Constitution...* (Brooklyn, 1888), pp. 25–65.

a Standing Army'. Dublin, Printed by A. Rhames, for T. Benson, at the Shakespear's Head, in Castle St, 1728. 8º. 231 pages.

3 Another edition of the same in 12º. 274 pages. Glasgow, Printed R. Urie, 1750.

4 *Democracy Vindicated. An Essay on the Constitution and Government of the Roman State; from the posthumous works of Walter Moyle;* with a preface and notes, by John Thelwall, Lecturer on Classical History. Norwich: Printed and Sold by J. March, Cockey-Lane, London: Sold by J. Smith. 1796, 8º. pp. iv and 41 (1s.).

5 *Essai sur le Gouvernement de Rome,* Par Walter Moyle; Traduit de l'Anglois [by Bertrand Barère]. Ouvrage utile aux Hommes d'État, et aux Philosophes. À Paris, Chez Leger, Libraire, quai des Augustins, nº. 44. De L'imprimerie de Marchant, l'Aîné. An. 1801. 8º. pp. viii and 112.

Other Works

Collected Works. Three volumes were printed, but collected by two different editors. In 1726, Thomas Sergeant, probably with the help of Moyle's brother Joseph, to whom he dedicated the volumes, brought out *The Works of Walter Moyle Esq; None of which were ever before Publish'd.* London, Printed by J. Darby, 1726, 2 vols. 8º. In the first volume was 'An Essay upon the Roman Government' and other pieces; in the second, the letters to Dr Prideaux, and about the Thundering Legion.

The Whole Works of W. Moyle, Esq., that were published by himself. To which is prefixed some account of his life and writings [by Anthony Hammond]. London, printed for J. Knapton, 1727. 8º. This contained the Xenophon, 'Essay on the Lacedaemonian Government', miscellaneous letters, a character of Andrew Fletcher. Boase and Courtney supply all details about both reprints and the controversy over certain items in *The Works.*

39

IV. *The English Republicans*

English republicans or Commonwealthmen were more renowned than numerous. The great puritans Milton, Vane and Baxter achieved fame in their lifetime and, even among those who do not read their works, are still names to conjure with. Among the 'politic statesmen' not primarily motivated by religious ideals and aspirations, Sidney and Harrington are the best known, and were certainly the most gifted and probably the most influential. For more than a century, wherever revolution was advocated in the western world, the name of Sidney was invoked as saint and martyr, justifying as he died revolt against tyranny. Harrington inspired many constitution makers, and his importance in America needs no further emphasis here. More recently, for reasons that might have surprised the author of *Oceana*, his work and that of his disciples has been investigated by students of socio-economic factors in history, and the Marxists have devoted serious study to the political literature of the English Interregnum.

Lesser men, for long widely read, were Edmund Ludlow, soldier and memorialist of republican vicissitudes; Marchamont Nedham, unsteady in loyalty to the good old cause, but one of its most original and brilliant exponents; Neville, often investigated by the Harringtonians; and such interesting but less popular writers as William Sprigge, author of *A Modest Plea for an Equal Commonwealth* (1659), declaiming against monarchy, tithe, the legal profession, established churches and current educational practice, and Henry Stubbe, physician, reputed atheist, and disciple who found *Oceana* 'wanting', too mild to guard against the re-establishment of old authorities, and who was prepared to limit civil rights for the time being to like-minded liberators of the country.

At the end of the seventeenth century another generation may be found in Fletcher, Molesworth, Trenchard and Moyle, all profound admirers of the earlier republicans and writers of famous tracts against the dangers of a standing army, the evils of ecclesiastical establishments, and other threats to liberty. Their polemics and interpretations of history and of the politics of the quarter-century in which they flourished often permeate the writings of later historians and political commentators not overtly, or even secretly, republican in sympathy. Less than a dozen slim pamphlets in the times of crisis provoked by James as heir to or possessor of the crown specifically proposed a republican constitution. In this later phase, amendment of the old and restored government along lines suggested by earlier republican treatises was the chief concern of the more prominent authors.

This republicanism in England found expression only in those two periods of the seventeenth century when circumstances suggested a possibility of implementing theories, and when, in the same context, authoritarian philosophers, by offering very different solutions to the problems of statecraft, provided stimulus to rebuttal and counter-proposal. During the dozen or so years following the defeat of Charles I, republican and levelling ideas began to be heard in the army council and to make their way to the public through the tracts flooding the presses. Milton and Nedham defended the Commonwealth established after the execution of the King. As time wore on, others, like Vane, resenting Cromwell's assumption of power, defended that short-lived republic against protectorial constitutionalists. Thomas Hobbes's *Leviathan*, putting forward entirely different responses to the crisis, in turn affected the composition of *Oceana*. With the death and removal of the Cromwells, the need for a stable regime brought a fresh crop of suggestions about a free state, but secured too meagre a following to prevent the restoration of the Stuarts in 1660 and the resulting apathy in political speculation for almost two decades. Yet Exclusion controversy, Revolution and Settlement once more inspired very important works. The *Patriarcha* of Robert Filmer appeared in 1680 to provide ammunition for the defenders of York's claims to the throne. Provoked by it and others who seemed to share its views, treatises by Sidney, Neville, Locke and others were written, if not all published immediately. After the Revolution both Locke and Sidney appeared and Neville and Harrington found a new public, a public also reading that shower of tracts produced by Moyle and his associates. Open opposition to monarchy was not often expressed, but many suggestions for bounding the power exercised were made in the republican tradition. This tradition continued through the eighteenth century, but the works that fed it were, for the most part, the fruits of the earlier period.

'Republican' is a term not easily defined. Loosely applied to many different and varied opponents of Stuart policy, it had no more clarity than the designation of Leveller with which it was occasionally and wrongly confused. On the continent, outside the oligarchic republics of Venice, Switzerland and the United Provinces, republican connoted almost any critic of established authority. These would include those who said that the people should rule and that the monarch himself should be under the law; those who served or supported any state not headed by a king; those who preferred elective to hereditary monarchy. Everywhere republican implied an aristocratic concept of 'people' or 'country'. Democracy was seldom or never discussed save as an anarchic condition. Sidney and some few others thought democracy better than tyranny, but believed that the propertied, the educated, well-born and responsible members of society should regulate its affairs and prevent the chief officer overstepping the due bounds of prerogative.

Even after the establishment of the American Republic, differences existed among the founding fathers, between John Adams on the one hand and men like Thomas Jefferson and John Taylor on the other. Adams, Jefferson reported to Taylor in 1814, considered any government which could be described as 'an empire of laws' a republic. To the Sage of Monticello, a republic implied a government by citizens acting directly and personally, according to rules set up by the majority among them. Most English writers from the time of Sir John Fortescue supported the rule of law, but few were ever republican in the sense marked out by Jefferson. Those Englishmen correctly labelled republican in the seventeenth century, and not primarily concerned with the rule of saints and sages, held a variety of views to be examined here. In some ways they endorsed theories widely shared by their contemporaries. In some others divergence was a matter of degree or emphasis only. The secular or classical republicans can be most readily distinguished by their fear of a strong executive, by often violent anticlericalism, by emphasis on virtue or public spirit, and on the necessity for renovation, renewal of principles, even adaptation to changing circumstance, and by advocacy of certain constitutional devices which they thought would secure the rule of law and the mixed government they so much admired.

At the same time they shared with other Englishmen a concern to make England great by encouraging population, by raising the national prosperity, in only some few instances accepting, with Moyle, a responsibility for the welfare of unemployed and underprivileged, and by colonial expansion and the promotion of commerce and industry. There cannot be discovered a typical republican imperial ideology, but it is at least worth noticing that Harrington remarked that Rome in her rise to power proceeded by colonies, that Neville approved this activity of that 'most glorious' government and only regretted that, in the acquisition of the mainland behind the city islands of Venice, the Serene Republic had used mercenaries for conquests and failed to send out their own people for settlement. Moyle devoted several paragraphs to an admiring exposition of Roman colonial policy and the benefits it brought by rewarding veterans, guarding frontiers, settling otherwise malcontent persons, and thus increasing the total population of useful citizens. Until Trenchard wrote his perceptive essay in *Cato's Letters* on the plantations, the republicans were, like their contemporaries, mercantilist proponents of wealth and power, but they stressed the benefits obtained by spreading English liberties abroad and the trust thus incurred to rule well.

Republican Proposals

If fear of tyrannical rule was the predominant republican tenet, then the proposals to restrict the executive officer were the most important. These restrictions took various forms. Resistance rights were stressed; a bad king or magistrate could be resisted. Civil war was a disease, but tyranny, as Machiavelli had written, was the death of a state. The revolt of a whole people could not, Sidney declared, be called a rebellion. Any man might kill a tyrant. A Cromwell was as distasteful as a Stuart and bitterly reviled as betrayer of that Commonwealth so briefly set up. All Englishmen, even the bishops if driven too far, were potentially opponents of arbitrary power, but republicans extolled a rationale of resistance, and this was naturally a favourite topic with their critics. Sidney was condemned for an unpublished defence of rebellion, and admirers of Milton's poetry long felt obliged to proclaim dissociation with his defence of tyrannicide. Harrington, probably because he wanted to interest Cromwell in the role of Lycurgus and the establishment of Oceana, dwelt little upon the matter, and Neville, because of his observation of the indecisiveness and futility of the civil wars, pretended to disown the rebellious theories of men like Sa and

43

Mariana. Moyle stated flatly, better a factious liberty than a settled tyranny.

By the time that Moyle wrote, resistance had assumed a different form in England, though overseas revolutionary theories were to continue to influence malcontents, and were perhaps the republicans' chief contribution to politics. In England Commonwealthmen, like most others, condemned party, faction, bandings and alliances, especially when these seemed to promote internal dissension and further the ends of ministers, monarchs and other ambitious men. On the other hand, without some allowance for dissidents, it would be impossible to suggest remedies for the ills of the state. Machiavelli wrote that parties served to invigorate politics; Molesworth, in describing the effects of Danish absolutism, noted the apathy induced by a general conformity in religion and statecraft. All the town clocks of Copenhagen chimed in unison with the palace. Party was bad, if it meant the organization of men to further executive power or private gain, but essential if the undue exercise of that same power or ambition were to be thwarted. The republicans had no conception of the desirability of compromise and unity in the interests of their party, and, even in their hey-day, undoubtedly lost any advantage they might temporarily have had, by differences that, if we study them now in the pages of Ludlow or others, seem unimportant. But they affirmed belief in the right of free expression, and in the natural right of everyone to oppose the establishment. Thus, in the long run, republican insistence on diversity helped to develop a climate of opinion favourable to the growth of the later English party systems.

Tyrants could be resisted, and ministers criticized, but, if tumults were not to be multiplied, explicit limitations upon king and magistrate should be declared and generally understood. A general presumption that kings will govern well, Sidney wrote, was not a sufficient security to the people. Yet, to many an admirer of the English constitution, it was just the familiar phrase that the king had all possible power to do good, and, if law-abiding, none to do ill, that they approvingly repeated. The republican wanted laws and clearly defined restrictions. Civil commotion was a lesser evil than the threat posed by ill-defined sovereignty. Neville proposed to deprive the king of the power of war and peace, control over the armed forces, the appointment of ministers and creation of peers, the management of public finance, and the calling and dissolving of parliament. During the next two centuries the English head of state continually lost authority, but never by agreement between parliament and king, and seldom by legislative enactment. Englishmen generally disliked republican insistence upon definition. They did not, they often averred, want a Venetian doge, or a written constitution. They felt free to impose on the king reduction of the armed forces, an act for triennial or septennial parliaments, or even attempt a peerage bill. Impeachment, the accusatory power of parliament curtailing royal choice of ministers, was almost never used after the Revolution settlement, though public opinion, and that part of it represented in the Commons, played an increasing role in the selection and retention of executive officers. The monarch continued to direct or influence greatly the conduct of foreign policy, and, though complaints about the standing army long retained a popular appeal, the republican formula was not adopted. Even in another way, the cry against placemen, courtiers and pensioners—that is, the republican interest in separation of power and rotation of office—never found in England any real support, except in a rather vague limitation of the numbers of officials in the Commons and in occasional discussion of more frequently elected parliaments.

It could be argued that a good deal of what the republicans wanted found its way into practice, if not into those more specific laws that Moyle and his friends seem to have thought desirable. Yet the spirit of the constitution was different. There was a prejudice against anything that might hamper effective action in emergency, even among those entirely sceptical of divine right and unwilling to recognize an absolute sovereignty. The ruler, it was felt, should not exercise arbitrary power, but he must be able to act quickly and successfully. Republics and elective monarchies like Poland, at times Sweden, even the respected Dutch government, had been in the past reduced to confusion and suffered defeat because of a failure to allow enough discretionary authority to their officers. Restrictions could make that decisiveness essential to victory impossible. The fear of government that so marked republicans was much less important among their contemporaries than dread of anarchy.

If the executive were to be limited by law, that law must in turn be protected. Harrington suggested a small council to watch, for a given period of years, the infant state as he had designed it. Ludlow conceived of the same necessity. The ephors of Sparta and medieval officials like the Aragonese justiciars were mentioned by republicans with approval. The defeat of that official's purpose in protecting Antonio Perez against Philip II's wishes, with the aid of royal forces, possession of a sister kingdom and utilization of inquisitorial agents, meant, it was often pointed out, the end of the famous liberties of Aragon. Neville had brought forward Harrington's plan to parliament in 1659, but, when he wrote the third Dialogue in *Plato Redivivus* in 1680, he was thinking not in terms of *Oceana*, but of the exigencies of a critical moment in the fortunes of the restored monarchy. He then suggested, as Moyle did explicitly later, that in England and under these circumstances parliament, like ephors of old in Sparta, would act as the guardian of liberty. Also relating to this question was the discussion about the independence of the judges and their security of tenure, one of the few limitations of royal power achieved with general approval.

Sidney discussed, as a deterrent to despotic action, the oath of office taken by magistrates, which he regarded as a contract. If the 'Discourses' were complete they would contain more about Sidney's contractual theories, but these seem to have sprung less from an interest in the origin of government than from a belief that men enjoyed a natural right to select the rulers they chose and to judge when they had violated the trust which had been given them. Possibly the use made of a contract theory by Hobbes frightened Sidney out of any great stress on such agreements. Neville bothered little with the matter and Moyle less, though the latter paid tribute to Locke's 'A.B.C. of Politicks'.

In the mid-seventeenth century, republicans were among the first to put forward the doctrine of the separation of powers. The separation praised by Nedham, Milton, Harrington and, later, Locke concerned function. Each aspect of government activity—legislative, executive and eventually judicial (though that was for a long while conceived of as essentially executive in character)—should be clearly differentiated. The law-making body should not encroach upon the ministerial. Undue power in any part was thus prevented: neither magistrate nor parliament could usurp authority. The proponents of the older theory of mixed government regarded the checks and balances of different interests, popular, aristocratic, and monarchical, as safeguarding liberty. Harrington emphasized the balance of property in the general equilibrium of the state; too great a concentration of function in any person or body was dangerous, but in sum it was the balance of power and interest that his proposals were designed to maintain. Executive and legislature should be separate, but the famous agrarian regulation and limitation of property was to rectify the balance of those older interests in a mixed government which had become, because of shifting wealth, unbalanced and unrealistic. Neville spoke in Richard Cromwell's Parliament of the old 'trinity' of king, lords, commons. Levellers and writers like Stubbe were reproached for promoting single assemblies to run the state. Earlier, property had been concentrated in royal hands; then it had been held by the nobles; now with changing times the commons controlled the greater part and should then have the weightier role in affairs. There was thus a continuance of the theory of mixed government, along with a development, not very much stressed until after the Revolution, of a doctrine of the separation of power and a much greater emphasis upon the 'balance'. In the next century the newer theory received attention, and in France and America serious attempts were to be made to implement constitutionally this particular panacea for political problems.

In various ways—by rebellion, by opposition and discussion, by limitations enacted into law or preserved by definite agreement, by constant vigilance concerning the balance of interest and the separation of powers—the republicans proposed to prevent the executive becoming too powerful. Probably, had they been able, the first generation of republicans would have liked to gain acceptance for a written constitution spelling out the safeguards of liberty and providing protectors alerted to infringements of good laws and customs. The principle of liberty was constant, but, as Sidney had pointed out, times changed and with the times fashions of dress and of armament, and modes of government. All Commonwealthmen dwelt upon the good old laws, upon the natural rights enjoyed from immemorial days, some expressing nostalgia for feudal privileges and contracts, or even for the stirring period of the Roman Republic. Yet they also realized that changes in the distribution of wealth, in scientific invention and information, in acquaintance with other continents, inevitably brought about alterations in society, in the ratio of rich and poor, noble and gentle, and thus in the structure of the constitution. Political science was difficult and needed close study, and methods to renew and increase liberty in the light of changed need and circumstance must be investigated.

Machiavelli had recommended stocktaking and was often quoted. Harrington and Neville recognized the desirability of new modelling. Sidney spoke scornfully of outmoded systems. Renewal involved not only the recalling of virtuous men to their duty, and to the challenge of a Cannae or similar catastrophe; it also included alteration and improvement. Thus *Oceana* was justified, and so, too, were Neville's later suggestions for changes which his friends, in reading the Dialogues, recognized as extensive and surprising. Thoughtful persons, good men with the interests of their country at heart, had an obligation to involve themselves in such proposals. Neville told at length the story of the aloofness of a contemporary, probably Sir William Pierrepont, and his refusal, even though he had the ability, estate and the means to be useful, to offer any advice on public affairs. This was a horrible example of what had perhaps kept England from a readier solution to her problems. This lack of patriotic involvement was perhaps also that which Halifax noticed when discussing the reasons why England could never be a Commonwealth. Virtue was not merely a moral life but a life of service, a classical and renaissance ideal very fully appreciated by English republicans, and a justification for some of their more revolutionary suggestions. Constant appeals to old rights and good customs were no more important, perhaps much less so, than the belief that good men could devise ways to save their country.

Long after interest in constitutional reform had died down in a general complacency at having survived the troubled seventeenth century, the republicans maintained concern in various specifics to simplify the law, to increase the independence of the electorate by the ballot, to urge more frequent parliaments. The Commonwealthmen and their disciples felt sure that some rectification of constituency and franchise was desirable. Though they also continued to discuss an agrarian they never evolved another programme, and no definite proposals were brought forward for interference in the distribution of landed property. The empire of wealth became so much more complex that to enlist a part of it in the public service, and to equalize the disabilities resulting from a minor or non-existent share in it, presented problems which have not yet found a solution. The drastic suggestions of Thomas Spence and William Ogilvie towards the end of the eighteenth century for nationalization of land owed much to republican theories, but had even less chance than *Oceana* of being seriously considered in the realm of practical politics. The importance of discussions about an agrarian lay in the reminder they afforded that undue wealth in any single concentration must upset the social and political balance, a not unimportant contribution as the race for wealth and power became increasingly ruthless. The seventeenth-century republicans believed in property; that it was theft never occurred to them, nor did they for the most part subscribe to Christian doctrines of communal ownership. What concerned them was a due balance, and a recognition of the responsibility entailed by landed possessions. Except with respect to the resources afforded by commerce for the aggrandizement of the state, the republicans in the mid-seventeenth century were not concerned with private mercantile wealth, though their later disciples, like Moyle and Hutcheson, were increasingly interested.

As already noticed, the republicans were in no sense democratic. All mankind, the people, the country, whichever they wrote about, meant the independent, the well-to-do, the literate. They believed in representation, but not on a numerical basis. The old lords, when they owned the better part of the kingdom, had well represented their tenantry and had curbed royal excesses. Now the commons must do the same for the country. Reforms in franchise and constituency might be advocated, but at no time did republicans propose manhood suffrage, or even that approximation of it suggested by the Levellers. Their chief concern was to ensure that all the propertied classes voted. That servants, fishermen, labouring men and 'rabble' should exercise such a privilege was never conceived by them.

Civil and religious liberty was a phrase constantly upon the lips of republicans. Definitions of religious liberty varied. Puritan republicans wished to reform the church, though that sometimes seemed to others simply a substitution of one set of prejudices and ceremonies for another. Yet the beliefs of a Vane, a Milton or a Baxter led to increased emphasis on the rights of the individual with respect to his own salvation, as well as to a continuing opposition to the established church and to the claims of papists in any land. The fanatics and sectaries wished to set up their own forms of religious worship, sometimes for their own benefit only, and with the idea that all others or most others might worship as they pleased. The classical republicans were anti-clerical and free-thinking. They associated bishops and popes with protestant and catholic authoritarianism, with passive obedience and non-resistance.

They resented the near monopoly enjoyed by the church in matters educational. The universities, they declared, were full of supporters of divine right. The privileges enjoyed by clergy in church and state enabled them to broadcast such doctrines. Moreover, the clergy were tenacious of their special position, and intolerant of dissent.

The Commonwealthmen therefore found almost nothing to praise in the professed churchmen. If they conformed, they still lacked interest in doctrinal and organizational differences. Sometimes, like Anthony Collins the free-thinker, they may have felt some form of worship necessary for the morals of the uneducated. Religious liberty was a cardinal doctrine, but belief in it in secular or classical republicans sprang as much from distrust of any law but the natural law of reason, and dislike of fanatic, presbyterian, fifth-monarchy-man, Laudian or papist, as from any interest in personal revelation or in rule by the good. The church, as it existed anywhere it was established, had a vested interest in ceremonies and catechisms, in tithe, in apostolic succession. They did not deny a long history behind many claims; what they would not accept was their sacred character. Marvell, Neville, Locke, Moyle, and the independent Whig Trenchard, were determined to point out the clerical concern with divine right and with the evils of persecution that it too often brought. They admired the unsalaried, unprivileged 'diviners' of the Roman Republic; they wished that priests and ministers would keep out of politics and attend to their proper functions of prayer, admonition to good works, and to morality. Implicit faith, Sidney wrote, belonged to fools. The attempt to decide judgement about political problems by appeals to sacred law and established custom was an infringement of liberty.

Sources of Republican Thought

Most republicans agreed in declaring the debt they owed to ancient and modern prudence. Favourite classical writers and renaissance commentary upon them inspired admiration for the constitutions of republican Rome and of Sparta. At the same time, theories about natural law, in England often to be identified with belief in the rights of Englishmen, throve on the reaction provoked by ecclesiastical and secular claims to an authority unchecked by traditional privilege and customary restrictions. Arguments about resistance to commands running, it was asserted, counter to the law of God and of Nature stimulated also plans for ideal commonwealths. Libertarian literature was produced in many different areas and by catholics and protestants, humanists, historians and lawyers. Some writers were purely anti-quarian in intention; others had uppermost in mind opposition to papal or royal decrees, criticism of new economic inequalities, dislike of innovations. How many republicans there were in sixteenth- and seventeenth-century Europe is unknown; certainly there was no movement comparable to that of the late eighteenth century. All the same, there are many indications of discussions of republican government, and everywhere those who favoured it seem to have used the same books and similar historical examples.

Literate Europeans enjoyed some acquaintance with Plato and Aristotle, Polybius, Livy, Tacitus and Sallust. How far the familiar quotation or allusion denoted a close study of Plutarch and Cicero for example, or merely derived from a common fund of anecdote and aphorism, is not always easy to determine. Some were enormously well read in the originals; others were deeply informed in the political and historical literature of the last two centuries. He who wished could easily find support at first or second hand for republican speculations. The common education of the day ensured a ready appreciation in their audience of classical analogy and example. Here it is more profitable to leave aside comment upon Polybius, Tacitus and their peers, and to examine briefly what may be called the books of authority produced by modern prudence and to discuss some current interpretations of history. This will also take for granted the knowledge of the Bible and of the history and government of the Hebrews.

Of modern authorities, incomparably the most important was Machiavelli, and English republicans freely admitted an enormous debt to the *Discourses*. Harrington praised the Florentine; Moyle dubbed him 'divine'; Neville's edition of *The Works* was both a tribute to the master of political science and a means of continuing and extending his influence. Machiavelli expressed a preference for a republic; he pointed out the valour of the population in the days of Rome's greatness, that is, during the Republic, and the encouragement of the people by the easy naturalization of strangers, and by colonial enterprise. The clergy in those happy days enjoyed no great wealth or special favour, a citizen army defended the republic and extended its dominion. When catastrophe came, virtuous men renewed the first principles of liberty, and restored the state. Whenever men argued the relative merits of forms of government, those whose preference was for a republic cited Machiavelli.

The role of the Italian is, to be sure, confusing. Machiavelli had a bad name for a supposed exaltation of reasons of state over morality, and to this was added a support of doctrines subversive of church and state. Opponents of republicanism made no distinction between classical, Christian, oligarchical and levelling theories, and Machiavelli's reputation was as low with them as it was high with thoughtful Commonwealthmen. His influence cannot be exaggerated.

Of the multitude of authors inspired by the controversies of the times, one calvinist and one catholic may be mentioned as typical of many others, and themselves highly regarded by the republicans. Francis Hottoman or Hotman, a French protestant, published the *Franco Gallia* in 1574, a tract which was to be reprinted, translated and studied for very many years thereafter. In it were described ancient Frankish or Gothic liberties, elective monarchies and estates with reference to the history of France, but in the context of the history of similar institutions in England, Spain, Poland, Germany and elsewhere. *Franco Gallia* was a bible of republican medieval history. Others of his compatriots, the author of the *Vindiciae contra tyrannos*, the historians of the civil wars in France, and many more, found readers in England, but Hottoman must serve here as the chief example and his work stands high on the list of authorities.

Emanuel Sa, like Juan Mariana a jesuit, and like him an advocate of tyrannicide, was referred to by Neville as 'foolish', but his influence, that of the French monarchomachi, apologists for king-killing, and of the Scot, George Buchanan, must be remembered, when Sidney's defence of rebellion is investigated. In each division of the Christian church in western Europe, resistance rights, especially with reference to heretical rulers, were loudly claimed, and in this literature could be found plenty of ammunition for the republicans' battle with tyranny in the seventeenth century.

English republicans paid tribute to some men who were not so obviously connected with political and religious controversy. Francis Bacon, a noted Machiavellian, was often mentioned admiringly and most probably achieved reputation less as a statesman than as an

empiricist, a supporter of free enquiry, and as a believer in the possi-
bilities of scientific progress. All this enforced belief in man's right and
duty to consider political problems. Bacon added nothing to republican
selection of constitutional reforms, but his attitude could be assumed to
support their investigations. Another great contemporary or near
contemporary was Hugo Grotius, whose authority was to be used on
both sides of English controversies. Grotius believed in a natural law
based upon immutable right reason and supported contractual theories
of government. In matters of religious liberty he ranked with the less
dogmatic of the contenders at Dort, and his proofs of the truth of
the Christian religion, though widely esteemed, proved particularly
attractive to the liberals of the succeeding generations like the new
lights of Scotland, and others. Hardly any treatise on politics was
written without some reference to the great Dutchman.

John Selden also enjoyed a reputation by no means confined to one
coterie or school. He himself remained a moderate royalist and tolerant
anglican to the end of his life. But he had played a prominent role in the
contest about Stuart prerogative and he had written reasonably about
tithe and the episcopal succession. Selden believed in parliamentary
government, that is, in royal power exercised in partnership with the
two Houses; he supported the rule of law and the preservation of
property; he never acknowledged the divine right of anything or
anyone. All who lived virtuously would, he thought, achieve salvation
whatever their particular religious affiliation. Research into Hebrew
history and government brought him additional fame. Both Harrington
and Neville, among many others, were familiar with his learned account
of the Jewish Sanhedrim, and from this derived ideas about the nature
of the senate or peers' house. Selden's preferences may have been
rather different from those of the English republicans, but like Bacon
his attitude was congenial. He opposed all pretensions to any but a
reasonable authority, and this carried weight with those who feared
untrammelled executive power.

To such writers many more could be added, but these were most
important and representative of the authors whose work stimulated
republicanism. Tracts produced during the Conciliar controversies may
have been studied but, if they were, the influence is not immediately
apparent. In the same way the treatises of the protestant reformers, and
of John Calvin in particular, were widely read, but direct evidence of

any special contribution to the thought of Harrington, Sidney and Neville is lacking save where some specific reference is made to that catholic domination from which they had rescued a part of Europe. The republicans departed much further from tradition and from the dictates of ecclesiastical authority than Calvin, and had no sympathy whatever with Genevan organization. Legal and constitutional books and documents were cited, and the law of the land, the Great Charter, and the Petition of Right, referred to with reverence. As much or more attention was paid to the lessons of ancient and gothic history as to legalistic exposition. Natural rights and laws were more frequently appealed to than the protection afforded by common law and Westminster courts.

Interpretation of History

The most effective arguments of the republicans were those derived from their reading and interpretation of history. This may well explain a part of their continued ability to attract readers throughout the eighteenth century. The Whig historian owes at least as much to them as to the lawyers and antiquarians. The virtues of Roman republicanism and the freedom enjoyed in the 'German woods' were widely believed in, long after the schemes advocated in dialogues and discourses had ceased to be taken seriously. On the other hand, the very academic character of the lessons taught may well have diminished effective popular appeal. It was from this that both English utilitarian and American reacted as the nineteenth century began.

Machiavelli and Bacon both pronounced the study of history essential to the understanding of politics. The Commonwealthmen read about ancient republics and never stopped admiring the durability of Sparta and the greatness of Rome. Moyle's *Essay*, inspired of course in part by the discussions of his preceptors Machiavelli, Harrington, Sidney and Neville, was also based on his own extensive reading, and, as already noticed, started a whole series of similar investigations of Roman history designed to guide contemporary statesmen to the right policy and to the avoidance of old errors. Every solution to English problems offered by the republicans could be found in the history of the greatest republic, and of course the horrid moral of decline and fall caused by the failure to observe good laws, act patriotically, and maintain austerity in the face of growing luxury, was easy to apply to current developments.

54

The republicans did not neglect the history of what we now call the middle ages. Sidney exhaustively examined the fortunes of those gothic kingdoms which succeeded to lands once ruled by Rome. Many pronouncements about the propriety of change in government were based on examples from countries where royal succession had been altered as occasion demanded. In these nations councils of nobles developed into the estates of the realm. Sidney pointed out the wide use of Monsieur in France, Signore in Italy, Herr in Holland and Baron in England. Neville also described the role of nobility, expressed some doubts about the supposed antiquity of the Commons, but allowed himself to be persuaded that in some form parliament had always existed. Fletcher dwelt upon the advantages of the people, that is, the nobles being armed to protect the country and secure their rights. Much of his tract against standing armies reads like a defence of the feudal system. Neville attached more importance to the fact that the nobles had lost their old precedency and that the commons were now their logical successors. Failure to adjust to this new situation had already proved fatal to peace.

Neville and Harrington, as they studied history and particularly recent history, saw an opportunity for new modelling or drastic alteration. Fletcher almost seems to have preferred to hark back. But almost all republicans were agreed on the astonishing changes that had taken place in Europe during the last two hundred years. The precise date for that transformation might vary; Neville fixed it at Bosworth in 1485; Fletcher in the several events of the fifteenth century associated with the revival of letters—the inventions of the printing press and the mariner's compass, the fall of Constantinople and the discoveries of Columbus. Others pointed to the grant of the *taille* to the French King as the Hundred Years War reached a critical stage, enabling him to keep at pleasure a mercenary army long after a victorious peace was concluded; others recalled the end of the liberties of Aragon. Any and all of these occasions gave rise to alterations fatal to ancient freedom and favourable to boundless prerogative. For Sidney and Neville, the recent revolution in Denmark, later so vividly described by Molesworth, also translator of the *Franco Gallia*, was the latest horrid example of these sad changes. Even more poignant to the two republicans was the betrayal of the English Commonwealth by Cromwell and his army.

Explanations of the disappearance of gothic liberty varied in detail but in general were remarkably similar. The same neglect they discovered in Rome of old laws and institutions, the development of new theories of authority, the growth of luxury and the decline of virtue, the increasing use of mercenary rather than citizen armies—all these had brought about the opportunity for unscrupulous rulers to seize power. An expanding economy provided kings with fresh sources of funds with which to hire troops and pursue independent courses. Everywhere authority had grown at the expense of liberty, and the dislocation of the social balance had left the people without protection from duly established institutions and persons.

The Commonwealthmen looked back to a freedom which had scarcely existed as they imagined it, whatever the country described. But in re-reading the republican tracts this consideration should not be allowed to conceal the continual references, not to the revival of gothic institutions, but to the necessity for devising others to suit the new age. Practice must adapt to changing circumstance even while principle remained constant. Rome's decline came not from a failure to return to the situation of the early republic but from a failure to fit the good habits then developed to an expanding empire. Misunderstanding of royal purpose in 1660 had led the Danes into the fatal mistake of abandoning elective monarchy and thus their bargaining power with the King. The republicans intended not to reverse historical process, but to observe and learn by it how best to circumvent the situations which over-ambitious monarch or indolent subject might create.

Influence and Significance

English political literature would be infinitely the poorer had the Commonwealthmen never written. Their work enjoyed a circulation in the British Isles, North America and France, and was studied until well into the nineteenth century. Webster and Barère preferred Moyle to Montesquieu; Jefferson and Adams admired Harrington and Sidney and listed with them Neville, Bacon, Locke, Milton, Nedham and Benjamin Hoadley. Gentz compared Sidney to Xenophon; Niebuhr continually re-read the *Discourses*. That republicans were read and often admired is demonstrable; the effects of that veneration upon political achievement is less easy to discover.

56

In England the republicans reinforced a national love of liberty, and in certain ways already noticed—the attitude to a standing army, the separation of powers, annual parliaments and extension of civil and religious liberty—provided favourite slogans and devices when the establishment seemed less than usually effective or more than justifiably powerful. They had some effect upon men seeking for solutions to national and social problems. Francis Hutcheson found in them support for many of his ideas. Thomas Spence found in them encouragement of his projects. That such men, and others afterwards, accepted the challenge of changed times, and developed quite different and novel ways of adaptation to them, is at least partially due to pronouncements not always understood in their contemporary context, but stimulating to lovers of liberty. Political theories must be examined, when their influence is considered, in the light of later readers and interpreters, as well as in that of the life and times which produced them. In spite of the apparent futility of their efforts, the English republicans can fairly be placed in the continuing liberal tradition of the western world. In this context the Good Old Cause of liberty against tyrants is never lost, and its prophets and martyrs always deserving of honour.

While the eighteenth-century Commonwealthmen continued to extend the areas of proposed reformation in all good faith, if with little result, it is also true that others in opposition to the current ministry, but in no way innovators or reformers, cried out against placemen, septennial parliaments and similar grievances and fill the parliamentary records. Writers, native and foreign, often assumed the actual existence of desired effects, like the separation of powers put forward originally by republicans, even when it was obviously ignored, or distorted, and contrary practice could be observed. Limitation of royal prerogative and extension of parliamentary authority came about without those checks on executive action which the republicans wished to see. Opposition, even resistance rights, as Halévy pointed out, were in a manner accepted, but as much from the circumstances of party rivalry as from those rights claimed by Sidney. At no time during the Interregnum, the Exclusion crisis, or the Revolution following the flight of James, were the republicans successful in constitutional achievement.

Abroad, in France and America, some parts of their programme were incorporated into confederacy and constitution. Serious attempts were

57

made to separate functions of government, prevent the development of party, and restrict executive power. When in France the republicans enjoyed a revival, the Revolution which brought them renewed popularity soon created its own ideology and its own definitions, of the people for example, very different from those of the Commonwealthmen. Numerical criteria and changed expectations unfolded along with increased emphasis upon democracy and posed problems for which the principles of the earlier republicans had offered no solution. Nor could these gifted Englishmen have foreseen the changed character of society as industry revolutionized much of their world. They had not conceived of government in the terms forced during the nineteenth and twentieth centuries upon statesmen and political theorists.

Though, like the French, American republicanism was, in the long run, to develop along lines very different from those taken for granted by their English predecessors, yet the constitution of 1787 was and remains the Commonwealthmen's most lasting memorial. The rule of law, secured by a written constitution, and eventually by a bill of rights; by checks and balances; by separation of powers; and these all in turn guarded by the ephors of a supreme court, would surely have delighted the seventeenth-century republicans. They would have been surprised of course, but perhaps not altogether disconcerted, by the greater participation of the people in policy decisions, by an extending franchise, and by the evolution of a less hierarchical society brought about by the indigenous circumstance of the New World. They would have commended the divorce of church and state, and would have approved the many restraints upon government at state and federal levels. Whether they would have approved the criticisms of Thomas Jefferson and John Taylor, or would have recognized the necessities perceived by the authors of *The Federalist*, none can tell, but certainly in the enactments of several state constitutions in 1776, as well as in the United States constitutional convention of 1787, the republicans would have found much for which they could justly claim credit.

Republican proposals in their own time and country remained unfulfilled. The Commonwealth of 1649 was established by the abolition of monarchy and the upper house, and by the election each year, in the Rump of the Long Parliament, of a Council of State. A new seal and new terms were used in official communications. After victories in Scotland and Ireland, Cromwell tired of the discussions in the Rump, rudely ejected it from St Stephen's and brought about the existence of the experimental Parliament of Saints. After a few argumentative months this too was disbanded and the Protectorate set up. With the removal of Richard, the Rump reassembled and elected a new Council of State until it was in turn overthrown by army dissidents. When these were overthrown, the Rump and a new Council briefly took over the government. This familiar story bears repetition here only to emphasize the fact that the republicans never tried out a new model, only temporary adjustments. Disestablishment of the church, reform of law, of constituency and franchise talked about in the army councils before the Commonwealth, found some expression in acts and ordinances of Commonwealth as well as Protectorate. But the rule of Oliver, whose control of the army enabled him to be at least partially effective, was more fruitful than that of the republicans. Harrington hoped to persuade the Protector to set up an *Oceana*: Neville attempted to gain consideration of the whole matter of government in 1659 by Richard Cromwell's Parliament and by the restored Rump; neither accomplished anything.

In suggesting the limits of the direct influence of the Commonwealth-men, we must also consider contemporary explanations of failure. Near the end of his life, in 1694, George Saville, marquis of Halifax, wrote *A Rough Draft of a New Model at Sea*, in which he examined the relative advantages of promotion in the navy of 'tarpaulins', common sailors, or 'gentlemen', and, as he did so, found it appropriate to explain the English form of government. England must be ruled, he wrote, by an absolute king, not to be confused with a despotism, or by a mixed monarchy, or by a commonwealth. The English could not now be ruled by the first, nor by the third, but would, he prophesied, continue, with the changes made necessary by time, to be governed by a 'bounded' monarchy. Perhaps his conversations with William III led him to expatiate at rather greater length on the reasons why England would not accept a republic, something which the Dutch ruler evidently believed a possibility. There was, Halifax explained, a general dislike of a commonwealth, and the 'herd' was entirely against it. The preparations necessary for effecting so great a change had never been made. Such a fabric of government demanded virtue, morality, diligence, or, he continued with the wry humour of the 'Trimmer', hypocrisy. These things being wanting, he deduced that 'A commonwealth is not fit for us, because we are not fit for a commonwealth'.

PLATO
REDIVIVUS:
OR, A
DIALOGUE
CONCERNING
Government,

Wherein, by Obſervations drawn from
other K I N G D O M S and
S T A T E S both Ancient and Modern, an Endeavour is uſed to diſ-
cover the preſent POLITICK
DISTEMPER of our OWN,
with the CAUSES, and RE-
MEDIES.

Non Ego ſum Vates, ſed Priſci conſcius ævi.
Pluribus exemplis hæc tibi Myſta Cano.
Res nolunt male adminiſtrari.

The Second Edition, with Additions.

LONDON,
Printed for *S. I.* and Sold by *R. Dew*, 1681.

Non ego sum vates, sed prisci conscius aevi,
Pluribus exemplis haec tibi mysta cano.
Res nolunt male administrari.

I am no prophet, but know about times past and, a priest of the mysteries, sing of many examples for you. ‡ A government cannot subsist long under an ill administration.

‡ Note to translation: this is Moyle's rendering (*The Whole Works*, p. 60) of the last line, said by him to have been a favourite saying of Harley's. Harley's Latin differs slightly from that appearing on the title-page of all editions of *Plato Redivivus* (except that of 1698, which omitted the whole quotation) and runs: *Res nolunt administrari diu.*

Contents

Political Discourses and Histories   *page* 65
   worth Reading

The Publisher to the Reader   67

The Argument   71

The First Dialogue   73

The Second Dialogue   79

The Third Dialogue   152

Political Discourses and Histories worth reading

[prefaced to the second edition of *Plato Redivivus*, 1681]

1. The Works of the famous Nicholas Machiavel, Citizen and Secretary of Florence, containing, 1. The History of Florence. 2. The Prince. 3. The Original of the Guelf and Ghibilin Factions. 4. The Life of Castruccio Castracani. 5. The Murther of Vitelli, &c. by Duke Valentino. 6. The State of France. 7. The State of Germany. 8. The Discourses on Titus Livius. 9. The Art of War. 10. The Marriage of Belphegor, a Novel. 11. Nicholas Machiavel's Letter, in Vindication of himself and his writings: All written in Italian, and from thence newly and faithfully Translated into English. In Folio, Price Bound, 16s. [Ed. H. Neville, 1675.]

2. I Ragguagli di Parnasso; or Advertisements from Parnassus, in two Centuries, with the Politick Touchstone, written Originally in Italian, By that Noble Roman Trajano Boccalini. Englished by the Earl of Monmouth: In Folio, Price bound 8s. [1674.]

3. The History of the Affairs of Europe, in this present age, but more particularly of the Republick of Venice, written in Italian, by Battista Nani, Cavalier and Procurator of St Mark: Englished by Sir Robert Honiwood, Knight; in Folio, price bound 12s. [1673.]

4. The History of the Government of Venice, wherein the Policies, Councils, Magistrates, and Laws of that State are fully related, and the use of the Balloting Box, exactly described: Written in the Year 1675, in Octav. Price bound 3s. [Abraham Nicolas Amelotte de la Houssaye, tr. 1677.]

5. The History of the Turkish Empire, from the year 1623, to the year 1677, containing the Reigns of the three last Emperours, viz. Sultan Morat, Sultan Ibrahim, and Sultan Mahomet 4th, his Son, the 13th Emperour now Reigning: By Paul Rycaut, Esq; late Consul of Smyrna. In Folio, Price bound 14s. [1680.]

6. The present State of the Ottoman Empire in 3 Books, containing the Maximes of the Turkish Polity, their Religion and Military Discipline, Illustrated with divers Figures. Written by Paul Rycaut, Esq; late Secretary to the English Ambassadour there, and since Consul of Smyrna. The Fourth Edition, in Octavo. Price bound 5s. [1672.]

7. The Memoires of Philip de Commines Lord of Argenton, containing the History of Lewis XI. and Charles VIII, Kings of France, with the most remarkable occurrences in their particular Reigns, from the Year 1464, to 1498, Revised and Corrected by Denis Godfrey, Councellour and Historiographer to the French King, and from his Edition lately Printed at Paris, newly Translated into English, in Octav. Price bound 5s. [1674.]

8. The History of France, under the Ministry of Cardinal Mazarine, viz. from the Death of King Lewes XIII, to the year 1664, wherein all the Affairs of State to that time are exactly Related: By Benjamine Priolo, and faithfully Englished, by Christopher Wase, Gent. in Octav. Price bound 4s. [1671.]

9. The Present State of the United Provinces of the Low Countries, as to the Government, Laws, Forces, Riches, Manners, Customes, Revenue, and Territory of the Dutch; Collected out of divers Authors: By W. A. Fellow of the Royal Society, the Second Edition in twelves: Price bound 2s. 6d. [Wm. Aglionby, 1670.]

10. The Present State of the Princes and Republicks of Italy, the Second Edition enlarged, with the manner of Election of Popes, and a Character of Spain. Written Originally in English by J. Gailhard, Gent. in twelves. Price bound 1s. 6d. [1668.]

11. The Policy and Government of the Venetians, both in Civil and Military Affairs: Written in French by the Sieur de la Hay, and faithfully Englished, in 12s. Price bound 1s. [1671.]

12. The Secret History of the Court of the Emperour Justinian, giving a true account of the Debaucheries thereof: Written in Greek, by Procopius of Cæsarea; faithfully Englished, in Octav. Price bound 1s. 6d. [1674.]

The Publisher to the Reader

Courteous Reader,

All the account I can give thee of this piece, is; that about the middle of October last[1] it was sent to me; accompanied with a letter without a name, and written in a hand altogether unknown to me; though different from the character of the dialogue itself, and the argument. The letter was very short; and contained only, that the writer having the fortune to meet with this discourse, (of which he denied to be the author,) he thought it very fit to be sent to me, to the end if I thought it could be of any advantage to me and no prejudice, I might publish it if I pleased and make my best of it. When I had opened it, and perceived that it treated of government, and of the present times; I (supposing it to be something of the nature of those scurrilous libels, which the press spawns every day) was extremely displeased with my servant, for receiving in my absence and in these dangerous days, such a packet; without taking any account or notice of the messenger who brought it: till he, to appease me, assured me, that the bearer did look like a gentleman, and had a very unsuitable garb to a trepan, and that he did believe he had seen him often at my shop, and that I knew him well. When I had begun to read it, and found no harm; I was resolved to peruse it in the company of a gentleman, a worthy friend of mine; who, to his exact skill and learning in the laws of his country, has added a very profound knowledge in all other literature; and particularly the excellence of platonic philosophy. When we had jointly gone through it, he was clearly of opinion; that although some might be angry with certain passages in it, yet the discourse reflecting upon no particular person, was very incapable of bringing me into any danger for publishing it; either from the state, or from any private man. When I had secured myself against the resulting loss, we went about the consideration of the other part of the distinction of the schools, which is lack of

[1] On the strength of this reference, Thomas Hollis, 'editor' of the fourth edition, asserts that Neville's tract appeared in October 1680, but the material in Crino (2) (*passim* and p. 255) suggests that both first and second editions appeared early in 1681. Three of Charles II's five Parliaments brought in exclusion bills to bar James of York from the throne, the Habeas Corpus (6 March–27 May 1679), the Westminster referred to here (21 October 1680–18 January 1681) and the Oxford (21–28 March 1681).

profit:[1] and I made some objections against the probability of vending this dialogue to profit; which, in things of my trade, is always my design, as it ought to be. My first fear in that behalf was, that this author would disgust the reader, in being too confident and positive in matters of so high a speculation. My friend replied; that the assurance he showed was void of all sauciness, and expressed with great modesty: and that he verily believed, that he meant very faithfully and sincerely towards the interest of England. My next doubt was; that a considerable part of this treatise being a repetition of a great many principles and positions out of *Oceana*, the author would be discredited for borrowing from another and the sale of the book hindered. To that my friend made answer; that before ever *Oceana* came out, there were very many treatises and pamphlets which alleged the political principle, that empire was founded in property, and discoursed rationally upon it: amongst the rest, one entitled *A Letter from An Officer in Ireland, to his Highness the Lord Protector* (which he then showed me) printed in 1653,[2] as I remember; which was more than three years before *Oceana* was written; and yet, said he, no man will aver that the learned gentleman who writ that book had stolen from that pamphlet: for whosoever sets himself to study politics, must do it by reading history, and observing in it the several turns and revolutions of government; and then the cause of such change will be so visible and obvious, that we need not impute theft to any man that finds it out: it being as lawful and as easy for any person, as well as for the author of *Oceana*, or that pamphlet, to read Thucydides, Polybius, Livy or Plutarch; and if he do so with attentiveness, he shall be sure to find the same things there that they have found. And if this were not lawful, when that any one person has written in any science, no man must write after him; for in polity, the orders of government; in architecture, the several orders of pillars, arches, architraves, cornices, &c; in physic, the causes, prognostics and crisis of diseases, are so exactly the same in all writers, that we may as well accuse all subsequent authors to have been

---

[1] 'Resulting loss'—from government action; 'lack of profit'—from poor sales.
[2] *A Copy of a Letter from an Officer of the Army in Ireland to his Highness, the Lord Protector...* (London, 1656) (B.M. press mark 4157/28) is signed R.G. and dated from Waterford, 24 June 1654, two years before publication. The tract has been ascribed to Neville himself, to John Wildman, or some other Harringtonian who had already read *Oceana*, published in the autumn of 1656 (Zagorin, *History of Political Thought*, p. 150 and n.). The style is not very reminiscent of Neville, but could perhaps be that of Edmund Ludlow.

but plagiaries of the antecedent. Besides this the learned gentleman added: that *Oceana* was written (it being thought lawful so to do in those times) to evince out of these principles, that England was not capable of any other government than a democracy; and this author out of the same maxims or aphorisms of politics, endeavours to prove, that they may be applied naturally and fitly to the redressing and supporting one of the best monarchies in the world, which is that of England. I had but one doubt more, and that was an objection against the title; which I resolved, at the first, not to mention; because I could salve it by altering the title page: But since I had opportunity, I acquainted the gentleman with it and it was, that certainly no man would ever buy a book that had in the front of it so insolent and presumptuous a motto, as *Plato Redivivus*; for that he must needs be thought not only vain in the highest degree, but void of sense and judgement too, who compares himself with Plato; the greatest philosopher, the greatest politician (I had almost said the greatest divine too) that ever lived. My counsellor told me, that he had as great a resentment of any injury done to Plato as I, as any man could have: but that he was hard to believe, that this man intended to compare himself to Plato, either in natural parts or learning; but only to show that he did imitate his way of writing, as to the manner of it, (though not the matter) as he has done exactly. For Plato ever writ these high matters in easy and familiar dialogues; and made the philosophers, and learned men of that age; as Simmias, Cebes, Timæus, Callias, Phaedon, &c, yea and Socrates himself, the interlocutors; although they never heard anything of it till the book came out; and although talking of state-affairs in a monarchy must needs be more offensive, than it was in the democracy where Plato lived; therefore our author has forborne the naming the persons who constitute this dialogue: yet he does make a pretty near representation and character of some persons, who (I dare swear) never heard of this discourse, nor of the author's design. This convinced me, and made me suffer the title to pass. So that I have nothing more to say to thee, courteous reader, but to desire thee to pardon the faults in printing; and also the plainness and easiness of the style, and some tautologies: which latter I could easily have mended, but that I thought the author did not let them pass out of neglect, but design; and intended that both they, and the familarity of the words and expressions, suited better with his purpose of disposing this matter

69

to be treated in ordinary conversation amongst private friends, than full periods and starched language would have done; which might have been impropriety. The next request I have to thee is: that if thou do believe this discourse to be a very foolish one, as it may be for aught I know, (for I am no fit judge of such matters) that thou wilt yet vouchsafe to suspend thy censure of it for a while, till the whole impression is vended; that so, although neither the public nor thyself may ever reap any benefit or profit by it, I may be yet so fortunate by thy favour as to do it: which will make me study thy content hereafter in something better, and in the mean time remain,

Thy Friend and Servant.

The Argument

A Noble Venetian,[1] (not one of the young fry, but a grave, sober person who had born office and magistracy in his own commonwealth,) having been some years since in France, with a near relation of his who was ambassador at that court, and finding himself out of employment; resolved to divert himself, by visiting some part of the world which he had never seen: and so passing through Germany, Flanders, and Holland, arrived in England, about the beginning of May last; bringing letters of recommendation to several English gentlemen, who had been travellers, and made friendship in his country: a custom, usually practised amongst such who travel into any part, where they have no habitude or acquaintance. Amongst the rest, he was addressed to one of the gentlemen who acts a part in this dialogue. Who, after he had waited upon him and served him for near two months, had certain necessary occasions, which called him for some time into the country: where he had not been above three weeks, before he heard, by mere accident, that the gentleman of Venice was fallen dangerous sick of a malignant fever: which made him post away immediately to London, to assist and serve him in what he might. But he found him almost perfectly restored to his health, by an eminent physician[2] of our nation; as renowned for his skill and cures at home, as for his writings both here and abroad: and who (besides his profound knowledge in all learning as well in other professions as his own) had particularly arrived to so exact and perfect a discovery of the formerly hidden parts of human bodies; that every one, who can but understand Latin, may by his means know more of anatomy, than either Hippocrates, or any

---

[1] 'A Noble Venetian' has not been identified, but Ludwig Bittner and Lothar Gross, *Repertorium der diplomatischen Vertreter*... (Berlin, 1936, p. 549), lists many noble names employed at Paris such as Contarini (1676–9), A. Giustiniani (1673–6).

[2] The Doctor is Richard Lower (1631–91), trained at Oxford, known as the 'Aesculapius of his age'. Lower attended Charles II, though he consorted with the politicians of the Grecian. His charity was famous and his publications numerous. *Tractatus de Corde* (1669; 4th ed. 1680) was among those books dispatched by Neville to Cosmo. Harvey was long since dead, and had, besides, studied at Padua, which the Doctor denies having done (see p. 107 below). Locke, another suggested 'Doctor', had by 1680 little by way of publication, and had been abroad already for many months.

71

of the ancients or moderns, did or do perceive: and if he had lived in the days of Solomon, that great philosopher would never have said, the heart of man is inscrutable. This excellent doctor being in the sick man's chamber, when the other English gentleman newly alighted, came to visit him; after some compliments and conversation of course, they began to talk of political matters: as you will better understand, by the introduction and by the discourse itself.

The First Dialogue

ENGLISH GENTLEMAN.[2] The sudden news I had of your sad distemper, and the danger you were in, has been the cause of a great deal of affliction to me; as well as of my present and speedy repair to London, some weeks sooner than I intended. I must confess I received some comfort to hear at my arrival of your amendment; and do take much more now to find you up, and as I hope recovered: which I knew would be a necessary consequence of your sending for this excellent physician, the Aesculapius of our age; it being the first request I had to make to you, if by seeing him here in your chamber I had not found it needless. For the destiny of us Englishmen depends upon him; and we either live or die infallibly, according to the judgement or good fortune we have when we are sick, either to call or not call him to our assistance.

NOBLE VENETIAN. I am infinitely obliged to you, for your care of me; but am sorry it has been so inconvenient to you, as to make you leave your affairs in the country sooner than you proposed to yourself to do. I wish I might be so fortunate in the course of my life, as to find an opportunity of making some part of an acknowledgement, for this and all the rest of your favours; but shall pray God it may not be in the same kind: but that your health may ever be so entire, that you never need so transcendent a charity, as I now receive from your goodness. And as to this incomparable doctor; although, I must confess, that all the good which has happened to me in this country, as well as the knowledge I have received of persons and things, does derive from you; yet I must make an exception, as to this one point: for if I can either read or hear, this gentleman's excellent writings, and the fame he worthily enjoys in my country, would have made it inexcusable in me to implore the help of any other. And I do assure you, that, before I left England, it was in my ambition to beg your mediation towards the bringing me into the acquaintance and favour of this learned person;

[1] In all editions before that of 1742, and the second Dublin reprint of 1758, this is 'The First Day' under which is 'The Introduction'. Dialogue II and Dialogue III were the 'second' and 'third' days.
[2] The English Gentleman is obviously Neville himself: see p. 75, n.1, below.

73

even before I had any thoughts of becoming the object of his care and skill, as now I am the trophy of both.

DOCTOR. Well, gentlemen, you are both too great to be flatterers, and I too little to be flattered; and therefore I will impute this fine discourse you both make about me, to the overflowing of your wit, and the having no object near you to vent it upon but me. And for you, sir, if my art fail me not, the voiding this mirth is a very good sign that you are in a fair way to a perfect recovery. And for my countryman here, I hope whilst he has this vent, that his hypochondriac distemper will be at quiet; and that neither his own thoughts, nor the ill posture of our public affairs, will make him hang himself, for at least this twelve-month. Only, gentlemen, pray take notice, that this does not pass upon me, nor do I drink it like milk (as the French phrase it;) being mindful of what a grave gentleman at Florence replied to a young esquire, (who answered his compliments with, 'Oh, sir, you flatter me,') —'The principle of flattery is that your equals understand you'.[1] That last word I cannot render well into Latin.

ENG. GENT. Well, doctor, we will not offend your modesty: the next time we do you justice, it shall be behind your back, since you are so severe upon us. But you may assure yourself, that my intention of recommending you to this gentleman, was for his own sake and not for yours: for you have too many patients already; and it were much better, both for you and us, that you had but half so many: for then we should have more of your writings, and sometimes enjoy your good conversation; which is worth our being sick on purpose for: and I am resolved to put my self sometimes into my bed, and send for you, since you have done coming to our coffee-house.[2]

But to leave this subject now, I hear you say, that this gentleman is in a perfect way of recovery: pray is he well enough to hear, without any prejudice to his convalescence, a reprehension I have to make him?

DOCT. Yes, yes, you may say what you will to him; for your reprimands will rather divert than trouble him, and prove more a cordial than a corrosive.

ENG. GENT. Then, sir, pray consider what satisfaction you can ever make me for the hard measure you have used towards me, in letting me learn from common fame and fortune, the news of your sickness,

---

[1] *I principi s'adulano, i pari vostri si coglionono*—freely translated.
[2] 'Our coffee-house'—probably the Grecian, frequented by both Neville and Lower.

and that not till your recovery; and for depriving me of the opportunity of paying the debt I owe to your own merit, and to the recommendation of those worthy persons in Italy, who did me the honour to address you to me. And this injury is much aggravated by the splendour of your condition, and greatness of your fortune; which makes it impossible for me ever to hope for any other occasion to express my faithful service to you, or satisfy any part of the duty I have to be at your devotion. To be sick in a strange country, and to distrust the sincerity and obedience of—

NOBLE VEN. Pray, sir, give me leave to interrupt you, and to assure you, that it was not any distrust of your goodness to me, of which I have had sufficient experience; nor any insensibleness how much your care might advantage me; much less any scruple I had of being more in your debt; which if it had been possible for me to entertain, it must have been thought of long since, before I had received those great obligations, which I never made any difficulty to accept of. It was not, I say, any of these considerations, which hindered me from advertising you of my distemper; but the condition and nature of it, which in a moment deprived me of the exercise of those faculties which might give me a capacity of helping myself in any thing. But otherwise I assure you that no day of my life shall pass, wherein I will not express a sense of your favours; and—

DOCT. Pray now, sir, permit me to interrupt you; for this gentleman, I dare say, looks for no compliments: but that which I have to say, is; that the desire you signified to me, to give you some account of our affairs here, and the turbulency of our present state, will be much better placed, if you please to address it to this gentleman, whose parts and studies have fitted him for such an employment; besides his having had a great share in the managing affairs of state here, in other times: and really no man understands the government of England better than he.[1]

ENG. GENT. Now doctor, I should tell you, those who are my equals understand me;[2] for so you yourself have baptized this kind of civility. But however, this is a province that I cannot be reasonably pressed to take upon me, whilst you are present; who are very well known to be as skilful in the nature and distemper of the body politic, as the whole nation confesses you to be in the concerns of the natural. And you would

[1] Neville had been on the Council of State (1651–2, 1659–60), and had been a member of parliament as a recruiter for the Long Parliament, and for Richard Cromwell's Parliament.
[2] *I pari miei si coglionono.*

have good store of practice in your former capacity, if the wise custom amongst the ancient Greeks were not totally out of use. For they, when they found any craziness or indisposition in their several governments, before it broke out into a disease, did repair to the physicians of state (who, from their profession, were called the seven wise men of Greece;) and obtained from them some good recipes, to prevent those seeds of distemper from taking root, and destroying the public peace. But in our days, these signs or forerunners of diseases in state are not foreseen, till the whole mass is corrupted; and that the patient is incurable, but by violent remedies. And if we could have perceived the first symptoms of our distemper, and used good alternatives, the curiosity of this worthy gentleman had been spared, as also his command to you to give him some light into our matters; and we unfortunate Englishmen had reposed in that quiet, ease, and security, which we enjoyed three hundred years since. But let us leave the contest who shall inform this gentleman, lest we spend the time we should do it in unprofitably, and let each of us take his part; for if one speak all, it will look like a studied discourse fitted for the press, and not a familiar dialogue. For it ought to be in private conversation, as it was originally in the planting the gospel; when there were two sorts of preaching: the one concionary,[1] which was used by the apostles and other missionaries, when they spoke to those who had never heard of the mysteries of Christian religion; possibly not so much, as of the Jewish law or the history of Christ; the duty of those was to hear, and not reply, or any way interrupt the harangue: but when the believers (called the church) assembled together, it was the custom of such of the auditors to whom any thing occurred, or (as saint Paul calls it) was revealed, to interpose and desire to be heard; which was called an interlocutory preaching, or religious conversation: and served very much to the instructing and edifying those who had long believed in Christ, and possibly knew as much of him as their pastor himself; and this is used still amongst many of our independent congregations.

DOCT. I have (besides the reason I alleged before, and which I still insist upon) some other cause to beg that you will please to give yourself the trouble of answering this gentleman's queries; which is, that I am very defective in my expressions in the Italian language: which though I understand perfectly, and so comprehend all that

---

[1] 'Concionary'—pertaining to an oratorical assembly or meeting.

either of you deliver; yet I find not words at hand to signify my own meaning, and am therefore necessitated to deliver my self in Latin, as you see. And I fear that our pronunciation being so different from that which is used in Italy, this worthy person may not so easily comprehend what I intend, and so be disappointed in the desire he has to be perfectly instructed in our affairs.[1]

NOBLE VEN. Really, sir, that is not all; for besides that, I confess your pronunciation of the Latin tongue to be very new to me, and for that reason I have been forced to be troublesome to you, in making you repeat things twice, or thrice. I say besides that, your Latinity, (as your writings show and all the world knows) is very pure and elegant: which it is notorious to all, that we in Italy scarce understand; gentlemen there never learning more Latin, than what is necessary to call for meat and drink, in Germany or Holland, where most of the hosts speak a certain Franck, compounded of Dutch, Latin, and Italian. And though some of us have Latin enough to understand a good author, (as you have of our language) yet we seldom arrive to speak any better than this Franck; or can without study comprehend good Latin, when we meet with it in discourse. And therefore it is your perfection in that tongue, and my ignorance in it, that makes me concur with you, in desiring this gentleman to take the pains of instructing my curiosity in Italian.

ENG. GENT. I shall obey you in this, and all things else, upon this condition, that both you and the doctor will vouchsafe to interrogate me, and by that means give me the method of serving you in this: and then that you will both please to interrupt and contradict me, when you think I say any thing amiss, or that either of you are of a different opinion; and to give me a good occasion of explaining myself, and possibly of being convinced by you, which I shall easily confess; for I hate nothing more than to hear disputes amongst gentlemen and men of sense, wherein the speakers seem (like sophisters in a college) to dispute rather for victory, than to discover and find out the truth.

DOCT. Well, all this I believe will be granted you; so that we have nothing to do now, but to adjourn, and name a time when to meet again. Which I, being this gentleman's physician, will take upon me to appoint: and it shall be tomorrow morning about nine of the clock, after he has slept well; as I hope he will, by means of a cordial I intend

---

[1] Latin was pronounced so differently by Englishmen, that continental Europeans had difficulty in following this common language! See W. Sidney Allen, *Vox Latina* (Cambridge, 1965), pp. 102 ff.

to send him immediately. In the mean time, not to weary him too much, we will take our leaves of him for this night.

NOBLE VEN. I shall expect your return with great impatience; and if your cordial be not very potent, I believe the desire of seeing you will make me wake much sooner than the hour you appoint: and I am very confident, that my mind as well as my body, will be sufficiently improved by such visits. It begins to be darkish; boy, light your torch, and wait on these gentlemen down.

BOTH. Sir, we wish you all good rest and health.

NOBLE VEN. And I, with a thousand thanks, the like to you.

The Second Dialogue

DOCT. Well, sir, how is it? have you rested well to night? I fear we come too early.

NOBLE VEN. Dear doctor, I find myself very well, thanks to your care and skill; and have been up above these two hours, in expectation of the favour you and this gentleman promised me.

DOCT. Well, then pray let us leave off compliments and repartees (of which we had a great deal too much yesterday) and fall to our business; and be pleased to interrogate this gentleman what you think fit.

NOBLE VEN. Then, sir, my first request to you is, that you will vouchsafe to acquaint me for what reasons this nation, which has ever been esteemed (and very justly) one of the most considerable people of the world; and made the best figure both in peace, treaties, war and trade; is now of so small regard, and signifies so little abroad? Pardon the freedom I take, for I assure you it is not out of disrespect, much less of contempt that I speak it: for since I arrived in England, I find it one of the most flourishing kingdoms in Europe, full of splendid nobility and gentry; the comeliest persons alive, valiant, courteous, knowing, and bountiful; and as well stored with commoners, honest, industrious, fitted for business, merchandise, arts, or arms; as their several educations lead them. Those who apply themselves to study, prodigious for learning, and succeeding to admiration in the perfection of all sciences: all this makes the riddle impossible to be solved; but by some skilful Oedipus, such as you are; whose pains I will yet so far spare, as to acknowledge, that I do in that little time I have spent here, perceive that the immediate cause of all this, is the disunion of the people and the governors; the discontentment of the gentry, and turbulency of the commonalty; although without all violence or tumult, which is miraculous. So that what I now request of you, is, that you will please to deduce particularly to me, the causes of this division; that when they are laid open, I may proceed (if you think fit to permit it) from the disease when known, to enquire after the remedies.

ENG. GENT. Before I come to make you any answer, I must thank you for the worthy and honourable character you give of our nation;

79

and shall add to it, that I do verily believe, that there are not a more loyal and faithful people to their prince in the whole world, than ours are; nor that fear more to fall into that state of confusion, in which we were twenty years since: and that, not only this parliament, which consists of the most eminent men of the kingdom, both for estates and parts; but all the inhabitants of this isle in general; even those (so many of them as have their understandings yet entire) which were of the anti-royal party in our late troubles, have all of them the greatest horror imaginable to think of doing any thing, that may bring this poor country into those dangers and uncertainties, which then did threaten our ruin.[1] And the rather for this consideration: that neither the wisdom of some who were engaged in those affairs, which I must aver to have been very great; nor the success of their contest, which ended in an absolute victory; could prevail so, as to give this kingdom any advantage; nay not so much as any settlement, in satisfaction and requital of all the blood it had lost, money it had spent, and hazard it had run. A clear argument why we must totally exclude a civil war from being any of the remedies, when we come to that point. I must add farther; that as we have as loyal subjects as are anywhere to be found, so we have as gracious and good a prince: I never having yet heard that he did or attempted to do, any the least act of arbitrary power, in any public concern; nor did ever take, or endeavour to take from any particular person the benefit of the law. And for his only brother, (although accidentally he cannot be denied to be a great motive of the people's unquietness,) all men must acknowledge him to be a most glorious and honourable prince: one who has exposed his life several times for the safety and glory of this nation; one who pays justly and punctually his debts, and manages his own fortune discreetly, and yet keeps the best court and equipage of any subject in Christendom; is courteous and affable to all; and in fine, has nothing in his whole conduct to be excepted against, much less dreaded; excepting, that he is believed to be of a religion contrary to the honour of God, and the safety and interest of this people, which gives them just apprehensions of their future condition. But of this matter we shall have occasion to speculate hereafter: in the mean time, since we have such a prince, and such subjects, we must needs want the ordinary cause of distrust and

---

[1] 'Twenty years since'—the Anarchy—Neville repeats his determination to avoid recourse to war, or recommending it.

division; and therefore must seek higher, to find out the original of this turbulent posture we are in.

DOCT. Truly you had need seek higher, or lower, to satisfy us; for hitherto you have but enforced the gentleman's question, and made us more admire what the solution will be.

ENG. GENT. Gentlemen, then I shall delay you no longer. The evil counsellors, the pensioner-parliament, the thorough-paced judges, the flattering divines, the busy and designing papists, the French counsels, are not the causes of our misfortunes;[1] they are but the effects, (as our present distractions are) of one primary cause; which is, the breach and ruin of our government: which, having been decaying for near two hundred years,[2] is in our age brought so near to expiration, that it lies agonizing; and can no longer perform the functions of a political life; nor carry on the work of ordering and preserving mankind. So that the shifts that our courtiers have within some years used are but so many tricks, or conclusions which they are trying to hold life and soul together a while longer: and have played handy-dandy[3] with parliaments, (and especially with the house of commons, the only part which is now left entire of the old constitution) by adjourning, and proroguing, and dissolving them; contrary to the true meaning of the law; as well in the reign of our late king, as during his majesty's that now is. Whereas indeed our counsellors (perceiving the decay of the foundation, as they must if they can see but one inch into the politics) ought to have addressed themselves to the king to call a parliament, the true physician, and to lay open the distemper there; and so have endeavoured a cure, before it had been too late: as I fear, it now is; I mean for the piecing and patching up the old government. It is true, as the divine Machiavel says, that diseases in government are like a marasmus[4] in the body natural, which is very hard to be discovered, whilst it is curable; and after it comes to be easy to discern, difficult (if not impossible) to be remedied: yet it is to be supposed that the counsellors are, or ought to be skilful physicians; and to foresee the seeds of state-distempers, time enough to prevent the death of the patient: else they ought in conscience to excuse themselves from that sublime employment, and

---

[1] Cf. Algernon Sidney, *Discourses*, chapter III, section 45.
[2] Neville dates the decline of the old constitution from Bosworth, 1485.
[3] 'Handy-dandy'—a child's game in which the player guesses which of the others' hands conceals the desired object.
[4] 'Marasmus'—a wasting away or decline.

betake themselves to callings more suitable to their capacities. So that although for this reason, the ministers of state here are inexcusable; and deserve all the fury, which must one time or other be let loose against them; (except they shall suddenly fly from the wrath to come, by finding out in time and advising the true means of setting themselves to rights) yet neither prince nor people are in the mean time to be blamed, for not being able to conduct things better; no more, than the waggoner is to answer for his ill guiding, or the oxen for their ill drawing the waggon; when it is with age and ill usage broken, and the wheels unserviceable; or the pilot and mariners, for not weathering out a storm; when the ship hath sprung a plank. And as in the body of man, sometimes the head and all the members are in good order, nay, the vital parts are sound and entire; yet if there be a considerable putrification in the humours, much more, if the blood (which the scripture calls the life) be impure and corrupted; the patient ceases not to be in great danger, and oftentimes dies without some skilful physician: and in the mean time the head and all the parts suffer, and are unquiet, full as much, as if they were all immediately affected: so it is in every respect with the body politic, or commonwealth, when their foundations are mouldered. And although in both these cases, the patients cannot (though the distemper be in their own bodies) know what they ail, but are forced to send for some artist to tell them; yet they cease not to be extremely uneasy and impatient, and lay hold oftentimes upon unsuitable remedies, and impute their malady to wrong and ridiculous causes. As some people do here, who think that the growth of popery is our only evil; and that if we were secure against that, our peace and settlement were obtained; and that our disease needed no other cure. But of this more when we come to the cure.

NOBLE VEN. Against this discourse, certainly we have nothing to reply: but must grant, that when any government is decayed, it must be mended; or all will ruin. But now we must request you to declare to us, how the government of England is decayed; and how it comes to be so. For I am one of those unskilful persons that cannot discern a state-marasmus, when the danger is so far off.

ENG. GENT. Then no man living can; for your government is this day the only school in the world, that breeds such physicians, and you are esteemed one of the ablest amongst them: and it would be manifest to all the world for truth, although there were no argument for it, but the admirable stability and durableness of your government; which has lasted above twelve hundred years entire and perfect. Whereas all the rest of the countries in Europe, have not only changed masters very frequently in a quarter of that time; but have varied and altered their polities very often. Which manifests that you must needs have ever enjoyed a succession of wise citizens, that have had skill and ability to forewarn you betimes of those rocks against which your excellently-built vessel might in time split.

NOBLE VEN. Sir, you over-value, not only me, but the wisdom of my fellow-citizens; for we have none of these high speculations, nor has scarce any of our body read Aristotle, Plato, or Cicero, or any of those great artists ancient or modern, who teach that great science of the governing and increasing great states and cities: without studying which science no man can be fit to discourse pertinently of these matters; much less to found, or mend a government, or so much as find the defects of it. We only study our own government; and that too chiefly to be fit for advantageous employments, rather than to foresee our dangers. Which yet, I must needs confess, some amongst us are pretty good at; and will in a harangue, made upon passing a law, venture to tell us what will be the consequence of it two hundred years hence. But of these things I shall be very prodigal in my discourse, when you have leisure and patience to command me to say any thing of our polity; in the mean time pray be pleased to go on with your edifying instruction.

ENG. GENT. Before I can tell you how the government of England came to be decayed, I must tell you what that government was; and what it now is. And I should say something too of government in general, but that I am afraid of talking of that subject before you who are so exact a judge of it.

NOBLE VEN. I thought you had been pleased to have done with this discourse. I assure you, sir, if I had more skill in that matter than ever I can pretend to, it would but serve to make me the fitter auditor of what you shall say on that subject.

ENG. GENT. Sir, in the course of my reasoning upon this point, I shall have occasion to insist and expatiate upon many things, which both myself and others have published in former times. For which I will only make this excuse; that the repetition of such matters is the more pardonable, because they will be at least new to you who are a

83

stranger to our affairs and writings. And the rather, because those discourses shall be applied to our present condition, and suited to our present occasions. But I will say no more; but obey you, and proceed. I will not take upon me to say, or so much as conjecture, how and when government began in the world; or what government is most ancient. History must needs be silent in that point: for that government is more ancient than history; and there was never any writer but was bred under some government; which is necessarily supposed to be the parent of all arts and sciences, and to have produced them. And therefore it would be as hard for a man to write an account of the beginning of the laws and polity of any country, except there were memory of it; (which cannot be before the first historiographer:) as it would be to any person, without records, to tell the particular history of his own birth.

DOCT. Sir, I cannot comprehend you: may not historians write a history of matters done before they were born? If it were so, no man could write but of his own times.

ENG. GENT. My meaning is, where there are not stories, or records, extant; for as for oral tradition, it lasts but for one age, and then degenerates into fable: I call any thing in writing, whereby the account of the passages or occurrences of former times is derived to our knowledge, a history; although it be not penned methodically, so as to make the author pass for a wit: and had rather read the authentic records of any country, that is a collection of their laws and letters concerning transactions of state and the like, than the most eloquent and judicious narrative that can be made.

NOBLE VEN. Methinks, sir, your discourse seems to imply, that we have no account extant of the beginning of governments. Pray what do you think of the books of Moses? Which seem to be penned on purpose to inform us how he, by God's command, led that people out of Egypt into another land; and in the way made them a government. Besides, does not Plutarch tell us, how Theseus gathered together the dispersed inhabitants of Attica, brought them into one city, and under one government of his own making? The like did Romulus in Italy, and many others in divers countries.

ENG. GENT. I never said, that we had not sufficient knowledge of the original of particular governments; but it is evident, that these great legislators had seen and lived under other administrations, and had the help of learned law-givers and philosophers; excepting the first,

84

who had the aid of God himself. So that it remains undiscovered yet, how the first regulation of mankind began: and therefore I will take for granted that which all the politicians conclude: which is, that necessity made the first government. For every man by the first law of nature (which is common to us and brutes) had, like beasts in a pasture, right to everything; and there being no property, each individual, if he were the stronger, might seize whatever any other had possessed himself of before, which made a state of perpetual war. To remedy which, and the fear that nothing should be long enjoyed by any particular person, (neither was any man's life in safety,) every man consented to be debarred of that universal right to all things; and confine himself to a quiet and secure enjoyment of such a part, as should be allotted him. Thence came in ownership, or property: to maintain which, it was necessary to consent to laws, and a government; to put them in execution.[1] Which of the governments now extant, or that have been formerly, was first, is not possible now to be known: but I think this must be taken for granted, that whatsoever the frame or constitution was first, it was made by the persuasion and mediation of some wise and virtuous person, and consented to by the whole number. And then, that it was instituted for the good and preservation of the governed; and not for the exaltation and greatness of the person or persons appointed to govern. The reason why I beg this concession is, that it seems very improbable, not to say impossible, that a vast number of people should ever be brought to consent to put themselves under the power of others, but for the ends above-said, and so lose their liberty without advantaging themselves in any thing. And it is full as impossible that any person (or persons so inconsiderable in number as magistrates and rulers are) should by force get an empire to themselves. Though I am not ignorant that a whole people have in imminent dangers, either from the invasion of a powerful enemy, or from civil distractions, put themselves wholly into the hands of one illustrious person for a time; and that with good success, under the best forms of government: but this is nothing to the original of states.

NOBLE VEN. Sir, I wonder how you come to pass over the consideration of paternal government, which is held to have been the beginning of monarchies.[2]

---

[1] Neville is recalling Hobbes, *Leviathan*, I, 13, 14, as well as Machiavelli, *Discourses*, I, 2.
[2] *Patriarcha*, by Robert Filmer, was published in 1680.

ENG. GENT. Really, I did not think it worth the taking notice of: for though it be not easy to prove a negative, yet I believe if we could trace all foundations of polities that now are, or ever came to our knowledge since the world began; we shall find none of them to have descended from paternal power. We know nothing of Adam's leaving the empire to Cain, or Seth: it was impossible for Noah to retain any jurisdiction over his own three sons; who were dispersed into three parts of the world, if our antiquaries calculate right: and as for Abraham, whilst he lived, as also his son Isaac, they were but ordinary fathers of families, and no question governed their own household as all others do. And when Jacob upon his death-bed did relate to his children the promise almighty God had made his grandfather; to make him a great nation, and give his posterity a fruitful territory; he speaks not one word of the empire of Reuben his first-born, but supposes them all equal. And so they were taken to be by Moses, when he divided the land to them by lot; and by God's command made them a commonwealth. So that I believe this fancy to have been first started, not by the solid judgement of any man, but to flatter some prince; and to assert, for want of better arguments, the divine right of monarchy.

NOBLE VEN. I have been impertinent in interrupting you, but yet now I cannot repent of it, since your answer has given me so much satisfaction; but if it be so as you say, that government was at first instituted for the interest and preservation of mankind, how comes it pass, that there are and have been so many absolute monarchies in the world, in which it seems that nothing is provided for, but the greatness and power of the prince?

ENG. GENT. I have presumed to give you already my reason, why I take for granted, that such a power could never be given by the consent of any people, for a perpetuity: for though the people of Israel did against the will of Samuel, and indeed of God himself, demand and afterwards choose themselves a king; yet he was never such a king as we speak of; for that all the orders of their commonwealth, the sanhedrim, the congregation of the people, the princes of the tribes, &c. did still remain in being: as has been excellently proved by a learned gentleman of our nation, to whom I refer you.[1] It may then be enquired

---

[1] The learned gentleman is John Selden (1584-1654), whose book, *De Synedriis et Praefecturis Juridicis Veterum Ebraeorum* (1650), was much used by Harrington in the section on the Commonwealth of Israel in *Oceana*, and by other students of Hebrew history.

into, how these monarchies at first did arise. History being in this point silent as to the ancient principalities, we will conjecture, that some of them might very well proceed from the corruption of better governments, which must necessarily cause a depravation in manners; (as nothing is more certain than that politic defects breed moral ones, as our nation is a pregnant example) this debauchery of manners might blind the understandings of a great many; destroy the fortunes of others, and make them indigent; infuse into very many a neglect and carelessness of the public good (which in all settled states is very much regarded) so that it might easily come into the ambition of some bold aspiring person, to affect empire; and as easily into his power, (by fair pretences with some, and promises of advantages with others,) to procure followers, and gain a numerous party, either to usurp tyranny over his own country, or to lead men forth to conquer and subdue another. Thus it is supposed that Nimrod got his kingdom: who in scripture is called, a great hunter before God; which expositors interpret, a great tyrant. The modern despotical powers have been acquired by one of these two ways. Either by pretending, by the first founder thereof, that he had a divine mission; and so gaining not only followers, but even easy access in some places without force, to empire, and afterwards dilating their power by great conquests; thus Mohamet and Genghis Khan began, and established the Saracen and Tartarian kingdoms: or by a long series of wisdom in a prince, or chief magistrate of a mixed monarchy, and his council, who by reason of the sleepiness and inadvertency of the people, have been able to extinguish the great nobility, or render them inconsiderable; and so by degrees taking away from the people their protectors, render them slaves. So the monarchies of France, and some other countries, have grown to what they are at this day; there being left but a shadow of the three states in any of these monarchies, and so no bounds remaining to the regal power. But since property remains still to the subjects; these governments may be said to be changed, but not founded or established: for there is no maxim more infallible and holding in any science, than this is in politics; that empire is founded in property. Force or fraud may alter a government; but it is property that must found and eternize it. Upon this undeniable aphorism we are to build most of our subsequent reasoning: in the meantime we may suppose, that hereafter the great power of the king of France may diminish much, when his enraged and oppressed subjects come to be commanded by a prince of less courage, wisdom, and military virtue; when it will be very hard for any such king to govern tyrannically a country,[1] which is not entirely his own.

DOCT. Pray, sir, give me leave to ask you by the way, what is the reason that here in our country where the peerage is lessened sufficiently, the king has not got as great an addition of power as accrues to the crown of France?

ENG. GENT. You will understand that, doctor, before I have finished this discourse: but to stay your stomach till then, you may please to know that in France the greatness of the nobility which has been lately taken from them, did not consist in vast riches and revenues; but in great privileges, and jurisdictions, which obliged the people to obey them: whereas our great peers in former times had not only the same great dependencies, but very considerable revenues besides, in demesnes, and otherwise. This vassalage over the people, which the peers of France had, being abolished, the power over those tenants, which before was in their lords, fell naturally and of course into the crown; although the lands and possessions divested of those dependencies did and do still remain to the owners: whereas here in England, though the services are for the most part worn out, and insignificant; yet for want of providence and policy in former kings, who could not forsee the danger afar off, entails have been suffered to be cut off; and so two parts in ten of all those vast estates, as well manors as demesnes, by the luxury and folly of the owners, have been within these two hundred years purchased by the lesser gentry and the commons; which has been so far from advantaging the crown, that it has made the country scarce governable by monarchy. But if you please, I will go on with my discourse about government, and come to this again hereafter.

NOBLE VEN. I beseech you, sir, do.

ENG. GENT. I cannot find by the small reading I have, that there were any other governments in the world anciently than these three: monarchy, aristocracy, and democracy. For the first; I have no light out of antiquity to convince me, that there were in old times any other monarchies, but such as were absolutely despotical. All kingdoms then, as well in Greece, (Macedon, Epirus, and the like, where it is said the princes exercised their power moderately) as in Asia, being altogether unlimited by any laws, or any assemblies of nobility or people. Yet I

[1] Louis XIV (1643–1715).

must confess, Aristotle, when he reckons up the corruptions of these three governments, calls tyranny the corruption of the monarchy: by which if he means a change of government, (as it is in the corruptions of the other two;) then it must follow, that the philosopher knew of some other monarchy at the first, which afterwards degenerated into tyranny; that is, into arbitrary power: (for so the word tyranny is most commonly taken, though in modern languages it signifies the ill exercise of power;) for certainly arbitrary government cannot be called tyranny, where the whole property is in the prince, (as we reasonably suppose it to have been in those monarchies); no more than it is tyranny for you to govern your own house and estate as you please. But it is possible Aristotle might not in this speak so according to terms of art, but might mean, that the ill government of a kingdom or family is tyranny. However we have one example, that puzzles politicians: and that is Egypt, where Pharaoh is called king; and yet we see, that till Joseph's time he had not the whole property: for the wisdom of that patriarch taught his master a way to make a new use of that famine, by telling him, that if they would buy their lives, and sell their estates (as they did afterwards, and preserve themselves by the king's bread) they shall serve Pharaoh: which shows that Joseph knew well, that empire was founded in property. But most of the modern writers in polity, are of opinion, that Egypt was not a monarchy till then; though the prince might have the title of king: as the Heraclides had in Sparta, and Romulus and the other kings had in Rome; both which states were instituted commonwealths. They give good conjectures for this their opinion, too many to be here mentioned; only one is, that originally (as they go about to prove) all arts and sciences had their rise in Egypt; which they think very improbable to have been under a monarchy. But this position, that all kings in former times were absolute, is not so essential to the intent I have in this discourse; which is to prove, that in all states, of what kind soever, this aphorism takes place: Dominion is founded in property. So that if there were mixed monarchies, then the king had not all the property; but those who shared with him in the administration of the sovereignty, had their part (whether it were the senate, the people, or both) or if he had no companions in the sovereign power, he had no sharers likewise in the dominion or possession of the land. For that is all we mean by property, in all this discourse; for as for personal estate, the subjects may enjoy it in the largest proportion, without being able to invade the empire: the prince may when he pleases take away their goods by his tenants and vassals, (without an army;) which are his ordinary force, and answers to our county force; but the subjects with their money cannot invade his crown.[1] So that all the description we need make of this kind or form of government, is, that the whole possession of the country, and the whole power lies in the hands and breast of one man; he can make laws, break and repeal them when he pleases, or dispense with them in the meantime when he thinks fit; interpose in all judicatories, in behalf of his favourites; take away any particular man's personal estate, and his life too, without the formality of a criminal process, or trial; send a dagger, or a halter to his chief ministers, and command them to make themselves away; and in fine, do all that his will, or his interest, suggests to him.

DOCT. You have dwelt long here upon an argumentation, that the ancients had no monarchies but what were arbitrary—

ENG. GENT. Pray give me leave to save your objections to that point, and to assure you first; that I will not take upon me to be so positive in that; for that I cannot pretend to have read all the historians and antiquaries that ever wrote; nor have I so perfect a memory as to remember, or make use of, in a verbal and transient reasoning, all that I have ever read: and then to assure you again, that I build nothing upon that assertion; and so your objection will be needless, and only take up time.

DOCT. You mistake me; I had no intent to use any argument or example against your opinion in that, but am very willing to believe that it may be so. What I was going to say was this, that you have insisted much upon the point of monarchy, and made a strange description of it; whereas many of the ancients, and almost all the modern writers, magnify it to be the best of governments.

ENG. GENT. I have said nothing to the contrary. I have told you in fact, what it is; which I believe none will deny. The philosopher said it was the best government; but with this restriction, where philosophers reigned:[2] and they had an example of it, in some few Roman emperors: but in the most turbulent times of the commonwealth, and factions between the nobility and the people, Rome was much more full

---

[1] Only landed property in the hands of subjects can threaten a monarch, not property in the form of financial wealth.

[2] Plato; *ubi philosophi regnant*: an example in Neville's mind, probably Marcus Aurelius.

of virtuous and heroic citizens, than ever it was under Aurelius or Antoninus. For the moderns that are of that judgement; they are most of them divines, not politicians: and something may be said in their behalf, when by their good preaching, they can infuse into their imaginary prince, (who seems already to have an image of the power of God), the justice, wisdom, and goodness too of the Deity.

NOBLE VEN. We are well satisfied with the progress you have hitherto made in this matter. Pray go on to the two other forms used amongst the ancients, and their corruptions; that so we may come to the modern governments, and see how England stands; and how it came to decay, and what must rebuild it.

ENG. GENT. You have very good reason to hasten me to that; for indeed, all that has been said yet, is but as it were a preliminary discourse to the knowledge of the government of England, and its decay: when it comes to the cure, I hope you will both help me, for both yourself and the doctor are a thousand times better than I at remedies. But I shall dispatch the other two governments. Aristocracy, or optimacy, is a commonwealth, where the better sort, (that is, the eminent and rich men,) have the chief administration of the government: I say, the chief; because there are very few ancient optimacies, but the people had some share: as in Sparta, where they had power to vote, but not debate; for so the oracle of Apollo, brought by Lycurgus from Delphos, settles it. But the truth is, these people were the natural Spartans: for Lycurgus divided the country or territory of Laconia into 39,000 shares; whereof 9,000 only of these owners were inhabitants of Sparta; the rest lived in the country: so that although Thucydides calls it an aristocracy, and so I follow him, yet it was none of those aristo-cracies usually described by the politicians; where the lands of the territory were in a great deal fewer hands. But call it what you will, wherever there was an aristocracy, there the property, or very much of the overbalance of it, was in the hands of the *Aristoi* or governors; be they more or fewer: for if the people have the greatest interest in the property, they will, and must have it in the empire. A notable example of it is Rome, the best and most glorious government that ever the sun saw; where the lands being equally divided amongst the tribes (that is, the people) it was impossible for the *patricii* to keep them quiet, till they yielded to their desires: not only to have their tribunes, to see that nothing passed into a law without their consent, but also to have it declared, that both the consuls should not only be chosen by the people (as they ever were, and the kings too before them) but that they might be elected too, when the people pleased, out of plebeian families.[1] So that now I am come to democracy. Which you see is a government where the chief part of the sovereign power, and the exercise of it, resides in the people: and where the style is, at the command of the people, by the authority of the senate. And it does consist of three fundamental orders; the senate proposing, the people resolving, and the magistrates executing. This government is much more powerful than aristocracy; because the latter cannot arm the people, for fear they should seize upon the government; and therefore are fain to make use of none but strangers and mercenaries for soldiers: which, as the divine Machiavel says, has hindered your commonwealth of Venice[2] from mounting up to heaven; whither those incomparable orders, and that venerable wisdom used by your citizens in keeping to them, would have carried you; if in all your wars, you had not been ill served.

DOCT. Well, sir, pray let me ask you one thing concerning Venice: how do you make out your empire is founded on property there? Have the gentlemen there, who are the party governing, the possession of the whole territory? does not property remain entire to the gentlemen, and other inhabitants in the several countries of Padua, Brescia, Vicenza, Verona, Bergamo, Cremona, Treviso, and Friuli; as also in the ultra-marine provinces and islands? And yet I believe you will not deny, but that the government of Venice is as well founded, and has been of as long continuance, as any that now is or ever was in the world.[3]

ENG. GENT. Doctor, I shall not answer you in this; because I am sure it will be better done by this gentleman, who is a worthy son of that honourable mother.

NOBLE VEN. I thought you had said, sir, that we should have done complimenting; but since you do command me to clear the objection made by our learned doctor, I shall presume to tell you first how our city began. The Goths, Huns, and Lombards coming with all the violence and cruelty imaginable to invade that part of Italy which we now call *Terra Firma*, [mainland] and where our ancestors did then inhabit; forced them in great numbers to seek a shelter amongst a

---

[1] Cf. Moyle, below, p. 238.
[2] Machiavelli, *The Prince*, chapter XII.
[3] Neville recommended nos. 3 and 4, 'Political Discourses', above, p. 65, on the Venetian government.

great many little rocks, or islands, which stood very thick in a vast lake, or rather marsh, which is made by the Adriatic sea; we call it *Laguna*, [the Lagoon] here they began to build, and getting boats, made themselves provisions of all kinds from the land; from whence innumerable people began to come to them, finding that they could subsist, and that the barbarous people had no boats to attack them, nor that they could be invaded either by horse or foot without them. Our first government, and which lasted for many years, was no more than what was practised in many country parishes in Italy, (and possibly here too,) where the clerk, or any other person, calls together the chief of the inhabitants to consider of parish-business; as choosing of officers, making of rates, and the like. So in Venice, when there was any public provision to be made by way of law, or otherwise, some officers went about to persons of the greatest wealth and credit, to intreat them to meet and consult; from whence our senate is called to this day *Consiglio de pregadi*, which in our barbarous idiom is as much as *Pregati* in Tuscan language. Our security increased daily; and so by consequence our number and our riches: for by this time there began to be another inundation of Saracens upon Asia Minor; which forced a great many of the poor people of Greece to fly to us for protection, giving us the possession of some islands, and other places upon the continent. This opened us a trade, and gave a beginning to our greatness: but chiefly made us consider what government was fittest to conserve ourselves, and keep our wealth; (for we did not then much dream of conquests, else without doubt we must have made a popular government.) We pitched upon an aristocracy: by ordering that those who had been called to council for that present year and for four years before, should have the government in their hands; and all their posterity after them forever: which made first the distinction between gentlemen and citizens. The people, who consisted of diverse nations, most of them newly come to inhabit there, and generally seeking nothing but safety and ease, willingly consented to this change; and so this state has continued to this day: though the several orders and councils have been brought in since, by degrees; as our nobility increased, and for other causes. Under this government we have made some conquests in Italy, and Greece: for our city stood like a wall between the two great torrents of Goths and Saracens; and as either of their empires declined, it was easy for us, without being very warlike, to pick up some pieces of each side. As for the government of these conquests: we did not think fit to divide the land among the nobility, for fear of envy, and the effects of it; much less did we think it advisable to plant colonies of our people, which would have given the power into their hands; but we thought it the best way for our government to leave the people their property, tax them what we thought fit, and keep them under by governors and citadels; and so in short make them a province. So that now the doctor's riddle is solved; for I suppose this gentleman did not mean that his maxim should reach to provincial governments.

ENG. GENT. No, sir; so far from that, that it is just contrary. For as in national or domestic government, where a nation is governed, either by its own people or its own prince, there can be no settled government, except they have the rule who possess the country: so in provincial governments, if they be wisely ordered, no man must have any the least share in the managing affairs of state, but strangers; or such as have no share or part in the possessions there; for else they will have a very good opportunity of shaking off their yoke.

DOCT. That is true; and we are so wise here (I mean our ancestors were) as to have made a law, that no native in Ireland can be deputy there.[1] But, sir, being fully satisfied in my demand by this gentleman, I beseech you to go on to what you have to say before you come to England.

ENG. GENT. I shall then offer two things to your observation; the first is, that in all times and places, where any great heroes or legislators have founded a government, (by gathering people together, to build a city, or to invade any country to possess it,) before they came to dividing the conquered lands, they did always very maturely deliberate under what form or model of government they meant to live; and accordingly made the partition of the possessions. Moses, Theseus, and Romulus, founders of democracies, divided the land equally. Lycurgus, who meant an optimacy, made a certain number of shares which he intended to be in the hands of the people of Laconia. Cyrus, and other conquering monarchs before him, took all for themselves and successors: which is observed in those eastern countries to this day; and which has made those countries continue ever since under the same government, though conquered and possessed very often by several nations. This

---

[1] Both the English Gentleman and the Doctor voice the opinion generally held at the time that English provinces, like Ireland and the colonies in America, must be governed only by men born in England.

brings me to the second thing to be observed; which is, 'that wherever this apportionment of lands came to be changed in any kind, the government either changed with it, or was wholly in a state of confusion'. And for this reason Lycurgus, the greatest politician that ever founded any government, took a sure way to fix property, by confounding it and bringing all into common: and so the whole number of the natural Spartans, who inhabited the city of Lacedemon, ate and drank in their several convives[1] together: and as long as they continued so to do, they did not only preserve their government entire (and that for a longer time than we can read of any commonwealth, that ever lasted amongst the ancients,) but held as it were the principality of Greece. The Athenians, for want of some constitutions to fix property as Theseus placed it, were in danger of utter ruin; which they had certainly encountered, if the good genius (as they then called it) of that people, had not raised them up a second founder, (more than 600 years after the first,) which was Solon. And because the history of this matter will very much conduce to the illustrating of this aphorism we have laid down, I will presume so much upon your patience as to make a short recital of it; leaving you to see it more at large, in Plutarch, and other authors.

The lands in the territory of Attica, which were in the possession of the common people, (for what reason history is silent) were for debt all mortgaged to the great men of the city of Athens; and the owners having no possibility of redeeming their estates, were treating to compound with their creditors and deliver up their lands to them. Solon (who was one of those state physicians we spoke of,) was much troubled at this, and harangued daily to the nobility and people against it; telling them first, that it was impossible for the Grecians to resist the Medes (who were then growing up to a powerful monarchy) except Athens, the second city of Greece, did countenance a democracy: that it was as impossible the people could keep their empire, except they kept their lands; nothing being more contrary to nature, than that those who possess nothing in a country should pretend to govern it. They were all sensible of his reasons, and of their own danger; but the only remedy (which was, that the great men should forgive the common people their debts) would not at all be digested. So that the whole city (now fully understanding their condition) were continually

---

[1] 'Convives'—banquets.

95

in an uproar; and the people flocked about Solon, whenever he came abroad, desiring him to take upon him the government and be their prince, and they would make choice of him the next time they assembled. He told them, No, he would never be a tyrant, especially in his own country: meaning, that he who had no more share than other of the nobles, could not govern the rest, without being an usurper or tyrant. But this he did to oblige his citizens; he frankly forgave all the debts that any of the people owed to him, and released their lands immediately: and this amounted to fifteen Attic talents of gold, (a vast sum in those days:) and betook himself to a voluntary exile; in which he visited Thales, and went to the oracle of Delphos, and offered up his prayers to Apollo for the preservation of his city. In return of which (as the people then believed) the hearts of the great ones were so changed and enlarged, that they readily agreed to remit all their debts to the people; upon condition, that Solon would take the pains to make them a new model of government, and laws suitable to a democracy; which he as readily accepted and performed. By virtue of which that city grew and continued long the greatest, the justest, the most virtuous, learned and renowned, of all in that age: drove the Persians afterwards out of Greece; defeated them both by sea and land, with a quarter of their number of ships and men; and produced the greatest wits and philosophers that ever lived upon earth. The city of Athens instituted a solemn feast in commemoration of that great generosity and self-denial of the nobility; who sacrificed their own interest to the preservation of their country: which feast was called the solemnity of the *Seisactheia*, (which signifies recision or abolition of debts,) and was observed with processions, sacrifices, and games, till the time of the Romans' dominion over them (who encouraged it) and even till the change of religion in Greece, and invasion of the Saracens.

The Romans, having omitted in their institution to provide for the fixing of property, and so the nobility (called *patricii*) beginning to take to themselves a greater share in the conquered lands than had been usual (for in the first times of the commonwealth under Romulus, and ever after, it was always practised to divide the lands equally amongst the tribes), this innovation stirred up Licinius Stolo, then tribune of the people, to propose a law (which, although it met with much difficulty, yet at last was consented to) by which it was provided, that no Roman citizen, of what degree soever, should possess above five hundred acres of land; and for the remaining part of the lands which should be conquered, it was ordered to be equally divided, as formerly, amongst the tribes. This found admittance (after much opposition) because it did provide but for the future; no man at that time being owner of more lands, than what was lawful for him to possess: and if this law had been strictly observed to the last, that glorious commonwealth might have subsisted to this day, for aught we know.[1]

DOCT. Some other cause would have been the ruin of it: what think you of a foreign conquest?

ENG. GENT. Oh doctor, if they had kept their poverty, they had kept their government and their virtue too; and then it had not been an easy matter to subdue them: Whom Jupiter wishes to destroy, he makes mad. Breach of rules and order causes division; and division, when it comes to be incurable, exposes a nation, almost as much as a tyrannical government does. The Goths and Vandals, had they invaded in those days, had met with the same success which befell the Cymbri and the Teutons. I must confess, a foreign invasion is a formidable thing, when a commonwealth is weak in territory and inhabitants, and that the invader is numerous and warlike; and so we see the Romans were in danger of utter ruin, when they were first attacked by the Gauls under Brennus. The like hazard may be feared, when a commonwealth is assaulted by another of equal virtue, and a commander of equal address and valour to any of themselves; thus the Romans ran the risk of their liberty and empire, in the war of Hannibal: but their power and their virtue grew to that height in that contest, that when it was ended, I believe that if they had preserved the foundation of their government entire, they had been invincible. And if I were alone of this opinion, I might be ashamed; but I am backed by the judgement of your incomparable countryman Machiavel: and no man will condemn either of us of rashness, if he first considers what small states, that have

---

[1] Agrarian laws, possibly dating back to the Licinio-Sextian laws of 387 B.C. arranging for the reclamation of some public lands and their distribution to poorer citizens, were revived and extended in a programme of agricultural reform by Tiberius Sempronius Gracchus the younger, and his brother Gaius, in the second half of the second century B.C. Their regulations disturbed established owners, and made them so unpopular with wealthy Romans that each in turn was murdered. Harrington, of course, made the regulation of landholding an essential basis for his *Oceana*. If the balance of property, and by this of course he meant *real* property, does not change, political power will remain constant, and the state stable. 'An agrarian' in both seventeenth- and eighteenth-century political writing must be understood to imply, not necessarily egalitarianism, but an attempt to prevent extremes, the possession of undue wealth by any one class or person.

stood upon right bottoms, have done to defend their liberty against great monarchs. As is to be seen in the example of the little commonwealth of Athens; which destroyed the fleet of Xerxes, consisting of a thousand vessels, in the straits of Salamis: and before, the land-army of Darius, of three hundred thousand, in the plains of Marathon, and drove them out of Greece: for though the whole confederates were present at the battle of Plataea, yet the Athenian army singly under their general Miltiades gained that renowned battle of Marathon.[1]

NOBLE VEN. I beseech you, sir, how was it possible, or practicable, that the Romans conquering so many and so remote provinces, should yet have been able to preserve their Agrarian Law, and divide all those lands equally to their citizens? or if it had been possible, yet it would have ruined their city, by sending all their inhabitants away; and by taking in strangers in their room, they must necessarily have had people less virtuous and less warlike; and so both their government and their military discipline must have been corrupted: for it is not to be imagined, but that the people would have gone with their families to the place where their lands lay: so that it appears that the Romans did not provide, in the making and framing their first polity, for so great conquests as they afterwards made.

ENG. GENT. Yes, surely they did: from their first beginning they were founded in war, and had neither land nor wives but what they fought for; but yet what you object were very weighty, if there had not been a consideration of that early: for as soon as that great and wise people had subdued the Samnites on the east, and brought their arms as far as the Greek plantations, in that part of Italy which is now called the kingdom of Naples; and westward, had reduced all the Tuscans under their obedience, as far as the river Arnus; they made that, and the river Volturnus, (which runs by the walls of Capua,) the two boundaries of their empire, which was called the abode of empire. These were the uttermost points attained; for what they conquered between these two rivers, was all confiscated and divided amongst the tribes; the rustic tribes being twenty-seven, and the urban tribes nine, which made thirty-six in all. The city tribes were like our companies in London, consisting of tradesmen. The country tribes were divided like shires; and there was scarce any landed man who inhabited in the city,

[1] Cf. Moyle, on the role of courageous and virtuous citizens in averting or repairing decadence, and Machiavelli, *Discourses*, III, 1 and 31.

but he was written in that tribe where his estate lay: so that the rustic tribes (though they had all equal voices) were of far more credit and reputation than the urban. Upon the days of the *Comitia*, which were very well known, as many as thought fit amongst the country tribes came to give their voices; though every tribe was very numerous of inhabitants, that lived in the city. Now the Agrarian did not extend to any lands conquered beyond this precinct, but they were left to the inhabitants; they paying a revenue to the commonwealth: all but those which were thought fit to be set out to maintain a Roman colony; which was a good number of Roman citizens, sent thither, and provided of lands and habitations: which being armed, did serve in the nature of a citadel and garrison to keep the province in obedience; and a Roman praetor, proconsul, or other governor, was sent yearly to head them, and brought forces with him besides.

Now it was ever lawful for any Roman citizen to purchase what lands he pleased in any of these provinces; it not being dangerous to a city to have their people rich, but to have such a power in the governing part of the empire, as should make those who managed the affairs of the commonwealth depend upon them; which came afterwards to be that which ruined their liberty, and which the Gracchi endeavoured to prevent when it was too late. For those illustrious persons, seeing the disorder that was then in the commonwealth, and rightly comprehending the reason, which was the intermission of the Agrarian, and by consequence the great purchases which were made by the men of Rome (who had enriched themselves in Asia and the other provinces) in that part of Italy which was between the two rivers before-mentioned, began to harangue the people, in hopes to persuade them to admit of the right remedy; which was to confirm the Agrarian Law with a retrospect; which although they carried, yet the difficulties in the execution proved so great, that it never took effect: by reason that the common people whose interest it was to have their lands restored, yet having long lived as clients and dependents of the great ones, chose rather to depend still upon their patrons than to hazard all for an imaginary deliverance: by which supineness in them, they were prevailed with rather to join (for the most part) with the oppressors of themselves and their country, and to cut the throats of their redeemers, than to employ their just resentment against the covetous violators of their government and property. So perished the two renowned Gracchi, one soon after the other; not for any crime, but for having endeavoured to preserve and restore their commonwealth: for which (if they had lived in times suitable to such an heroic undertaking, and that the virtue of their ancestors had been yet in any kind remaining) they would have merited and enjoyed a reputation equal to that of Lycurgus, or Solon; whereas as it happened they were sometime after branded with the name of sedition, by certain wits, who prostituted the noble flame of poetry (which before had wont to be employed in magnifying heroic actions) to flatter the lust and ambition of the Roman tyrants.

NOBLE VEN. Sir, I approve what you say in all things; and in confirmation of it, shall further allege the two famous princes of Sparta, Agis and Cleomenes: which I couple together, since Plutarch does so. These (finding the corruption of their commonwealth, and the decay of their ancient virtue, to proceed from the neglect and in-observance of their founder's rules, and a breach of that equality which was first instituted;) endeavoured to restore the laws of Lycurgus, and divide the territory anew; their victory in the Peloponnesian war, and the riches and luxury brought into their city by Lysander, having long before broken all the orders of their commonwealth, and destroyed the proportions of land allotted to each of the natural Spartans. But the first of these two excellent patriots perished by treachery, in the beginning of his enterprise: the other began and went on with in-comparable prudence and resolution; but miscarried afterwards, by the iniquity of the times, and baseness and wickedness of the people. So infallibly true it is, that where the policy is corrupted, there must necessarily be also a corruption and depravation of manners; and an utter abolition of all faith, justice, honour, and morality. But I forget myself, and entrench upon your province: there is nothing now remains to keep you from the modern policies, but that you please to shut up this discourse of the ancient governments, with saying something of the corruptions of aristocracy and democracy. For I believe both of us are satisfied that you have abundantly proved your assertion: and that when we have leisure to examine all the states or policies that ever were, we shall find all their changes to have turned upon this hinge of property; and that the fixing of that with good laws in the beginning or first institution of a state, and the holding to those laws afterwards, is the only way to make a commonwealth immortal.

ENG. GENT. I think you are very right: but I shall obey you; and do presume to differ from Aristotle, in thinking that he has not fitly called those extremes (for so I will style them) of aristocracy and democracy, corruptions: for that they do not proceed from the alteration of property, which is the only corruptor of politics. For example, I do not find that oligarchy, or government of a few, which is the extreme of an optimacy, ever did arise from a few men getting into their hands the estates of all the rest of the nobility: for had it begun so, it might have lasted, which I never read of any that did. I will therefore conclude, that they were all tyrannies; for so the Greeks called all usurpations, whether of one or more persons: and all those that I ever read of, as they came in either by craft or violence, (as the thirty tyrants of Athens; the fifteen of Thebes; and the *Decemviri* of Rome, though these at first came in lawfully:)[1] so they were soon driven out; and ever, were either assassinated, or died by the sword of justice: and therefore I shall say no more of them; not thinking them worth the name of a government. As for the extreme of democracy, which is anarchy, it is not so: for many commonwealths have lasted for a good time under that administration (if I may so call a state so full of confusion.) An anarchy then is when the people not contented with their share in the administration of the government, (which is the right of approving, or disapproving of laws, of leagues, and of making of war and peace, of judging in all causes upon an appeal to them, and choosing all manner of officers) will take upon themselves the office of the senate too, in managing subordinate matters of state, proposing laws originally, and assuming debate in the market-place, making their orators their leaders: nay, not content with this, will take upon them to alter all the orders of the government when they please; as was frequently practised in Athens, and in the modern state of Florence. In both these cities, whenever any great person who could lead the people, had a mind to alter the government, he called them together, and made them vote a change. In Florence they called it: To call the people to a parliament and to reform the government,[2] which is summoning the people into the market-place to resume the government; and did then presently institute a new one, with new orders, new magistracies, and the like.

[1] *Decemviri*—ten magistrates at times appointed to define or create laws, but in 450 B.C. very tyrannically inclined: Machiavelli, *Discourses*, I, 35.
[2] *Chiamar il populo a parlamento, e ripigliar lo stato.*

Now that which originally causes this disorder, is the admitting (in the beginning of a government, or afterwards) the meaner sort of people, who have no share in the territory, into an equal part of ordering the commonwealth: these being less sober, less considering, and less careful of the public concerns; and being commonly the major part; are made the instruments oft-times of the ambition of the great ones, and very apt to kindle into faction. But notwithstanding all the confusion which we see under an anarchy, (where the wisdom of the better sort is made useless by the fury of the people;) yet many cities have subsisted hundreds of years in this condition: and have been more considerable, and performed greater actions, than ever any government of equal extent did; except it were a well-regulated democracy. But it is true, they ruin in the end; and that never by cowardice or baseness, but by too much boldness and temerarious undertakings; as both Athens and Florence did: the first undertaking the invasion of Sicily, when their affairs went ill elsewhere; and the other, by provoking the Spaniard and the pope. But I have done now; and shall pass to say something of the modern policies.[1]

NOBLE VEN. Before you come to that, sir, pray satisfy me in a point, which I should have moved before but that I was unwilling to interrupt your rational discourse. How came you to take it for granted, that Moses, Theseus, and Romulus were founders of popular governments? As for Moses, we have his story written by an infallible pen. Theseus was ever called king of Athens, though he lived so long since that what is written of him is justly esteemed fabulous: but Romulus certainly was a king; and that government continued a monarchy, though elective, under seven princes.

ENG. GENT. I will be very short in my answer; and say nothing of Theseus, for the reason you are pleased to allege: but for Moses, you may read in holy writ, that when, by God's command he had brought the Israelites out of Egypt, he did at first manage them by acquainting the people with the estate of their government; which people were called together with the sound of a trumpet, and are termed in scripture the Congregation of the Lord. This government he thought might serve their turn in their passage; and that it would be time enough to make them a better, when they were in possession of the land of

---

[1] Thucydides records the expedition to Sicily, 415–413 B.C.: and see Machiavelli, *The Prince*, chapter XXI.

Canaan: especially having made them judges and magistrates at the insistence of his father-in-law Jethro; which are called in authors, Jethronic magistracy.[1] But finding that this provision was not sufficient, he complained to God, of the difficulty he had to make that state of affairs hold together. God was pleased to order him, to let seventy elders be appointed for a senate; but yet the Congregation of the Lord continued still and acted: and by the several soundings of the trumpets, either the senate, or popular assembly were called together, or both. So that this government was the same with all other democracies; consisting of a principal magistrate, a senate, and a people assembled together: not by representation, but in a body. Now for Romulus: it is very plain, that he was no more than the first officer of the commonwealth (whatever he was called,) and that he was chosen (as your Doge is,) for life. And when the last of those seven kings usurped the place; that is, did reign without the people's command and exercise the government tyrannically; the people drove him out, (as all people in the world that have property will do in the like case, except some extraordinary qualifications in the prince preserve him for one age) and afterwards appointed in his room two magistrates, and made them annual; which two had the same command as well in their armies, as in their cities; and did not make the least alteration besides; excepting that they chose an officer that was to perform the king's function, in certain sacrifices which Numa appointed to be performed by the king; lest the people should think their religion was changed: this officer was called high priest. If you are satisfied; I will go on to the consideration of our modern states.

NOBLE VEN. I am fully answered; and besides am clearly of opinion, that no government, whether mixed monarchy or commonwealth, can subsist without a senate: as well from the turbulent state of the Israelites under Moses, till the Sanhedrim was instituted; as from a certain kingdom of the Vandals in Africa; where, after their conquest of the natives, they appointed a government consisting of a prince and a popular assembly; which latter, within half a year, beat the king's brains out; he having no bulwark of nobility, or senate, to defend him from them. But I will divert you no longer.

---

[1] Jethro, the father-in-law of Moses, suggested to him the appointment and use of others to help in administration (*Exodus* xviii). The magistracy so formed was a stage between the single rule of Moses, and the establishment of the Sanhedrim and the Commonwealth of Israel.

ENG. GENT. Sir, you are very right; and we should have spoken something of that before, if it had been the business of this meeting to discourse of the particular models of government: but intending only to say so much of the ancient policy as to show what Government in general is, and upon what basis it stands; I think I have done it sufficiently to make way for the understanding of our own; at least, when I have said something of the policies which are now extant; and that, with your favour, I will do. I shall need say little now of those commonwealths, which however they came by their liberty, either by arms or purchase, are now much-what under the same kind of policy as the ancients were. In Germany, the free towns, and many princes, make up the body of a commonwealth, called the empire; of which the emperor is head. This general union has its diets or parliaments, where they are all represented; and where all things concerning the safety and interest of Germany in general, or that belong to peace and war, are transacted. These diets never intermeddle with the particular concerns or policies of those princes or states that make it up, leaving to them their particular sovereignties. The several imperial cities, or commonwealths, are divided into two kinds; Lübeck's Law, and Cologne's Law:[1] which being the same exactly with the ancient democracies and optimacies, I will say no more of them. The governments of Switzerland, and the seven provinces of the Low-Countries, were made up in haste; to unite them against persecution and oppression, and to help to defend themselves the better: which they both have done very gallantly and successfully. They seem to have taken their pattern from the Grecians; who, when their greatness began to decline, and the several tyrants who succeeded Alexander began to press hard upon them, were forced to league themselves (yet in several confederacies, as that of the Aetolians, that of the Achaeans, &c.) for their mutual defence. The Swiss consist of thirteen sovereignties; some cities, which are most aristocratical; and some provinces, which have but a village for their head township. These are all democracies; and are governed all, by the owners of land: who assemble, as our freeholders do, at the county-court. They have their general diets, as in Germany.

The government of the United Provinces has for its foundation the

---

[1] Neville refers here to mercantile codes followed by Hanseatic cities linked to Lübeck (one famous law was that of 1614) and Cologne.

Union of Utrecht; made in the beginning of their standing upon their guard against the cruelty and oppression of the Spaniard, and patched up in haste; and seeming to be composed only for necessity as a state of war, has made modern statesmen conjecture, that it will not be very practicable in time of peace and security. At their general diet (which is called the States General) do intervene the deputies of the seven provinces, in what number their principals please: but all of them have but one vote, which are by consequence seven; and every one of the seven has a negative: so that nothing can pass without the concurrence of the whole seven. Every one of these provinces have a council or assembly of their own, called the States Provincial, who send and instruct their deputies to the states general; and perform other offices belonging to the peace and quiet of the province. These deputies to the states provincial, are sent by the several cities of which every province consists, and by the nobility of the province, which has one voice only. The basis of the government lies in these cities; which are each of them a distinct sovereignty: neither can the states of the province, much less the states general, entrench in the least upon their rights, nor so much as intermeddle with the government of their cities, or administration of justice; but only treat of what concerns their mutual defence, and their payments towards it. Every one of these cities is a sovereignty; governed by an optimacy, consisting of the chief citizens: which upon death are supplied by new ones elected by themselves. These are called the *Urnuscaperie*, or *Herne*;[1] which council has continued to govern those towns, time out of mind: even in the times of their princes, who were then the sovereigns: for without the consent of him, or his deputy, called stadtholder, nothing could be concluded in those days. Since, they have instituted an artificial minister of their own, whom they still call stadtholder; and make choice of him in their provincial assemblies, and for form sake defer something to him, as the approbation of their *Skepen* and other magistrates, and some other matters. This has been continued in the province of Holland, which is the chief province, in the succession of the princes of Orange; and in the most of the others too: the rest have likewise chosen some other of the house of Nassau. This government (so oddly set together, and so composed of a

---

[1] See no. 9, 'Political Discourses', above, p. 66. The councils of most cities in the United Provinces were increasingly closed oligarchies. *Urnuscaperie*, or *unus caperie*, may be *Vroedschappen*, that is, council of towns; *Herne*, lords or councillors.

state intended for a monarchy; and which as almanacs calculated for one meridian are made in some sort to serve for another, is by them continued in these several aristocracies) may last for a time: till peace and security, together with the abuse which is like to happen in the choice of the *Herne*, when they shall elect persons of small note into their body upon vacancies, for kindred or relation, rather than such as are of estate and eminency, or that otherwise abuse their power in the execution of it: and then it is believed, and reasonably enough, that those people (great in wealth, and very acute in the knowledge of their own interest) will find out a better form of government; or make themselves a prey to some great neighbour-prince in the attempting it: and this in case they in the meantime escape conquest from this great and powerful king of France, who at this time gives law to Christendom. I have nothing now left to keep me from the modern monarchies, but the most famous commonwealth of Venice; of which it would be presumption for me to say anything, whilst you are present.

NOBLE VEN. You may very safely go on if you please: for I believe strangers understand the speculative part of our government better than we do; and the doctrine of the ballot, which is our chief excellency: for I have read many descriptions of our frame, which have taught me something in it which I knew not before; particularly, Donato Gianotti the Florentine, to whom I refer those who are curious to know more of our orders. For we that manage the mechanical part of the government, are like horses who know their track well enough, without considering east or west, or what business they go about. Besides, it would be very tedious, and very needless, to make any relation of our model, with the several councils that make it up; and would be that which you have not done in treating of any other government. What we have said is enough to show what beginning we had; and that serves your turn: for we who are called nobility, and who manage the state, are the descendants of the first inhabitants; and had therefore been a democracy, if a numerous flock of strangers (who are contented to come and live among us as subjects) had not swelled our city, and made the governing party seem but a handful. So that we have the same foundations that all other aristocracies have, who govern but one city; and have no territory, but what they govern provincially. And our people, not knowing where to have better justice, are very well contented to live amongst us; without any share in the managing of affairs. Yet we have power to adopt whom we please into our nobility: and I believe that in the time of the Roman greatness, there were five for one of the inhabitants who were written in no tribe, but looked upon as strangers, and yet that did not vitiate their democracy; no more than our citizens and common people can hurt our optimacy. All the difficulty in our administration, has been to regulate our own nobility, and to bridle their faction and ambition; which can alone breed a disease in the vital part of our government: and this we do, by most severe laws; and a very rigorous execution of them.

DOCT. Sir, I was thinking to interpose concerning the propriety of lands in the territory of Padua; which, I hear, is wholly in the possession of the nobility of Venice.

NOBLE VEN. Our members have very good estates there, yet nothing but what they have paid very well for; no part of that country, or of any other province, having been shared amongst us as in other conquests. 'Tis true, that the Paduans having ever been the most revengeful people of Italy, could not be deterred from those execrable and treacherous murders which were every day committed, but by a severe execution of the laws as well against their lives as estates: and as many of their estates as were confiscated, were (during our necessities in the last war with the Turks)[1] exposed to sale, and sold to them that offered most; without any consideration of the persons purchasing. But it is very true, that most of them came into the hands of our nobility; they offering more than any other; by reason that their sober and frugal living, and their being forbidden all manner of traffic, makes them have no way of employing the money which proceeds from their parsimony; and so they can afford to give more than others, who may employ their advance to better profit elsewhere. But I perceive, doctor, by this question, that you have studied at Padua.

DOCT. No really, sir, the small learning I have was acquired in our university of Oxford; nor was I ever out of this island.

NOBLE VEN. I would you had, sir; for it would have been a great honour to our country to have contributed anything towards so vast a knowledge as you are possessor of: but I wish that it were your country, or at least the place of your habitation, that so we might partake not

---

[1] John Evelyn, *Diary*, ed. E. S. DeBeer (6 vols. Oxford, 1955), II, 471–2, notes disturbances in Padua. The war with the Ottomans raged 1645–69. Padua University was attended by Harvey and other famous Englishmen. Note in next paragraph the Doctor's denial of being at Padua.

only of your excellent discourse sometimes, but be the better for your skill; which would make us immortal.

DOCT. I am glad to see you so well that you can make yourself so merry: but I assure you I am very well here. England is a good wholesome climate for a physician. But, pray let our friend go on to his modern monarchies.

ENG. GENT. This is all I have now to do. Those monarchies are two, absolute, and mixed. For the first kind, all that we have knowledge of except the empire of the Turks, differ so little from the ancient monarchies of the Assyrians and Persians; that having given a short description of them before, it will be needless to say any more of the Persian, the Mogul, the king of Burma,[1] China, Prester John; or any other the great men under those princes, as the satraps of old: being made so, only by their being employed and put into great places and governments by the sovereign. But the monarchy of the grand seignior is something different. They both agree in this, that the prince is, in both, absolute proprietor of all the lands, (excepting in the kingdom of Egypt, of which I shall say something anon;) but the diversity lies in the administration of the property: the other emperors as well ancient as modern using to manage the revenue of the several towns and parishes, as our kings or the kings of France do; that is, keep it in their hands, and administer it by officers: and so you may read that Xerxes king of Persia allowed the revenue of so many villages to Themistocles; which assignations are practised at this day, both to public and to private uses, by the present monarchs. But the Turks, when they invaded the broken empire of the Arabians, did not at first make any great alteration in their policy: till the house of Ottoman, the present royal family, did make great conquests in Asia, and afterwards in Greece: whence they might possibly take their present way of dividing their conquered territories; for they took the same course which the Goths and other modern people had used with their conquered lands in Europe, upon which they planted military colonies, by dividing them amongst the soldiers for their pay or maintenance. These shares were called by them timars, which signifies benefices: and differed in this only from the European knights-fees, that these last originally were hereditary, and so property was maintained; whereas amongst the Ottomans, they were merely at will; and they enjoyed their shares whilst they remained the

[1] Pegu, or Burma.

108

Sultan's soldiers, and no longer; being turned out both of his service, and of their timars, when he pleases. This doubtless had been the best and firmest monarchy in the world, if they could have stayed here, and not had a mercenary army besides; which have often (like the praetorians in the time of the Roman tyrants) made the palace and the seraglio the shambles of their princes; whereas if the timariots, as well spahis (or horse) as foot, had been brought together to guard the prince by courses (as they used to do king David) as well as they are to fight for the empire; this horrid flaw and inconvenience in their government had been wholly avoided. For though these are not planted upon entire property, as David's were; (those being in the nature of trainedbands;) yet the remoteness of their habitations from the court and the factions of the great city, and their desire to repair home and to find all things quiet at their return, would have easily kept them from being infected with that cursed disease of rebellion against their sovereign, upon whose favour they depend for the continuance of their livelihood: whereas the janizaries [infantry] are for life, and are sure to be in the same employment under the next successor: so sure, that no grand seignior can, or dares go about to disband them; the suspicion of intending such a thing having caused the death of more than one of their emperors.[1] But I shall go to the limited monarchies.

DOCT. But pray, before you do so, inform us something of the Roman emperors: had they the whole dominion or property of the lands of Italy?

ENG. GENT. The Roman emperors I reckon amongst the tyrants: for so amongst the Greeks were called those citizens who usurped the government of their commonwealths, and maintained it by force, without endeavouring to found or establish it, by altering the property of lands, as not imagining that their children could ever hold it after them; in which they were not deceived: so that it was plain that the Roman empire was not a natural but a violent government. The reasons why it lasted longer than ordinarily tyrannies do, are many. First, because Augustus the first emperor kept up the senate, and so for his time cajoled them with this bait of imaginary power; which might not have sufficed neither to have kept him from the fate of his uncle, but that there had been so many revolutions and bloody wars between,

[1] Neville, like most contemporaries, relied on the two works by Paul Rycaut (nos. 5 and 6, 'Political Discourses', above, pp. 65-6).

that all mankind was glad to repose and take breath for a while under any government that could protect them. And he gained the service of these senators the rather, because he suffered none to be so but those who had followed his fortune in the several civil wars; and so were engaged to support him for their own preservation: besides, he confiscated all those who had at any time been proscribed, or sided in any encounter against him; which, considering in how few hands the lands of Italy then were, might be an over-balance of the property in his hands. But this is certain; that whatever he had not in his own possession, he disposed of at his pleasure; taking it away, as also the lives of his people, without any judicial proceedings, when he pleased. That the confiscations were great, we may see by his planting above sixty thousand soldiers upon lands in Lombardy; that is, erecting so many beneficia, or timars: and, if any man's lands lay in the way, he took them in for neighbourhood, without any delinquency. 'Mantua, unfortunately, was much too near Cremona'.[1] And it is very evident, that if these beneficia had not afterwards been made hereditary, that empire might have had a stabler foundation; and so a more quiet and orderly progress than it after had: for the court-guards called the praetorians, did make such havoc of their princes, and change them so often, that this (though it may seem a paradox) is another reason why this tyranny was not ruined sooner. For the people, who had really an interest to endeavour a change of government, were so prevented by seeing the prince whom they designed to supplant, removed to their hand, that they were puzzled what to do; taking in the meantime great recreation to see those wild beasts hunted down themselves, who had so often preyed upon their lives and estates: besides that, most commonly the frequent removes of their masters, made them scarce have time to do any mischief to their oppressed subjects in particular, though they were all slaves in general. This government of the later Romans is a clear example of the truth and efficacy of these politic principles we have been discoursing of. First, that any government (be it the most unlimited and arbitrary monarchy) that is placed upon a right basis of property, is better both for prince and people, than to leave them a seeming property still at his devotion; and then for want of fixing the foundation, expose their lives to those dangers and hazards, with which so many tumults and insurrections, which must necessarily happen,

---

[1] Virgil, *Eclogue*, IX. 28: *Mantua vae miserae nimium vicina Cremonae.*

will threaten them daily. And in the next place, that any violent constraining of mankind to a subjection, is not to be called a government; nor does salve either the politic or moral ends, which those eminent legislators amongst the ancients proposed to themselves, when they set rules to preserve the quiet and peace, as well as the plenty, prosperity and greatness of the people; but that the politics, or art of governing, is a science to be learned and studied by counsellors and statesmen be they never so great,[1] or else mankind will have a very sad condition under them, and they themselves a very perplexed and turbulent life, and probably a very destructive and precipitous end of it.

DOCT. I am very glad I gave occasion to make this discourse: now I beseech you, before you go to the mixed monarchies, not to forget Egypt.

ENG. GENT. 'Twas that I was coming to, before you were pleased to interrogate me concerning the Roman empire. The Egyptians are this day, for aught I know, the only people that enjoy property, and are governed as a province, by any of the eastern absolute princes. For whereas Damascus, Aleppo, and most of the other cities and provinces of that empire, whose territory is divided into timars, are governed by a bashaw,[2] who for his guards has some small number of janizaries or soldiers; the bashaw of Egypt, or of Grand Cairo, has ever an army with him: and divers forts are erected; which is the way European princes use in governing their provinces; and must be so where property is left entire, except they plant colonies as the Romans did. The reason why Selim, who broke the empire of the Mamelukes, and conquered Egypt,[3] did not plant timars upon it, was the laziness and cowardliness of the people, and the great fruitfulness of the soil, and deliciousness of the country, which has mollified and rendered effeminate all the nations that ever did inhabit it. So that a resolution was taken to impose upon them, first, the maintaining an army by a tax; and then to pay a full half of all the fruits and product of their lands to the grand seignior, which they are to cultivate and improve. This is well managed by the bashaws and their officers; and comes to an incredible sum: the goods being sold, the money is conveyed in specie to the port, and is the greatest part of that prince's revenue. And it is believed, that if all the lands had been entirely confiscated, and that

---

[1] Cf. Sidney, *Discourses*, chapter II, section viii.
[2] Bashaw or pasha, etc.   [3] Selim's victory, A.D. 1517.

the grand seignior had managed them by his officers, he would not have made a third part so much of the whole, as he receives now annually for one half: not only because those people are extremely industrious, where their own profit is concerned; but for that it is clear, if they had been totally divested of their estates, they would have left their country; and made that which is now the most populous kingdom of the world, a desert: as is all the rest of the Turkish dominions, except some cities. And if the people had removed as they did elsewhere, there would not only have wanted hands to have cultivated and improved the lands, but mouths to consume the product of it; so that the prince's revenue by the cheapness of victual, and the want of labourers, would have almost fallen to nothing.

NOBLE VEN. Pray God this be not the reason that this king of France leaves property to his subjects; for certainly he has taken example by this province of Egypt: his subjects having a tax (which for the continuance of it, I must call a rent or tribute) imposed upon them, to the value of one full half of their estates; which must ever increase, as the lands improve.

ENG. GENT. I believe, sir, there is another reason; for the property there, being in the nobility and gentry, which are the hands by which he manages his force both at home and abroad, it would not have been easy or safe for him to take away their estates.—But I come to the limited monarchies. They were first introduced (as was said before) by the Goths, and other northern people. Whence those great swarms came, as it was unknown to Procopius himself who lived in the time of their invasion,[1] and who was a diligent searcher into all the circumstances of their concernments, so it is very needless for us to make any enquiry into it: thus much being clear, that they came man woman and child, and conquered and possessed all these parts of the world; which were then subject to the Roman empire, and since Christianity came in have been so to the Latin church; till honest John Calvin[2] taught some of us the way how to deliver ourselves from the tyrannical yoke, which neither we nor our forefathers were able to bear. Whence those people had the government they established in these parts after their conquest;

---

[1] Procopius, sixth-century Byzantine historian, recommended, no. 12, 'Political Discourses', above, p. 66.

[2] John Calvin (1509–64), the reformer, rather surprisingly praised by the free-thinking anti-clerical Neville, but Neville was protestant, in spite of all the arguments of his Italian friends.

that is, whether they brought it from their own country, or made it themselves; must needs be uncertain, since their original is wholly so: but it seems very probable that they had some excellent persons among them, though the ignorance and want of learning in that age has not suffered any thing to remain that may give us any great light; for it is plain, that the government they settled, was both according to the exact rules of politics, and very natural and suitable to that division they made of their several territories. Whenever then these invaders had quieted any province, and that the people were driven out or subdued, they divided the lands: and to the prince they gave usually a tenth part, or thereabouts; to the great men, or *comites regis*, as it was translated into Latin, every one, as near as they could, an equal share. These were to enjoy an hereditary right in their estates; as the king did in his part, and in the crown. But neither he, nor his peers or companions, were to have the absolute disposal of the lands so allotted them: but were to keep a certain proportion to themselves for their use; and the rest was ordered to be divided amongst the freemen, who came with them to conquer. What they kept to themselves was called demesnes, in English and French; and in Italian, *beni allodiali.* The other part which they granted to the freemen, was called a feud: and all these estates were held of these lords hereditarily, only the tenants were to pay a small rent annually; and at every death or change an acknowledgement in money, and in some tenures the best beast besides. But the chief condition of the feud or grant, was, that the tenant should perform certain services to the lord; of which one (in all tenures of freemen) was to follow him armed to the wars, for the service of the prince and defence of the land. And upon their admittance to their feuds, they took an oath to be true vassals and tenants to their lords; and to pay their rents, and perform their services; and upon failure to forfeit their estates. And these tenants were divided, according to their habitations, into several manors; in every one of which there was a court kept, twice every year; where they all were to appear, and to be admitted to their several estates, and to take the oath above mentioned. All these peers did likewise hold all their demesnes, as also all their manors, of the prince: to whom they swore allegiance and fealty. There were besides these freemen or franklins, other tenants to every lord, who were called villeins; who were to perform all servile offices, and their estates were all at the lord's disposal when he pleased: these consisted mostly of such of the former inhabitants of these countries, as were not either destroyed or driven out; and possibly of others who were servants amongst them, before they came from their own countries. Perhaps thus much might have been unnecessary to be said; considering that these lords, tenants, and courts, are yet extant in all the kingdoms in Europe: but that to a gentleman of Venice, where there are none of these things, and where the Goths never were, something may be said in excuse for me.

NOBLE VEN. 'Tis true, sir, we fled from the Goths betimes; but yet in those countries which we recovered since in *Terra Firma*, we found the footsteps of these lords, and tenures, and their titles of counts: though being now provinces to us, they have no influence upon the government; as, I suppose, you are about to prove they have in these parts.

ENG. GENT. You are right, sir; for the governments of France, Spain, England, and all other countries where these people settled, were framed accordingly. It is not my business to describe particularly the distinct forms of the several governments in Europe, which do derive from these people, (for they may differ in some of their orders and laws, though the foundation be in them all the same) this would be unnecessary, they being all extant and so well known: and besides, little to my purpose; excepting to show where they have declined from their first institution, and admitted of some change. France, and Poland, have not, nor as I can learn, ever had any freemen below the nobility; that is, had no yeomen; but all are either noble, or villeins: therefore the lands must have been originally given, as they now remain, into the hands of these nobles. But I will come to the administration of the government in these countries; and first say wherein they all agree, or did as least in their institution; which is, that the sovereign power is in the states assembled together by the prince, in which he presides; these make laws, levy money, redress grievances, punish great officers, and the like. These states consist in some places of the prince and nobility only, as in Poland; and anciently in France, before certain towns, for the encouraging of trade, procured privileges to send deputies: which deputies are now called the third estate: and in others, consist of the nobility and commonalty; which latter had, and still have the same right to intervene and vote, as the great ones have both in England, Spain, and other kingdoms.

DOCT. But you say nothing of the clergy: I see you are no great friend to them, to leave them out of your politics.[1]

ENG. GENT. The truth is, doctor, I could wish there had never been any: the purity of Christian religion, as also the good and orderly government of the world, had been much better provided for without them; as it was in the apostolical time, when we hear nothing of clergy: but my omitting their reverend lordships was no neglect, for I meant to come to them in order; for you know that the northern people did not bring Christianity into these parts, but found it here, and were in time converted to it; so that there could be no clergy at the first. But if I had said nothing at all of this race, yet I had committed no solecism in the politics: for the bishops and great abbots intervened in the states here, upon the same foundation that the other peers do; viz. for their great possessions, and the dependence their tenants and vassals have upon them: although they being a people of that great sanctity and knowledge, scorn to intermix so much as titles with us profane lay-idiots; and therefore will be called, lords spiritual. But you will have a very venerable opinion of them, if you do but consider how they came by these great possessions, which made them claim a third part of the government. And truly not unjustly, by my rule; for I believe they had no less (at one time) than a third part of the lands, in most of these countries.

NOBLE VEN. Pray, how did they acquire these lands? was it not here by the charitable donation of pious Christians, as it was elsewhere?

ENG. GENT. Yes, certainly, very pious men! some of them might be well-meaning people, but still such as were cheated by these holy men: who told them perpetually, both in public and private, 'that they represented God upon earth, being ordained by authority from him who was his viceroy here; and that what was given to them, was given to God; and he would repay it largely, both in this world, and the next.' This wheedle made our barbarous ancestors, newly instructed in the Christian faith, (if this religion may be called so, and sucking in this foolish doctrine more than the doctrine of Christ) so zealous to these vipers, that they would have plucked out their eyes to serve them; much more bestow, as they did, the fruitfullest and best situate of their possessions upon them. Nay, some they persuaded to take

[1] The anti-clericalism of the following passage provoked much adverse criticism and comment.

upon them their callings; vow chastity, and give all they had to them; and become one of them; amongst whom, I believe, they found no more sanctity, than they left in the world. But this is nothing to another trick they had: which was to insinuate into the most notorious and execrable villains with which that age abounded; men, who being princes, (and other great men, for such were the tools they worked with) had treacherously poisoned or otherwise murdered their nearest relations, fathers, brothers, wives, to reign or enjoy their estates: these they did persuade into a belief, 'that if they had a desire to be saved notwithstanding their execrable villainies, they need but part with some of those great possessions (which they had acquired by those acts:) to their bishoprics or monasteries, and they would pray for their souls; and they were so holy and acceptable to God, that he would deny them nothing:' which they immediately performed; so great was the ignorance and blindness of that age! And you shall hardly find in the story of those times, any great monastery, abbey or other religious house in any of these countries, (I speak confidently as to what concerns our own Saxons,) that had not its foundation from some such original.

DOCT. A worthy beginning, of a worthy race!

**NOBLE VEN.[1] Sir, you maintain a strange position here, that it had been better there had been no clergy. Would you have had no gospel preached, no sacraments, no continuance of Christian religion in the world? Or do you think that these things could have been without a succession of the true priesthood, or (as you call it, of true ministry) by means of ordination? Does not your own church hold the same?

ENG. GENT. You will know more of my church, when I have told you what I find the word church to signify in scripture; which is to me, the only rule of faith, worship, and manners: neither do I seek these additional helps, of fathers, councils, or ecclesiastical history; much less tradition: for since it is said in the word of God itself, 'that Antichrist did begin to work even in those days;' I can easily believe that he had brought his work to some perfection, before the word church was by him applied to the clergy. I shall therefore tell you what I conceive that church, clergy, and ordination, signified in the apostolical times. I find then the word, church, in the New Testament taken but in

---

[1] **...* addition to the second edition, presumably printed with the Parliament about to gather at Oxford in mind.

two senses: the first, for the universal invisible church, called sometimes of the first-born; that is, the whole number of the true followers of Christ in the world, wherever resident, or into what part soever dispersed. The other signification of church, is an assembly; which though it be sometimes used to express any meetings (even unlawful and tumultuous ones) as well in scripture, as profane authors; yet it is more frequently understood of a gathering together to the duties of prayer, preaching, and breaking of bread: and the whole number so congregated is, both in the acts of the apostles and in their holy epistles, called the Church. Nor is there the least colour for appropriating that word to the pastors and deacons; who, since the corruptions of Christian religion, are called clergy. Which word in the Old Testament is used, sometimes for God's whole people, and sometimes for the tribe of Levi, out of which the priests were chosen; for the word signifies a lot; so that tribe is called God's lot, because they had no share allotted them when the land was divided, but were to live upon tithe, and serve in the functions of their religion, and be singers, porters, butchers, bakers, and cooks, for the sacrifices &c. So that this tribe was styled clergy but figuratively; and the allegory passed into the New Testament: where the saints are sometimes called clergy; but never the pastors or deacons: who were far from pretending, in those days, to come in the place of the Aaronical priesthood. The word ordination, in scripture, signifies lifting up of hands; and is used, first, for the giving a suffrage, which in all popular assemblies was done by stretching out the hand (as it is in the common hall of London:)[1] in the next place, it is applied to the order or decree made by the suffrage so given; which was then (and is yet too in all modern languages) called an ordinance; and the suffrage itself ordination: which word proves that the first Christian churches were democratical; that is, that the whole congregation had the choice in this, as well as the sovereign authority in all excommunications, and all other matters whatsoever that could occur: for in all aristocratical commonwealths the word for choice is *Keirothesia*, or imposition of hands, (for so the election of all magistrates and officers was made,) and not *Keirotonia* [stretching forth of hands— as in voting for M.P.s for example]. These pastors and other officers did not pretend to be, by virtue of such choice, of a peculiar profession

---

[1] At the Common Hall of London, 29 July 1680, the Livery assembled for the annual election of sheriffs and desired the Lord Mayor, Sir Robert Clayton, to beseech Charles II to call the parliament.

different from other men; as their followers have done since Antichrist's reign; but were only called and appointed (by the congregation's approval of their gifts or parts) to instruct or feed the flock; visit the sick; and perform all other offices of a true minister (that is, servant) of the gospel. At other times, they followed the business of their own trades and professions: and the Christians in those times (which none will deny to have been the purest of the church) did never dream that a true pastor ought to pretend to any succession, to qualify him for the ministry of the word; or that the idle and riduculous ceremonies used in your church, (and still continued in that which you are pleased to call mine,) were any way essential or conducing to capacitate a person to be a true preacher or dispenser of the Christian faith. And I cannot sufficiently admire why our clergy, who very justly refuse to believe the miracle which is pretended to be wrought in transubstantiation; because they see both the wafer and the wine to have the same substance, and the same accidents after the priest has mumbled words over those elements as they had before; yet will believe, that the same kind of spell or charm in ordination can have the efficacy to metamorphose a poor lay-idiot, into a heavenly creature: notwithstanding that we find in them the same human nature, and the same necessities of it, to which they were subject before such transformation; nay, the same debauch, profaneness, ignorance, and disability to preach the gospel.

NOBLE VEN. Sir, this discourse is very new to me. I must confess I am much inclined to join with you in believing, that the power priests exercise over mankind, with the jurisdiction they pretend to over princes and states, may be a usurpation; but that they should not have a divine call to serve at the altar, or that any person can pretend to perform those sacred functions without being duly ordained, seems very strange.

ENG. GENT. I am not now to discourse of religion: it is never very civil to do so in conversation of persons of a different belief; neither can it be of any benefit towards a Roman Catholic; for if his conscience should be never so clearly convinced, he is not yet master of his own faith; having given it up to his church, of whom he must ask leave to be a convert, which he will be sure never to obtain. But if you have the curiosity when you come amongst the learned in your own country (for amongst our ordination-mongers, there is a great scarcity of letters and other good parts) you may please to take the Bible, which you acknowledge to be the word of God as well as we; and intreat some of them to show you any passage, the plain and genuine sense of which can any way evince this succession, this ordination, or this priesthood, we are now speaking of: and when you have done, if you will let your own excellent reason and discourse judge, and not your priest, (who is too much concerned in point of interest) I make no doubt but you will be convinced that the pretence to the dispensing of divine things by virtue of a human constitution, and so ridiculous a one too as the ordination practised by your bishops and ours, (who descend and succeed from one and the same mother) is as little justifiable by scripture and reason, and full as great a cheat and usurpation, as the empire which the ecclesiastics pretend to over the consciences and persons of men, and the exemption from all secular power.

NOBLE VEN. Well, sir, though neither my faith nor my reason can come up to what you hold, yet the novelty and the grace of this argument has delighted me extremely: and if that be a sin, as I fear it is, I must confess it to my priest; but I ask your pardon first, for putting you upon this long deviation.*

ENG. GENT. Well, this digression is not without its use: for it will shorten our business, (which is grown longer than I thought it would have been;) for I shall mention the clergy no more: but whenever I speak of peerage, pray take notice, that I mean both lords spiritual and temporal; since they stand both upon the same foot of property. But if you please, I will fall immediately to discourse of the government of England; and say no more of those of our neighbours, than what will fall in by the way, or be hinted to me by your demands: for the time runs away, and I know the doctor must be at home by noon, where he gives daily charitable audience to an infinity of poor people; who have need of his help, and who send or come for it, not having the confidence to send for him, since they have nothing to give him: though he be very liberal too of his visits to such, where he has any knowledge of them. But I spare his modesty, which I see is concerned at the just testimony I bear to his charity. The sovereign power of England then is in king, lords, and commons. The parliaments, as they are now constituted (that is, the assigning a choice to such a number of boroughs, as also the manner and form of elections and returns) did come in, as I suppose, in the time of Henry the third; where now our statute-book begins. And I must confess I was inclined to believe, that before that time, our yeomanry or commonalty had not formally assembled in parliament, but been virtually included and represented by the peers, upon whom they depended: but I am fully convinced, that it was otherwise, by the learned discourses lately published by Mr Petyt of the Temple, and Mr Atwood of Grays-Inn; being gentlemen whom I do mention, *honoris causa* [in order to honour].[1] And really they deserve to be honoured, that they will spare some time from the mechanical part of their callings (which is to assist clients with counsel, and to plead their causes, which I acknowledge likewise to be honourable) to study the true interest of their country; and to show how ancient the rights of the people in England are: and that in a time, when neither profit nor countenance can be hoped for, from so ingenious an undertaking. But I beg pardon for the deviation.

Of the three branches of sovereign power which politicians mention, which are enacting laws, levying of taxes, and making war and peace, the two first of them are indisputably in the parliament; and when I say parliament, I ever intend, with the king. The last, has been usually exercised by the prince; if he can do it with his own money. Yet because even in that case it may be ruinous to the kingdom, by exposing it to an invasion, many have affirmed that such a power cannot be (by the true and ancient free government of England) supposed to be entrusted in the hands of one man; and therefore we see in divers kings' reigns the parliament has been consulted, and their advice taken in those matters that have either concerned war or leagues; and that if it has been omitted, addresses have been made to the king by parliaments, either to make war, or peace; according to what they thought profitable to the public. So that I will not determine whether that power which draws such consequences after it, be by the genuine sense of our laws in the prince or no; although I know of no statute, or written record, which makes it otherwise. That which is undoubtedly the king's right or prerogative, is to call and dissolve parliaments; to preside in them; to approve of all acts made by them; and to put in execution, as supreme or sovereign magistrate (in the intervals of parliaments, and during their sitting) all laws made by them, as also the common law. For which cause he has the nomination of all inferior officers and ministers

---

[1] Neville's doubts about the position of the commons before the reign of Henry III were well-founded, but evidently overruled by his friends William Petyt (1636–1707), author of *The Ancient Right of the Commons of England Asserted* (London, 1680), and W. Atwood (d. 1705), *Jani Anglorum Facies Nova* (London, 1680).

under him, excepting such as by law or charter are eligible otherwise; and the power of the sword, to force obedience to the judgements given both in criminal and civil causes.

DOCT. Sir, you have made us a very absolute prince: what have we left us? If the king have all this power, what do our liberties or rights signify, whenever he pleases?

ENG. GENT. This objection, doctor, makes good what I said before, that your skill did not terminate in the body natural, but extended to the politic: for a more pertinent interrogatory could never have been made by Plato or Aristotle. In answer to which, you may please to understand; that when these constitutions were first made, our ancestors were a plain-hearted, well-meaning people, without court-reserves, or tricks; who having made choice of this sort of government, and having power enough in their hands to make it take place, did not foresee or imagine, that any thoughts of invading their rights could enter into the prince's head. Nor do I read that it ever did, till the Norman line came to reign: which coming in by treaty,[1] it was obvious there was no conquest made upon any but Harold; in whose stead William the first came, and would claim no more after his victory, than what Harold enjoyed: excepting, that he might confiscate (as he did) those great men who took part with the wrong title; and Frenchmen were put into their estates. Which though it made in this kingdom a mixture between Normans and Saxons, yet produced no change or innovation in the government; the Norman peers being as tenacious of their liberties, and as active in the recovery of them to the full, as the Saxon families were.

Soon after the death of William, (and possibly, in his time,) there began some invasions upon the rights of the kingdom; which begat grievances, and afterwards complaints and discontents: which grew to that height, that the peers were fain to use their power, that is, arm their vassals to defend the government; whilst the princes of that age, first king John, and then Henry the third, got force together. The barons called in Lewis the dauphin, (whilst the king would have given away the kingdom to the Saracens, as he did to the pope) and armed their own creatures; so that a bloody war ensued, for almost forty years off and on, as may be read in our history. The success was, that the barons or peers obtained, in the close, two charters or laws for the ascertaining

[1] Neville believed the Norman conquest of 1066 effected no innovation in government.

their rights; by which, neither their lives, liberties, or estates, could ever be in danger any more from any arbitrary power in the prince: and so the good government of England, which was before this time (like the law of nature) only written in the hearts of men; came to be expressed in parchment and remain a record in writing; though these charters gave us no more, than what was our own before. After these charters were made, there could not choose but happen some encroachment upon them; but so long as the peers kept their greatness, there was no breaches but what were immediately made up in parliament: which whenever they assembled, did in the first place confirm the charters, and made very often interpretations upon them, for the benefit of the people; witness the statute *de Tallagio non concedendo*,[1] and many others.

But to come nearer the giving the doctor an answer, you may please to understand, that not long after the framing of these forementioned charters, there did arise a grievance not foreseen or provided for by them; and it was such an one that had beaten down the government at once, if it had not been redressed in an orderly way. This was the intermission of parliaments; which could not be called but by the prince; and he not doing of it, they ceased to be assembled for some years. If this had not been speedily remedied, the barons must have put on their armour again: for who can imagine, that such brisk assertors of their rights could have acquiesced in an omission that ruined the foundation of the government? which consisting of king, lords, and commons, and having at that time marched near five hundred years upon three legs, must then have gone on hopping upon one; which could it have gone forward (as was impossible, whilst property continued where it was) yet would have ridden but a little way. Nor can it be wondered at, that our great men made no provision against this grievance in their charters: because it was impossible for them to imagine that their prince, who had so good a share in this government, should go about to destroy it, and to take that burden upon himself; which, by our constitution was undeniably to be divided between him and his subjects. And therefore divers of the great men of those times speaking with that excellent prince king Edward the first about it, he (to take away from his people all fear and apprehension that he intended to

---

[1] The Confirmation of 1297 (25 Ed. I, see S of R I, 123), popularly supposed to secure the right of parliament to assent to taxes before their levy.

change the ancient government,) called speedily a parliament, and in it consented to a declaration of the kingdom's right in that point: without the clearing of which, all our other laws had been useless, and the government itself too; of which the parliament is (at the least) as essential a part as the prince. So that there passed a law in that parliament, that one should be held every year; and oftener, if need be:[1] which like another Magna Charta, was confirmed by a new act made in the time of Edward the third, that glorious prince. Nor were there any sycophants in those days, who durst pretend loyalty by using arguments to prove that it was against the royal prerogative, for the parliament to entrench upon the king's right of calling and dissolving of parliaments: as if there were a prerogative in the crown, to choose whether ever a parliament should assemble, or no. I would desire no more, if I were a prince, to make me grand seignior. Soon after this last act, the king, by reason of his wars with France and Scotland, and other great affairs, was forced sometimes to end his parliaments abruptly, and leave business undone; (and this not out of court-tricks, which were then unknown:) which produced another act not long after, by which it was provided; that no parliament should be dismissed, till all the petitions were answered. That is, in the language of those times, till all the bills (which were then styled petitions) were finished.

DOCT. Pray, sir, give me a little account of this last act you speak of; for I have heard in discourse from many lawyers, that they believe there is no such.

ENG. GENT. Truly, sir, I shall confess to you, that I do not find this law in any of our printed statute-books. But that which first gave me the knowledge of it, was what was said about three years ago in the house of commons, by a worthy and learned gentleman, who undertook to produce the record in the reign of Richard the second: and since, I have questioned many learned counsellors about it, who tell me there is such a one: and one of them, who is counted a prerogative lawyer, said it was so; but that the act was made in factious times.[2] Besides, I think it will be granted, that for some time after, (and particularly in the reigns of Henry the fourth, Henry the fifth, and Henry the sixth) it was

---

[1] Edward I was credited by Neville and many contemporaries with a statute about annual parliaments, but those of his grandson (4 Ed. III. c. 14. and 36 Ed. III. c. 10.) were probably the first that can be authenticated.

[2] *The Bulstrode Papers* (London, 1897), pp. 284–5 (Wed. 14 Apr. 1675), records the debate, which fell on a day omitted by Grey.

usual for a proclamation to be made in Westminster-hall, before the end of every session: That all those that had any matter to present to the parliament, should bring it in before such a day; for otherwise, the parliament at that day should determine. But if there were nothing at all of this, nor any record extant concerning it; yet I must believe that it is so by the fundamental law of this government, which must be lame and imperfect without it. For it is all one to have no parliaments at all but when the prince pleases, and to allow a power in him to dismiss them when he will; that is, when they refuse to do what he will. So that if there be no statute, it is certainly because our wise ancestors thought there needed none, but that by the very essence and constitution of the government it is provided for. And this we may call (if you had rather have it so) the common law; which is of as much value (if not more) than any statute, and of which all our good acts of parliament, and Magna Charta itself, is but declaratory. So that your objection is sufficiently answered in this, that though the king is entrusted with the formal part of summoning and pronouncing the dissolution of parliaments, which is done by his writ; yet the laws (which oblige him as well as us) have determined how and when he shall do it: which is enough to show, that the king's share in the sovereignty, (that is, in the parliament,) is cut out to him by the law, and not left at his disposal. Now I come to the king's part in the intervals of parliament.

NOBLE VEN. Sir, before you do so, pray tell us what other prerogatives the king enjoys in the government; for otherwise, I who am a Venetian, may be apt to think that our Doge, who is called our prince, may have as much power as yours.[1]

ENG. GENT. I am in a fine condition amongst you, with my politics: the doctor tells me, I have made the king absolute; and now you tell me, I have made him a doge of Venice. But when your prince has power to dispose of the public revenue; to name all officers ecclesiastical and civil, that are of trust and profit in the kingdom; and to dispose absolutely of the whole militia, by sea, and land; then we will allow him to be like ours, who has all these powers.

[1] Comparison of a limited monarch to the doge may well go back to the sixteenth century. Zera S. Fink, *The Classical Republicans* (Evanston, 1945), p. 46, cites an example 25 Dec. 1648. Neville was to be reproached for his attempt to reduce the English King to this position. The analogy continues down to Disraeli, *Vindication of the English Constitution* (1835), if not further.

DOCT. Well, you puzzle me extremely! For when you had asserted the king's power to the height, in calling and dissolving parliaments, you gave me such satisfaction, and showed me wherein the law had provided that this vast prerogative could not hurt the people, that I was fully satisfied; and had not a word to say: now you come about again, and place in the crown such a power, which in my judgement is inconsistent with our liberty.

ENG. GENT. Sir, I suppose you mean chiefly the power of the militia; which was, I must confess, doubtful, before a late statute declared it to be in the king.[1] For our government has made no other disposal of the militia, than what was natural; viz. that the peers in their several counties, or jurisdictions, had the power of calling together their vassals: either armed for the wars, or only so as to cause the law to be executed by serving writs; and in case of resistance, giving possession: which lords amongst their own tenants did then perform the two several offices of lord-lieutenant, and sheriff; which latter was but the earl's deputy, as by his title of *vice-comes* does appear. But this latter being of daily necessity; and justice itself (that is, the lives, liberties and estates of all the people in that county) depending upon it; when the greatness of the peers decayed, (of which we shall have occasion to speak hereafter,) the electing of sheriff was referred to the county-court: where it continued, till it was placed where it now is by a statute.[2] For the other part of the militia; which is, the arming the people for war, it was *de facto* exercised by commission from the king, to a lord-lieutenant (as an image of the natural lord) and other deputies: and it was tacitly consented to, though it were never settled by statute, (as I said before,) till his majesty's happy Restoration.

But to answer you I shall say, that whatever powers are in the crown, whether by statute or by old prescription, they are, and must be understood to be entrusted in the prince for the preservation of the government, and for the safety and interest of the people: and when either the militia, which is given him for the execution and support of the law, shall be employed by him to subvert it, (as in the case of

[1] 13 Car. II. c. 6. was an act declaring the control of the militia to rest in the King and it was followed by two, 14 Car. II. c. 3. and 15 Car. II. c. 4., providing for the administration.
[2] On election of sheriffs, 28 Ed. I. c. 8; on appointment, 5 Ed. II. c. 17, 9 Ed. II. c. 2, 14 Ed. III. c. 7, 23 Hen. VI. c. 7 & 9.

ship-money it was;)[1] or the treasure shall be misapplied, and made the revenue of courtiers and sycophants, (as in the time of Edward the second;) or worthless or wicked people shall be put into the greatest places, (as in the reign of Richard the second,) in this case, though the prince here cannot be questionable for it, (as the kings were in Sparta, and your doges I believe would be;) yet it is a great violation of the trust reposed in him by the government: and a making that power, which is given him by law, unlawful in the execution. And the frequent examples of justice inflicted in parliament upon the king's ministers, for abusing the royal power, show plainly that such authority is not left in his hands to use as he pleases. Nay, there have befallen sad troubles and dangers to some of these princes themselves, who have abused their power to the prejudice of the subjects; which although they are no way justifiable, yet may serve for an instruction to princes, and an example not to hearken to ruinous counsels: for men when they are enraged do not always consider justice, or religion; passion being as natural to man, as reason and virtue: which was the opinion of divine Machiavel.[2]

To answer you then, I say, that though we do allow such powers in the king; yet since they are given him for edification and not destruction, and cannot be abused without great danger to his ministers, and even to himself: we may hope that they can never be abused but in a broken government. And if ours be so (as we shall see anon), the fault of the ill execution of our laws is not to be imputed either to the prince or his ministers; excepting that the latter may be, as we said before, justly punishable for not advising the prince to consent to the mending the frame: of which we shall talk more hereafter. But in the meantime I will come to the king's other prerogatives: as having all royal mines; the being served first before other creditors where money is due to him; and to have a speedier and easier way than his subjects, to recover his debts and his rents; &c. But to say all in one word, when there arises any doubt whether anything be the king's prerogative or no, this is the way of deciding it: viz. To consider whether it be for the good and protection of the people, that the king have such a power; for the definition of prerogative is a considerable part of the common law, by

[1] Neville refers of course to Ship Money, levied 1634, and the famous case arising from refusals to pay it in 1637, for which see Cobbett, *State Trials*, III, 826-1283.
[2] Machiavelli, *Discourses, passim*; III, 43, etc.

which power is put into the prince for the preservation of his people. And if it be not for the good of his subjects, it is not prerogative, nor law; for our prince has no authority of his own, but what was first entrusted in him by the government, of which he is head: nor is it to be imagined that they would give him more power than what was necessary to govern them. For example, the power of pardoning criminals condemned, is of such use to the lives and estates of the people, that without it many would be exposed to die unjustly. As lately a poor gentleman, who by means of the harangue of a strepitous [talkative] lawyer was found guilty of murder, for a man he never killed; or if he had, the fact had been but man-slaughter; and he had been inevitably murdered himself, if his majesty had not been graciously pleased to extend his royal mercy to him: as he did likewise vouchsafe to do to a gentleman convicted for speaking words he never uttered; or if he had spoken them, they were but foolishly not maliciously spoken.[1] On the other side, if a controversy should arise, as it did in the beginning of the last parliament, between the house of commons and the prerogative lawyers, about the choice of their speaker; these latter having interested his majesty in the contest, and made him, by consequence, disoblige, at the beginning, a very loyal, and a very worthy parliament: and for what? For a question, which if you will decide it the right way, will be none; for setting aside the precedents, and the history when the crown first pretended to any share in the choice of a speaker, (which argument was very well handled by some of the learned patriots then;) I would have leave to ask, what man can show, and what reason can be alleged, why the protection and welfare of the people should require that a prerogative should be in the prince to choose the mouth of the house of commons; when there is no particular person in his whole dominion that would not think it against his interest if the government had given the king power to nominate his bailiff, his attorney, or his referee in any arbitration? Certainly there can be no advantage either to the sovereign or his subjects, that the person whose office, it is to put their deliberations into fitting words, and express all their requests to his majesty, should not be entirely in their own election and appointment: which there is the more reason for too, because the speakers for many years past have received instructions from the court; and have broken

---

[1] The royal prerogative of pardon for crimes against the King was frequently exercised, but I have been unable to discover the examples given by Neville.

the privileges of the house, by revealing their debates, adjourning them without a vote; and committed many other misdemeanours, by which they have begotten an ill understanding between the king and his house of commons, to the infinite prejudice both of his majesty's affairs and his people.[1] Since I have given this rule to judge prerogative by, I shall say no more of it: for as to what concerns the king's office in the intervals of parliament, it is wholly ministerial; and is barely to put in execution the common law, and the statutes made by the sovereign power (that is, by himself and the parliament) without varying one tittle; or suspending, abrogating, or neglecting the execution of any act whatsoever: and to this he is solemnly sworn at his coronation. And all his power in this behalf is in him by common law; which is reason itself: written as well in the hearts of rational men, as in the lawyers' books.

NOBLE VEN. Sir, I have heard much talk of the king's negative voice in parliaments; which in my opinion is as much as a power to frustrate, when he pleases, all the endeavours and labours of his people, and to prevent any good that might accrue to the kingdom by having the right to meet in parliament: for certainly, if we in Venice had placed any such prerogative in our duke, or in any of our magistracies, we could not call ourselves a free people.

ENG. GENT. Sir, I can answer you, as I did before: that if our kings have such a power, it ought to be used according to the true and genuine intent of the government; that is, for the preservation and interest of the people; and not for the disappointing the counsels of a parliament towards reforming grievances, and making provision for the future execution of the laws. And whenever it is applied to frustrate those ends, it is a violation of right, and infringment of the king's coronation-oath; in which there is this clause, that he shall confirm the laws, (which, in the Latin of those times, is laws which the people shall choose.) I know some critics, who are rather grammarians than lawyers, have made a distinction between *elegerim* and *elegero*: and will have it, that the king swears to such laws as the people 'shall have chosen': and not to those they 'shall choose'. But in my opinion, if that clause had been intended only to oblige the king to execute the laws made already, it might have been better expressed by 'preserve the laws' than by 'confirm the laws',

---

[1] Grey, *Debates*, VI, 403–39, 6 Mar. 1678–9, debates on speaker. Parliament was prorogued, reassembled and then elected not Sir Edward Seymour, the first choice whom Charles II rejected, but Sergeant Gregory (Grey, VII, 15 Mar. 1678–9, 1–4).

(or customs): besides that he is by another clause in the same oath sworn to execute all the laws. But I shall leave this controversy undecided: those who have a desire to see more of it, may look into those quarrelling declarations pro and con about this matter, which preceded our unhappy civil wars. This is certain, that there are not to be found any statutes that have passed, without being presented to his majesty, or to some commissioned by him; but whether such addresses were intended for respect and honour to his majesty, as the speaker of the house of commons and the lord mayor of London are brought to him, I leave to the learned to discourse. Only thus much we may affirm; that there never were yet any parliamentary requests, which did highly concern the public, presented to any king and by him refused, but such denials did produce very dismal effects: as may be seen in our histories ancient and late: it being certain, that both the barons' wars, and our last dismal combustions, proceeded from no other cause than the denial of the princes then reigning to consent to the desires of the states of the kingdom. And such has been the wisdom and goodness of our present gracious prince; that in twenty years, and somewhat more (for which time we have enjoyed him, since his happy Restoration) he has not exercised his negative voice towards more than one public bill; and that too, was to have continued in force (if it had passed into an act) but for six weeks; being for raising the militia for so long time:[1] and as for the private bills, which are matters of mere grace, it is unreasonable his majesty should be refused that right that every Englishman enjoys, which is not to be obliged to dispense his favours but where he pleases. But for this point of the negative vote; it is possible that when we come to discourse of the cure of our political distemper, some of you will propose the clearing and explanation of this matter, and of all others which may concern the king's power and the people's rights.[2]

NOBLE VEN. But pray, sir, have not the house of peers a negative voice in all bills? How come they not to be obliged to use it for the public good?

ENG. GENT. So they are, no doubt; and the commons too: but there is a vast difference between a deliberative vote, which the peers have

[1] On militia bill, see Grey, VI, 300-20, 30 Nov.-4 Dec. 1678; Gilbert Burnet, *History*, ed. O. Airy (2 vols. Oxford, 1900), I, ii, 178.
[2] Neville rarely talks of 'people's rights', as here and in next speech.

with their negative; and that in the crown, to blast all without deliberating. The peers are co-ordinate with the commons in presenting and hammering of laws; and may send bills down to them, as well as receive any from them; excepting in matters wherein the people are to be taxed. And in this our government imitates the best and most perfect commonwealths that ever were: where the senate assisted in the making of laws; and by their wisdom and dexterity, polished, filed, and made ready things for the more populous assemblies; and sometimes by their gravity and moderation, reduced the people to a calmer state; and by their authority and credit stemmed the tide, and made the waters quiet, giving the people time to come to themselves. And therefore if we had no such peerage now, upon the old constitution; yet we should be necessitated to make an artificial peerage or senate instead of it. Which may assure our present lords, that though their dependencies and power are gone, yet we cannot be without them: and that they have no need to fear an annihilation by our reformation, as they suffered in the late mad times. But I shall speak a word of the people's rights; and then show how this brave and excellent government of England came to decay.

The people by the fundamental laws, (that is, by the constitution of the government of England) have entire freedom in their lives, properties, and their persons: neither of which can in the least suffer, but according to the laws already made; or to be made hereafter in parliament, and duly published. And to prevent any oppression that might happen in the execution of these good laws, (which are our birthright) all trials must be by twelve men of our equals, and of our neighbourhood. These in all civil causes judge absolutely, and decide the matter of fact, upon which the matter of law depends: but if where matter of law is in question, these twelve men shall refuse to find a special verdict at the direction of the court, the judge cannot control it; but their verdict must be recorded. But of these matters, as also of demurrers, writs of error, and arrests of judgement, &c. I have discoursed to this gentleman (who is a stranger) before now; neither does the understanding of the execution of our municipal laws at all belong to this discourse. Only it is to be noted, that these juries, or twelve men, in all trials or causes which are criminal, have absolute power, both as to matter of law, and fact, (except the party by demurrer confess the matter of fact, and take it out of their hands.) And the first question the officer asks the foreman, when they all come in to deliver their verdict, is this; is he guilty in manner and form as he is indicted, or not guilty? Which shows plainly, that they are to examine and judge, as well whether, and how far the fact committed is criminal, as whether the person charged has committed that fact. But though by the corruption of these times (the infallible consequences of a broken frame of government) this office of the juries and right of Englishmen have been of late questioned, yet it has been strongly and effectually vindicated by a learned author of late, to whom I refer you for more of this matter.[1]

I shall say no more of the rights of the people, but this one thing; that neither the king, nor any by authority from him, has any the least power of jurisdiction over any Englishman, but what the law gives them: and that although all commissions and writs go out in the king's name, yet his majesty has no right to issue out any writ (with advice of his council, or otherwise) excepting what come out of his courts; nor to alter any clause in a writ, or add anything to it. And if any person shall be so wicked as to do any injustice to the life, liberty, or estate of any Englishman, by any private command of the prince, the person aggrieved, or his next of kin (if he be assassinated) shall have the same remedy against the offender, as he ought to have had by the good laws of this land, if there had been no such command given: which would be absolutely void and null, and understood not to proceed from that royal and lawful power which is vested in his majesty, for the execution of justice and the protection of his people.

DOCT. Now I see you have done with all the government of England; pray before you proceed to the decay of it, let me ask you what you think of the Chancery: whether you do not believe it a solecism in the politics to have such a court amongst a free people. What good will Magna Charta, the Petition of Right, or St Edward's laws do us to defend our property, if it must be entirely subjected to the arbitrary disposal of one man, whenever any impertinent or petulant person shall put in a bill against you? How inconsistent is this tribunal with all that has been said in defence of our rights, or can be said? Suppose the prince should, in time to come, so little respect his own honour and the interest of his people, as to place a covetous or revengeful person

---

[1] Probably a reference to William Penn (1644–1718), 'Truth rescued from Imposture' (1670), *Works* (2 vols. London, 1726), I, 486–521, where Penn, in light of recent case of Penn and Mead-Bushell's case, discusses the English jury, 'judges of law and fact'.

in that great judicatory; what remedy have we against the corruption of registers, who make what orders they please; or against the whole hierarchy of knavish clerks? Whilst not only the punishing and reforming misdemeanours depend upon him, who may without control be the most guilty himself; but that all the laws of England stand there arraigned before him, and may be condemned when he pleases. Is there, or ever was there any such tribunal in the world before, in any country?

ENG. GENT. Doctor, I find you have had a suit in chancery: but I do not intend to contradict or blame your orthodox zeal in this point. This court is one of those buildings that cannot be repaired, but must be demolished. I could inform you how excellently matters of equity are administered in other countries; and this worthy gentleman could tell you of the venerable *Quarantia* [court of the forty judges] in his city, where the law as well as the fact, is at the bar, and subject to the judges, and yet no complaint made or grievance suffered. But this is not the place for it, this is but the superstructure: we must settle the foundation first. Everything else is as much out of order as this: trade is gone; suits are endless; and nothing amongst us harmonious. But all will come right when our government is mended; and never before, though our judges were all angels. This is the first question and when you have this, all other things shall be added unto you. When that is done, neither the Chancery (which is grown up to this since our ancestors' time) nor the spiritual courts, nor the cheats in trade, nor any other abuses, no not the giant popery itself, shall ever be able to stand before a parliament; no more than one of us can live, like a salamander, in the fire.[1]

NOBLE VEN. Therefore, sir, pray let us come now to the decay of your government; that we may come the sooner to the happy restoration.

ENG. GENT. This harmonious government of England being founded as has been said upon property, it was impossible it should be shaken so long as property remained where it was placed: for if, when the ancient owners the Britons fled into the mountains, and left their lands to the invaders (who divided them, as is above related) they had made an Agrarian Law to fix it; then our government, and by con-

[1] Chancery was many times attacked during the Interregnum, e.g. William Cole, *A Rod for the Lawyers* (London, 1659).

132

sequence our happiness, had been for aught we know immortal. For our constitution, as it was really a mixture of the three, (which are monarchy, aristocracy, and democracy, as has been said) so the weight and predominancy remained in the optimacy; who possessed nine parts in ten of the lands, and the prince but about a tenth part. In this I count all the peoples' shares to the peers, and therefore do not trouble myself to enquire what proportion was allotted to them; for although they had an hereditary right in their lands, yet it was so clogged with tenures and services, that they depended, as to public matters, wholly on their lords: who by them could serve the king in his wars; and in time of peace, by leading the people to what they pleased, could keep the royal power within its due bounds; and also hinder and prevent the people, from invading the rights of the crown. So that they were the bulwarks of the government; which in effect was much more an aristocracy, than either a monarchy or democracy: and in all governments, where property is mixed, the administration is so too; and that part which has the greater share in the lands, will have it too in the jurisdiction. And so in commonwealths, the senate or the people have more or less power, as they have more or fewer possessions, as was most visible in Rome, where in the beginning, the *patricii* could hardly bring the people to any thing; but afterwards, when the Asiatic conquests had enriched the nobility to that degree, that they were able to purchase a great part of the lands in Italy, the people were all their clients, and easily brought even to cut the throats of their redeemers the Gracchi, who had carried a law for restoring them their lands.

But enough of this before. I will not trouble myself, nor you, to search into the particular causes of this change which has been made in the possessions here in England, but it is visible that the fortieth part of the lands which were at the beginning in the hands of the peers and church, is not there now: besides that not only all villainage is long since abolished, but the other tenures are so altered and qualified, that they signify nothing towards making the yeomanry depend upon the lords.[1] The consequence is: that the natural part of our government, which is power, is by means of property in the hands of the people; whilst the artificial part, or the parchment in which the form of government is

---

[1] Neville is reiterating the theory held by Harrington, Sidney, and others that the balance of the constitution had been upset by property changes, and the disappearance of an effective feudal system, marked by the abolition of Court of Wards, 1660.

written, remains the frame. Now art is a very good servant and help to nature, but very weak and inconsiderable, when she opposes her, and fights with her; it would be a very uneven contest between parchment and power. This alone is the cause of all the disorder you heard of, and now see in England; and of which every man gives a reason according to his own fancy, whilst few hit the right cause. Some impute all to the decay of trade; others to the growth of popery: which are both great calamities, but they are effects, and not causes. And if in private families there were the same causes, there would be the same effects: suppose now you had five or six thousand pounds a year, (as it is probable you have,) and keep forty servants; and at length by your neglect, and the industry and thrift of your domestics, you sell one thousand to your steward, another to your clerk of the kitchen, another to your bailiff, till all were gone: can you believe that these servants, when they had so good estates of their own, and you nothing left to give them, would continue to live with you, and to do their service as before?

It is just so with a whole kingdom. In our ancestors' times, most of the members of our house of commons thought it an honour to retain to some great lord, and to wear his blue coat: and when they had made up their lord's train, and waited upon him from his own house to the lords' house, and made a lane for him to enter, and departed to sit themselves in the lower house of parliament, as it was then (and very justly) called; can you think that anything could pass in such a parliament, that was not ordered by the lords? Besides, these lords were the king's great council in the intervals of parliaments, and were called to advise of peace and war; and the latter was seldom made without the consent of the major part: if it were, they would not send their tenants; which was all the militia of England, besides the king's tenth part. Can it be believed, that in those days the commons should dislike anything the lords did in the intervals, or that they would have disputed their right to receive appeals from courts of equity, if they had pretended to it in those days, or to mend money-bills? And what is the reason, but because the lords themselves at that time represented all their tenants (that is, all the people) in some sort?[1] And although the house of commons did assemble to present their grievances, yet all great affairs

---

[1] Neville regards the Lords as having been the great council and, since they had then held land as tenants-in-chief, it was truly representative.

of high importance concerning the government, were transacted by the lords; and the war which was made to preserve it, was called the barons' wars, not the war of both houses: for although in ancienter times the word baron was taken in a larger sense, and comprehended the franklins or freemen; yet who reads any history of that war, shall not find that any mention is made of the concurrence of any assembly of such men: but that Simon Montford, earl of Leicester, and others of the great ones, did by their power and interest manage that contest.

Now if this property which is gone out of the peerage into the commons, had passed into the king's hands, as it did in Egypt in the time of Joseph; as was before said, the prince had had a very easy and peaceable reign over his own vassals: and might either have refused, justly, to have assembled the parliament any more; or if he had pleased to do it, might have for ever managed it as he thought fit. But our princes have wanted a Joseph: that is, a wise counsellor; and instead of saving their revenue, which was very great and their expenses small; and buying in those purchases, which the vast expenses and luxury of the lords made ready for them; they have alienated their own inheritance. So that now the crown-lands, that is, the public patrimony, is come to make up the interest of the commons: whilst the king must have a precarious revenue out of the peoples' purses; and be beholden to the parliament for his bread in time of peace: whereas the kings their predecessors never asked aid of his subjects, but in time of war and invasion. And this alone (though there were no other decay in government) is enough to make the king depend upon his people: which is no very good condition for a monarchy.

NOBLE VEN. But how comes it to pass that other neighbouring countries are in so settled a state in respect of England? does their property remain the same it was, or is it come into the hands of the prince? You know you were pleased to admit, that we should ask you, in passing, something of other countries.[1]

ENG. GENT. Sir, I thank you for it, and shall endeavour to satisfy you. I shall say nothing of the small princes of Germany; who keep in a great measure their ancient bounds, both of government and property: and if their princes now and then exceed their part; yet it is in time of troubles and war, and things return into their right channel of assembling the several states, which are yet in being everywhere. But

---

[1] Again note 'Political Discourses and Histories worth reading', above, pp. 65-6.

Germany lying so exposed to the invasion of the Turks on the one side, and of the French on the other; and having ever had enough to do to defend their several liberties against the encroachments of the house of Austria (in which the imperial dignity is become in some sort hereditary) if there had been something of extraordinary power exercised of late years, I can say in war law is silent: but besides their own particular states, they have the diet of the empire, which never fails to mediate and compose things; if there be any great oppression used by princes to their subjects, or from one prince or state to another. I shall therefore confine myself to the three great kingdoms, France, Spain, and Poland:[1] for as to Denmark[2] and Sweden, the first has lately changed its government, and not only made the monarchy hereditary, which was before elective; but has pulled down the nobility, and given their power to the prince: which how it will succeed, time will show. Sweden remains in point of constitution, and property, exactly as it did anciently; and is a well-governed kingdom. The first of the other three, is France; of which I have spoken before, and shall only add: that though it be very true, that there is property in France, and yet the government is despotical at this present; yet it is one of those violent states, which the Grecians called tyrannies. For if a lawful prince (that is, one who being so by law, and sworn to rule according to it) breaks his oaths and his bonds, and reigns arbitrarily, he becomes a tyrant and an usurper, as to so much as he assumes more than the constitution has given him: and such a government, being as I said violent, and not natural, but contrary to the interest of the people, cannot be lasting when the adventitious props which support it fail; and whilst it does endure, must be very uneasy both to prince and people: the first being necessitated to use continual oppression, and the latter to suffer it.

DOCT. You are pleased to talk of the oppression of the people under the king of France, and for that reason, call it a violent government; when, if I remember, you did once today extol the monarchy of the Turks for well-founded and natural: are not the people in that empire as much oppressed as in France?

1 Moses Pitt, London, *The English Atlas* (Oxford, 1680), I, which opens with description of Poland and its government.
2 The Danish Revolution of 1660 greatly impressed Englishmen. In 1694 Robert Molesworth published an *Account of Denmark* in which chapter VII described the loss of liberty at that time.

ENG. GENT. By no means: unless you will call it oppression for the grand seignior to feed all his people out of the product of his own lands: and though they serve him for it, yet that does not alter the case; for if you set poor men to work and pay them for it, are you a tyrant? Or rather, are not you a good commonwealths-man, by helping those to live who have no other way of doing it but by their labour? But the king of France knowing that his people have, and ought to have property; and that he has no right to their possessions; yet takes what he pleases from them, without their consent, and contrary to law: so that when he sets them on work he pays them what he pleases, and that he levies out of their own estates. I do not affirm that there is no government in the world, but where rule is founded in property; but I say there is no natural fixed government, but where it is so. And when it is otherwise, the people are perpetually complaining, and the king in perpetual anxiety; always in fear of his subjects, and seeking new ways to secure himself: God having been so merciful to mankind, that he has made nothing safe for princes, but what is just and honest.

NOBLE VEN. But you were saying just now, that this present constitution in France will fall when the props fail; we in Italy, who live in perpetual fear of the greatness of that kingdom, would be glad to hear something of the decaying of those props: what are they, I beseech you?

ENG. GENT. The first is the greatness of the present king: whose heroic actions and wisdom has extinguished envy in all his neighbour-princes, and kindled fear; and brought him to be above all possibility of control at home: not only because his subjects fear his courage, but because they have his virtue in admiration; and amidst all their miseries cannot choose but have something of rejoicing, to see how high he has mounted the empire and honour of their nation. The next prop, is the change of their ancient constitution; in the time of Charles the seventh, by consent: for about that time the country being so wasted by the invasion and excursions of the English, the states, then assembled, petitioned the king that he would give them leave to go home, and dispose of affairs himself; and order the government for the future, as he thought fit. Upon this, his successor Lewis the eleventh, being a crafty prince, took an occasion to call the states no more; but to supply them with an assembly of notables: which were certain men of his own nomination, like Barebone's parliament here, but that they were of

137

better quality. These in succeeding reigns, (being the best men of the kingdom,) grew troublesome and intractable; so that for some years the edicts have been verified, (that is, in our language, bills have been passed) in the grand chamber of the parliament at Paris, commonly called the audience chamber: who lately, (and since the imprisonment of president Brouselles, and others, during this king's minority,) have never refused or scrupled any edicts whatsoever.[1] Now whenever this great king dies; and the states of the kingdom are restored; these two great props of arbitrary power are taken away.

Besides these two, the constitution of the government of France itself, is somewhat better fitted than ours, to permit extraordinary power in the prince. For the whole people there possessing lands are gentlemen; (that is, infinitely the greater part;) which was the reason why in their assembly of estates, the deputies of the provinces (which we call here knights of the shire) were chosen by, and out of the gentry: and sat with the peers in the same chamber, as representing the gentry only, called *Petite noblesse*. Whereas our knights here (whatever their blood is) are chosen by commoners; and are commoners: our laws and government taking no notice of any nobility, but the persons of the peers; whose sons are likewise commoners, even their eldest, whilst their fathers live. Now gentry are ever more tractable by a prince, than a wealthy and numerous commonalty; out of which our gentry (at least those we call so) are raised from time to time: for whenever either a merchant, lawyer, tradesman, grazier, farmer, or any other gets such an estate, as that he or his son can live upon his lands without exercising of any other calling, he becomes a gentleman. I do not say, but that we have men very nobly descended amongst these; but they have no pre-eminence, or distinction, by the laws or government. Besides this, the gentry in France are very needy, and very numerous: the reason of which is, that the elder brother in most parts of that kingdom has no more share in the division of the paternal estate than the cadets or younger brothers; excepting the principal house, with the orchards and gardens about it: which they call *Vol de Chappon*, as who should say as far as a capon can fly at once. This house gives him the title his father had, who was called seignior, or baron, or count of that place; which if he sells, he parts with his baronship: and for aught I

---

[1] Pierre Brouselles (1576–1654), of the Parlement of Paris, opposed edict taxing crown tenants, during the period of the Frondes in France.

know becomes in time *roturier*, or ignoble. This practice divides the lands into so many small parcels, that the possessors of them being noble, and having little to maintain their nobility, are fain to seek their fortune; which they can find nowhere so well as at the court; and so become the king's servants and soldiers; for they are generally courageous, bold, and of a good mien. None of these can ever advance themselves but by their desert; which makes them hazard themselves very desperately: by which means great numbers of them are killed; and the rest come in time to be great officers, and live splendidly upon the king's purse: who is likewise very liberal to them; and according to their respective merits, gives them often, in the beginning of a campaign, a considerable sum to furnish out their equipage. These are a great prop to the regal power: it being their interest to support it; lest their gain should cease, and they be reduced to be poor *Provinciaux*, that is country-gentlemen, again. Whereas if they had such estates as our country-gentry have, they would desire to be at home at their ease; whilst these (having ten times as much from the king as their own estates can yield them, which supply must fail if the king's revenue were reduced) are perpetually engaged to make good all exorbitances.

DOCT. This is a kind of governing by property too: and it puts me in mind of a gentleman of good estate in our country, who took a tenant's son of his to be his servant; whose father not long after dying, left him a living of about ten pound a year. The young man's friends came to him, and asked him why he would serve, now he had an estate of his own able to maintain him? His answer was, that his own lands would yield him but a third part of what his service was worth to him in all: besides, that he lived a pleasant life; wore good clothes; kept good company; and had the conversation of very pretty maids, that were his fellow-servants; which made him very well digest the name of being a servant.

ENG. GENT. This is the very case; but yet service, in both these cases, is no inheritance. And when there comes a peaceable king in France who will let his neighbours be quiet, or one that is covetous; these fine gentlemen will lose their employments, and their king his prop: and the rather, because these gentlemen do not depend (as was said before) in any kind upon the great lords whose standing interest is at court; and so cannot in a change, be by them carried over to advance the court-designs, against their own good and that of their country. And thus much is sufficient to be said concerning France.

As for Spain; I believe there is no country (excepting Sweden) in Christendom, where the property has remained so entirely the same it was at the beginning: and the reason is, the great and strict care that is taken to hinder the lands from passing out of the old owners' hands. For except it be by marriages, no man can acquire another man's estate; nor can any grandee, or *titulador*, or any other hidalgo there, alienate or engage his paternal or maternal estate, otherwise than for his life; nor can alter tenures, or extinguish services, or dismember manors: for to this the prince's consent must be had, which he never gives till the matter be debated in the council chamber: which is no junta, or secret war council; but one wherein the great men of the kingdom intervene, and wherein the great matters concerning the preservation of the government are transacted, not relating to foreign provinces or governments, but to the kingdom of Castile and Leon; of which only I speak now. It is true, there have been one or two exceptions against this severe rule, since the great calamities of Spain; and two great lordships have been sold, the Marquisate de Monastero to a Genoese contractor, and another to Sebastian Cortiza a Portuguese of the same profession: but both these have bought the entire lordships, without curtailing or altering the condition in which these two great estates were before; and notwithstanding, this has caused so much repining amongst the natural *Godos* (as the Castilians call themselves still for glory) that I believe this will never be drawn into an example hereafter.[1] Now the property remaining the same, the government does so too; and the king's domestic government, over his natural Spaniards, is very gentle, whatever it be in his conquered provinces: and the kings there have very great advantages of keeping their great men (by whom they govern) in good temper, by reason of the great governments they have to bestow upon them, both in Europe and the Indies; which changing every three years, go in an age through all the grandees, which are not very numerous. Besides, Castile having been in the time of king Roderigo over-run and conquered by the Moors (who governed there despotically, some hundreds of years, before it could be recovered again by the old inhabitants who fled to the

---

[1] Spanish finances were in poor condition in the seventeenth century and foreign financiers were thus able to profit by it in acquiring Spanish property. *Godos*—goth; or visigoth.

mountains;) when they were at length driven out, the count of Castile found a tax set upon all commodities whatsoever by the Moors in their reign, called *alcabala*; which was an easy matter to get continued, when their old government was restored, by the *cortes* or assembly of the states: and so it has continued ever since, as the excise has done here; which being imposed by them who drove and kept out the king, does now since his happy Restoration remain a revenue of the crown. This *alcabala*, or excise, is a very great revenue; and so prevented, for some time, the necessities of the crown, and made the prince have the less need of asking relief of his people, the ordinary cause of disgust: so that the *cortes*, or assembly of the states, has had little to do of late; though they are duly assembled every year, but seldom contradict what is desired by the prince; for there are no greater idolaters of their monarch in the world than the Castilians are, nor who drink deeper of the cup of loyalty. So that in short the government in Spain is, as ours was in queen Elizabeth's time; or in the first year after his now majesty's return; when the parliament for a time complemented the prince, who had by that means both his own power and the peoples': which days I hope to see again, upon a better and more lasting foundation.

But before I leave Spain, I must say a word of the kingdom of Aragon; which has not at all times had so quiet a state of their monarchy, as Castile has enjoyed. For after many combustions which happened there concerning their charters and privileges, which are their fundamental laws; the king one day coming to his seat in parliament, and making his demands as was usual, they told him that they had a request to make to him first: and he withdrawing thereupon, (for he had no right of sitting there to hear their debates) they fell into discourse how to make their government subsist against the encroachments of the prince upon them; and went very high in their debates, which could not choose but come to the king's ear, who walked in a gallery in the same palace to expect the issue: and being in great passion, was seen to draw out his dagger very often, and thrust it again into the sheath; and heard to say, 'this will cost blood'! Which coming to the knowledge of the estates, they left off the debate; and sent some of their number to him, to know what blood it should cost, and whether he meant to murder anybody. He drew out his dagger again, and pointing it to his breast, he said, 'the blood of the king' leaving them in doubt, whether he meant that his subjects would kill him, or that he would do it himself. However, that parliament ended very peaceably: and a famous settlement was there and then made, by which a great person was to be chosen every parliament, who should be as it were an umpire between the king and his people; for the execution of the laws, and the preservation of their government, their laws and privileges; which are their courts of justice, and their charters. This officer was called, the Justiciar of Aragon and his duty was to call together the whole power of the kingdom, whenever any of the aforesaid rights were by open force violated or invaded, and to admonish the king whenever he heard of any clandestine counsels among them to that effect. It was likewise made treason, for any person of what quality soever, to refuse to repair upon due summons to any place where this Justiciar should erect his standard; or to withdraw himself without leave; much more, to betray him, or to revolt from him. Besides, in this *cortes* or parliament, the old oath which at the first foundation of their state was ordered to be taken by the king at his admittance, was again revived; which is in these words: 'We who are as good as you, and more powerful, do choose you our king; upon condition that you preserve our rights and privileges: and otherwise, we do not choose you.' Notwithstanding all this, Philip the second, being both king of Castile and Aragon, picked a quarrel with the latter, by demanding his secretary Antonio Perez, who fled from the king's displeasure thither, being his own country; and they refusing to deliver him (it being expressly contrary to a law of Aragon, that a subject of that kingdom should be against his will carried to be tried elsewhere:) the king took that occasion, to invade them with the forces of his kingdom of Castile, (who had ever been rivals and enemies to the Aragonese;) and they, to defend themselves under their Justiciar, who did his part faithfully and courageously; but the Castilians being old soldiers, and those of Aragon but county-troops, the former prevailed: and so this kingdom, in getting that of Castile by a marriage but an age before, lost its own liberty and government; for it is since made a province and governed by a vice-roy from Madrid, although they keep up the formality of their *cortes* still.[1]

DOCT. No man living that knew the hatred and hostility that ever was between the English and Scots, could have imagined in the

---

[1] The 'lost liberties of Aragon' after the time of the clash between Philip II and Antonio Perez were often referred to by Englishmen as a horrible example of royal triumph at the expense of estates or parliaments.

years 1639 and 1640, (when our king was with great armies of English upon the frontiers of Scotland, ready to invade that kingdom) that this nation would not have assisted, to have brought them under; but it proved otherwise.[1]

ENG. GENT. It may be, they feared, when Scotland was reduced to slavery, and the province pacified and forces kept up there, such forces and greater might have been employed here to reduce us into the same condition; an apprehension, which at this time sticks with many of the common people, and helps to fill up the measure of our fears and distractions. But the visible reason, why the English were not at that time very forward to oppress their neighbours, was the consideration that they were to be invaded for refusing to receive from hence certain innovations in matters of religion, and the worship of God, which had not long before been introduced here; and therefore the people of this kingdom were unwilling to perpetuate a mongrel church here, by imposing it upon them. But I do exceedingly admire when I read our history, to see how zealous and eager our nobility and people here were anciently to assert the right of our crown to the kingdom of France; whereas it is visible, that if we had kept France (for we conquered it entirely and fully) to this day, we must have run the fate of Aragon; and been, in time, ruined and oppressed by our own valour and good fortune. A thing that was foreseen by the Macedonians, when their king Alexander had subdued all Persia and the East; who weighing how probable it was, that their prince having the possession of such great and flourishing kingdoms, should change his imperial residence and inhabit in the centre of his dominions, and from thence govern Macedon; by which means the Grecians, who by their virtue and valour had conquered and subdued the barbarians, should in time (even as an effect of their victories) be oppressed and tyrannized over by them: and this precautious foresight in the Greeks (as was fully believed in that age) hastened the fatal catastrophe of that great prince.

DOCT. Well, I hope this consideration will forearm our parliaments, that they will not easily suffer their eyes to be dazzled any more with the false glory of conquering France.

NOBLE VEN. You need no great cautions against conquering France, at this present; and I believe your parliaments need as little admonition

[1] Note analogy of Castile, fully royal, and Aragon, with Scotland (or Ireland) and England on the eve of the Civil War.

143

against giving of money towards new wars or alliances; that fine wheedle having lately lost them enough already: therefore, pray, let us suffer our friend to go on.

ENG. GENT. I have no more to say of foreign monarchies, but only to tell you; that Poland is both governed and possessed by some[1] very great persons or potentates, called palatines, and under them by a very numerous gentry. For the king is not only elective, but so limited, that he has little or no power but to command their armies in time of war; which makes them often choose foreigners of great fame for military exploits: and as for the commonalty or countrymen, they are absolutely slaves, or villains. This government is extremely confused; by reason of the numerousness of the gentry: who do not always meet by way of representation as in other kingdoms; but sometimes, for the choice of their king and upon other great occasions, collectively in the field; as the tribes did at Rome: which would make things much more turbulent if all this body of gentry did not wholly depend for their estates upon the favour of the palatines their lords, which makes them much more tractable. I have done with our neighbours beyond sea; and should not without your command have made so long a digression in this place: which should indeed have been treated of before we come to speak of England, but that you were pleased to divert me from it before: however, being placed near the portraiture of our own country, it serves better (as contraries set nearby) to illustrate it. But I will not make this deviation longer by apologizing for it; and shall therefore desire you to take notice: that as in England by degrees property came to shift from the few to the many, so the government is grown heavier and more uneasy both to prince and people; the complaints more in parliament; the laws more numerous, and much more tedious and prolix: to meet with the tricks and malice of men, which works in a loose government: for there was no need to make acts verbose, when the great persons could presently force the execution of them. The law of Edward the first for frequent parliaments, had no more words than 'a parliament shall be holden every year;' whereas our act for a triennial parliament,[2] in the time of king Charles the first, contained several sheets of paper: to provide against a failure in the execution of that law. Which if the power had remained in the lords, would have been need-

---

[1] See p. 136, n. 1, above. Poland was sometimes admired, sometimes pitied, at this period, one of the last elective kingdoms.

[2] Triennial acts: 16 Car. I. c. 1., 16 Car. II. c. 1.

144

less; for some of them, in case of intermission of assembling the parliament, would have made their complaints and address to the king, and have immediately removed the obstruction; which, in those days, had been the natural and easy way: but now that many of the lords, (like the bishops which the popes make at Rome in heathen lands,) are merely grown titular; and purchased for nothing but to get their wives' place; it cannot be wondered at if the king slight their addresses, and the court-parasites deride their honourable undertakings for the safety of their country.[1] Now the commons succeeding, as was said, in the property of the peers, and church; (whose lands, five parts of six, have been alienated; and mostly is come into the same hands, with those of the king and peers;) have inherited likewise, according to the course of nature, their power: but being kept from it by the established government, (which not being changed by any lawful acts of state, remains still in being formally, whereas virtually it is abolished) so that for want of outward orders and provisions, the people are kept from the exercise of that power, which is fallen to them by the law of nature: and those who cannot by that law pretend to the share they had, do yet enjoy it by virtue of that right which is now ceased; as having been but the natural effect of a cause that is no longer in being: and you know, the cause removed, the effect is gone. I cannot say that the greater part of the people do know this their condition, but they find very plainly that they want something which they ought to have; and this makes them lay often the blame of their unsettledness upon wrong causes: but however, are altogether unquiet and restless in the intervals of parliament; and when the king pleases to assemble one, spend all their time in complaints of the inexecution of the law; of the multiplication of an infinity of grievances; of misspending the public monies; of the danger our religion is in by practices to undermine it and the state, by endeavours to bring in arbitrary power; and in questioning great officers of state, as the causes and promoters of all these abuses: in so much, that every parliament seems a perfect state of war; wherein the commons are tugging and contending for their right, very justly and very honourably, yet without coming to a point. So that the court sends them packing; and governs still worse and worse in the vacancies, being necessitated thereunto by their despair of doing any good in parliament;

---

[1] Bishops appointed for title, not diocesan duties, abroad; lords who obtained titles, not for services but for status for their families.

and therefore are forced to use horrid shifts to subsist without it, and to keep it off: without ever considering, that if these counsellors understood their trade, they might bring the prince and people to such an agreement in parliament, as might repair the broken and ship-wrecked government of England; and in this secure the peace, quiet and prosperity of the people, the greatness and happiness of the king, and be themselves not only out of present danger, (which no other course can exempt them from,) but be renowned to all posterity.

NOBLE VEN. I beseech you, sir, how comes it to pass, that neither the king, nor any of his counsellors could ever come to find out the truth of what you discourse? for I am fully convinced it is as you say.

ENG. GENT. I cannot resolve you that; but this is certain, they have never endeavoured a cure, though possibly they might know the disease: as fearing that though the effects of a remedy would be, as was said, very advantageous both to king and people, and to themselves; yet possibly, such a reformation might not consist with the merchandize they make of the prince's favour; nor with such bribes, gratuities and fees as they usually take for the dispatch of all matters before them. And therefore our counsellors have been so far from suggesting any such thing to their master, that they have opposed and quashed all attempts of that kind: as they did the worthy proposals made by certain members of that parliament in the beginning of king James's reign, which is yet called the undertaking parliament.[1] These gentlemen considering what we have been discoursing of, viz. that our old government is at an end; had framed certain heads, which, if they had been proposed by that parliament to the king, and by him consented to, would, in their opinion, have healed the breach: and that if the king would perform his part, that house of commons would undertake for the obedience of the people. They did believe that if this should have been moved in parliament before the king was acquainted with it, it would prove abortive; and therefore sent three of their number to his majesty: sir James Croft, grandfather or father to the present bishop of

---

[1] Neville is now leading up to the explanation of his proposed remedies, and discusses by way of introduction the Parliament of 1614. See, inter alia, Thomas Birch, Court and Times of James I (2 vols. London, 1848), I, 314–35; CSPD, 1611–18, ed. Mary Green (London, 1858), pp. 234, 261, 273, 344. Sir James Croft (misprinted in all editions, Acroft), knighted 1603, satisfied Parliament 5 April that he had not worked against the public interest. He was the uncle of Herbert Croft (1603–91), bishop of Hereford. Thomas Harley (1548–1631), twice sheriff of Hereford, and Sir Henry Neville (d. 1616), Neville's grandfather, were other undertakers here praised.

Hereford; Thomas Harley, who was ancestor to the honourable family of that name in Herefordshire; and sir Henry Neville, who had been ambassador from queen Elizabeth to the French king. These were to open the matter at large to the king, and to procure his leave that it might be proposed in parliament: which, after a very long audience and debate, that wise prince consented to; with a promise of secrecy in the meantime, which they humbly begged of his majesty. However, this took vent; and the earl of Northampton, of the house of Howard, (who ruled the roost in that time) having knowledge of it, engaged sir R. Weston, afterwards lord treasurer and earl of Portland, to impeach these undertakers in parliament, before they could move their matters: which he did the very same day; accompanying his charge (which was endeavouring to alter the established government of England) with so eloquent an invective, that if one of them had not risen, and made the house acquainted with the whole series of the affair, they must have been in danger of being impeached by the commons, but however it broke their design, which was all that Northampton and Weston desired; and prevented posterity from knowing any of the particulars of this reformation: for nothing being moved, nothing could remain upon the journal.

So that, you see, our predecessors were not ignorant altogether of our condition; though the troubles which have befallen this poor kingdom since, have made it much more apparent; for since the determination of that parliament, there has not been one called, (either in that king's reign, or his son's, or since,) that has not been dissolved abruptly; whilst the main businesses, and those of most concern to the public, were depending and undecided. And although there has happened in this interim a bloody war, which in the close of it, changed the whole order and foundation of the polity of England; and that it has pleased God to restore it again by his majesty's happy return, so that the old government is alive again: yet it is very visible that its deadly wound is not healed; but that we are to this day tugging with the same difficulties, managing the same debates in parliament, and giving the same disgusts to the court and hopes to the country, which our ancestors did before the year 1640; whilst the king has been forced to apply the same remedy of dissolution to his two first parliaments, that his father used to his four first and king James to his three last, contrary to his own visible interest and that of his people: and this for want of having counsellors about him of abilities and integrity enough to discover to him the disease of his government, and the remedy. Which I hope, when we meet tomorrow morning you will come prepared to enquire into; for the doctor says, he will advise you to go take the air this afternoon in your coach.

NOBLE VEN. I shall think it very long till the morning come: But before you go, pray give me leave to ask you something of your civil war here. I do not mean the history of it, (although the world abroad is very much in the dark as to all your transactions of that time for want of a good one) but the grounds or pretences of it; and how you fell into a war against your king.

ENG. GENT. As for our history, it will not be forgotten. One of those who was in employment from the year '40 to '60, has written the history of those twenty years; a person of good learning and elocution: and though he be now dead, yet his executors are very unwilling to publish it so soon, and to rub a sore that is not yet healed.[1] But the story is writ with great truth and impartiality; although the author was engaged, both in councils and arms, for the parliament's side. But for the rest of your demand, you may please to understand, that our parliament never did, as they pretended, make war against the king: for he by law can do no wrong, and therefore cannot be quarrelled with. The war they declared was undertaken to rescue the king's person out of those men's hands who led him from his parliament, and made use of his name to levy a war against them.

NOBLE VEN. But does your government permit, that in case of a disagreement between the king and his parliament, either of them may raise arms against the other?

ENG. GENT. It is impossible that any government can go farther than to provide for its own safety and preservation whilst it is in being, and therefore it can never direct what shall be done when itself is at an end; there being this difference between our bodies natural and politic, that the first can make a testament to dispose of things after his death, but not the other. This is certain, that wherever any two coordinate powers do differ, and there be no power on earth to reconcile them otherwise, nor any umpire; they will, in fact, fall together by the ears. What can be done in this case justly, look into your own countryman

[1] The memorialist must be Bulstrode Whitelocke (1605–75), whose work was published in 1682.

148

Machiavel, and into Grotius; who in his book *De Jure Belli ac Pacis*, [*Of War and Peace*] treated of such matters long before our wars. As for the ancient politicians, they must needs be silent in the point, as having no mixed governments amongst them; and as for me, I will not rest myself in so slippery a place. There are great disputes about it in the parliament's declarations before the war; and something considerable in the king's answer to them; which I shall specify immediately, when I have satisfied you how our war began: which was in this manner.

The Long Parliament, having procured from the king his royal assent for their sitting till they were dissolved by act;[1] and having paid and sent out the Scottish army, and disbanded our own; went on in their debates for the settling and mending our government. The king, being displeased with them for it; and with himself for putting it out of his power to dissolve them, now the business which they pretended for their perpetuation was quite finished; takes an unfortunate resolution to accuse five principal men of the commons house, and one of the peers, of high-treason: which he prosecuted in a new unheard of way, by coming with armed men into the commons house of parliament, to demand their members. But nothing being done, by reason of the absence of the five; and tumults of discontented citizens flocking to Whitehall and Westminster; the king took that occasion to absent himself from his parliament. Which induced the commons house to send commissioners to Hampton Court, to attend his majesty with 'a remonstrance of the state of the kingdom;' and an humble request to return to his parliament, for the redressing those grievances which were specified in that remonstrance. But the king otherwise counselled, goes to Windsor; and thence northwards, till he arrived at York: where he summons in the militia, that is, the trained bands of the county; and besides, all the gentry: of which there was a numerous appearance. The king addressed himself to the latter with complaints against a prevailing party in parliament, which intended to take the crown from his head: that he was come to them, his loving subjects, for protection: and, in short, desired them to assist him with monies to defend himself by arms. Some of these gentlemen petitioned his majesty to return to his parliament; the rest went about the debate of

---

[1] 16 Car. I. c. 1. and c. 7. Neville relates the familiar story of the five members and the coming of civil war.

the king's demands; who, in the meantime, went to Hull, to secure the magazine there; but was denied entrance by a gentleman whom the house had sent down to prevent the seizing it: who was immediately declared a traitor, and the king fell to raising of forces. Which coming to the knowledge of the house, they made this vote; 'That the king, seduced by evil counsel, intended to levy war against his parliament and people, to destroy the fundamental laws and liberties of England, and to introduce an arbitrary government; &c.' This was the first time they named the king, and the last. For in all their other papers, and in their declaration to arm for their defence, (which did accompany this vote,) they name nothing but malignant counsellors.

The king's answer to these votes and this declaration, is that which I mentioned: wherein his majesty denies any intention of invading the government; with high imprecations upon himself and posterity, if it were otherwise; and owns, that they have right to maintain their laws and government. This is to be seen in the paper itself, now extant: and this gracious prince never pretended, (as some divines have done for him,) that his power came from God, and that his subjects could not dispute it, nor ought he to give any account of his actions (though he should enslave us all) to any but him. So that our war did not begin upon a point of right; but upon a matter of fact. For without going to lawyers or casuists to be resolved, those of the people who believed that the king did intend to destroy our liberties, joined with the parliament; and those who were of opinion that the prevailing party in parliament did intend to destroy the king or dethrone him, assisted vigorously his majesty with their lives and fortunes. And the question, you were pleased to ask, never came: for both parties pretended and believed they were in the right; and that they did fight for, and defend the government. But I have wearied you out.—

NOBLE VEN. No sure, sir! But I am infinitely obliged to you for the great care you have taken and still have used to instruct me; and beg the continuance of it for tomorrow morning.

ENG. GENT. I shall be sure to wait upon you at nine o'clock: but I shall beseech both of you to bethink yourselves what to offer; for I shall come with a design to learn, not to teach: nor will I presume in such a matter to talk all, as you have made me do today; for what I have yet to say in the point of cure is so little, that it will look like the mouse to the mountain of this day's discourse.

DOCT. It is so in all arts; the corollary is short: and in ours, particularly. Those who write of the several diseases incident to human bodies, must make long discourses of the causes, symptoms, signs and prognostics of such distempers; but when they come to treat of the cure, it is dispatched in a few recipes.

ENG. GENT. Well, sir, for this bout, I humbly take my leave of you.— Nay, sir, you are not in a condition to use ceremony.

DOCT. Sir, I forbid you this door; pray retire.—To stand here, is worse than to be in the open air.

NOBLE VEN. I obey you both.

DOCT. I shall wait on you in the evening.

The Third Dialogue

NOBLE VEN. Gentlemen, you are very welcome: what, you are come both together!

DOCT. I met this gentleman at the door but methinks we sit looking one upon another, as if all of us were afraid to speak.

ENG. GENT. Do you think we have not reason, in such a subject as this is? How can any man, without hesitation, presume to be so confident as to deliver his private opinion in a point, upon which for almost two hundred year[1] (for so long our government has been crazy) no man has ventured? and when parliaments have done anything towards it, there have been animosities, and breaches, and at length civil wars?

NOBLE VEN. Our work today, is to endeavour to show, how all these troubles may be prevented for the future, by taking away the cause of them; which is the want of a good government: and therefore it will not be so much presumption in you, as charity, to declare yourself fully in this matter.

ENG. GENT. The cure will follow naturally, if you are satisfied in the disease and in the cause of the disease. For if you agree that our government is broken; and that it is broken, because it was founded upon property, and that foundation is now shaken: it will be obvious, that you must either bring property back to your old government, and give the king and lords their lands again; or else you must bring the government to the property, as it now stands.

DOCT. I am very well satisfied in your grounds: but because this fundamental truth is little understood amongst our people; and that in all conversations men will be offering their opinions of what the parliament ought to do at their meeting; it will not be amiss to examine some of those expedients they propose: and to see whether some, or all of them, may not be effectual towards the bringing us to some degree of settlement; rather than to venture upon so great a change and alteration, as would be necessary to model our government anew.

ENG. GENT. Sir, I believe there can be no expedients proposed in parliament, that will not take up as much time and trouble; find as much

[1] Note 'two hundred' again; government 'crazy', that is, under Tudors and Stuarts.

152

difficulty in passing with the king and lords; and seem as great a change of government, as the true remedy would appear: at least I speak as to what I have to propose. But however, I approve your method: and if you will please to propose any of those things, I shall either willingly embrace them; or endeavour to show reason, why they will be of little fruit in the settling our state.

DOCT. I will reduce them to two heads, (besides the making good laws for keeping out arbitrary power, which is always understood;) the hindering the growth of popery, and consequently the providing against a popish successor; and then declaring the duke of Monmouth's right to the crown, after it has been examined and agreed to in parliament.

ENG. GENT. As for the making new laws, I hold it absolutely needless; those we have already against arbitrary power being abundantly sufficient, if they might be executed: but that being impossible (as I shall show hereafter) till some change shall be made, I shall postpone this point. And for the first of your other two, I shall divide and separate the consideration of the growth of popery, from that of the succession. I am sorry that in the prosecution of this argument, I shall be forced to say something that may not be very pleasing to this worthy gentleman, we being necessitated to discourse with prejudice of that religion which he professes; but it shall be with as little ill breeding as I can, and altogether without passion or invectives.

NOBLE VEN. It would be very hard for me to suspect anything from you that should be disobliging: but pray, sir, go on to your political discourse. For I am not so ignorant myself but to know, that the conservation of the national religion (be it what it will) is essential to the well ordering a state. And though in our city the doctrinals are very different from what are professed here; yet as to the government of the state, I believe you know, that the pope or his priests have as little influence upon it, as your clergy have here, or in any part of the world.

ENG. GENT. I avow it fully, sir; and with the favour you give, will proceed. It cannot be denied but that, in former times, popery has been very innocent here to the government; and that the clergy and the pope were so far from opposing our liberties, that they both sided with the barons to get a declaration of them by means of Magna Charta. It is true also that if we were all papists, and that our state were the same both as to property and empire as it was four hundred years ago, there would be but one inconvenience to have that religion national again in

153

England: which is, that the clergy, since such, had and will have a share in the sovereignty; and inferior courts in their own power, called ecclesiastical.[1] This is, and ever will be, a solecism in government; besides a manifest contradiction to the words of Christ our Saviour, who tells us his kingdom is not of this world. And the truth is, if you look into the scriptures, you will find that the apostles did not reckon that the religion they planted should be national in any country; and therefore have given no precepts to the magistrate to meddle in matters of faith and the worship of God: but preached, that Christians should yield them obedience in all lawful things. There are many passages in holy writ which plainly declare, that the true believers and saints should be but a handful, and such as God had separated, and as it were taken out of the world; which would not have been said by them, if they had believed that whole nations and people should have been true followers of Christ and of his flock: for certainly none of them are to be damned; and yet Christ himself tells us, that few are saved; and bids us strive to get in at the strait gate. And therefore I conceive it not to be imaginable, that either Christ or his apostles did ever account, that the true religion should be planted in the world by the framing of laws, catechisms, or creeds; by the sovereign powers and magistrates, whether you call them spiritual or temporal: but that it should have a progress suitable to its beginning. For it is visible that it had its original from the power and spirit of God; and came in against the stream: not only without a Numa Pompilius, or a Mohamet, to plant and establish it, by humane constitutions and authority;[2] but had all the laws of the world to oppose it, and all the bloody tyrants of that age to persecute it, and to inflict exquisite torments on the professors of it. In Nero's time (which was very early) the Christians were offered a temple in Rome, and in what other cities they pleased, to be built to Jesus Christ; and that the Romans should receive him into the number of their gods; but our religion being then in its purity, this was unanimously refused; for that such a God must have no companions, nor needed no temples; but must be worshipped in spirit and truth. The successors to these good Christians were not so scrupulous: for

[1] While Neville was to maintain that the danger of popery could be prevented by proper constitutional changes, and while he deplored the penal laws which bore very hardly on so many worthy gentry, he was in general anti-clerical, that is, against the clergy having any role in government, in the courts, and so on.

[2] Cf. Moyle, below, pp. 210-25, on Numa; first edition of *Plato Redivivus* had Pythagoras for Mohamet.

within some ages after, the priests to get riches and power, and the emperors to get and keep the empire, (for by this time the Christians were grown numerous and powerful,) combined together to spoil our holy religion, to make it fit for the government of this world; and to introduce into it all the ceremonious follies and superstitions of the heathen; and (which is worse) the power of priests, both over the persons and consciences of men. I shall say no more of this; but refer you to innumerable authors who have treated of this subject: particularly to a French minister, who has written a book entitled, *La Religion catholique apostolique Romaine instituée par Nume Pompile*;[1] and to the incomparable Machiavel in his posthumous Letter, printed lately in our language with the translation of his works.[2] But I have made a long digression: and to come back again, shall only desire you to take notice, when I say that anciently popery was no inconvenience in this kingdom, I mean only politically, as the government then stood; and do not speak at all of the prejudice which men's souls did and will ever receive from the belief of those impious tenets, and the want of having the true gospel of Jesus Christ preached unto them, living in perpetual superstition and idolatry. But the consideration of these matters is not so proper to my present purpose, being to discourse only of government. Notwithstanding therefore, as I said before, that popery might have suited well enough with our old constitution; yet as to the present estate which inclines to popularity, it would be wholly as inconsistent with it, and with the power of the keys and the empire of priests, (especially where there is a foreign jurisdiction in the case,) as with the tyranny and arbitrary power of any prince in the world. I will add thus much in confirmation of the doctor's assertion, that we ought to prevent the growth of popery; since it is now grown a dangerous faction here against the state.

[1] *The Apostolic Roman Catholic Religion Founded by Numa Pompilius.* The title is given as in the text: no tract of this title can be traced in English, French, or Swiss libraries, but the idea was much in the air and had been so for some time: that is, that Numa's ceremonies, pagan of course, were those used by the Roman church. Two tracts were likely to have been known to Neville: Jonas Poirée (*fl.* 1646–69), *Vitis Degeneris, A Treatise of Ancient Ceremonies* (Amsterdam 1646), translated by Thomas Douglas, who dedicated the first edition to Charles I. Second edition corrected, London, 1668. On similar lines but making much more of Numa, *Les Conformetez des cérémonies* by Pierre Mussard (1630–89) (Amsterdam, 1667). This was to be translated, and undoubtedly, as one eighteenth-century commentator remarked, inspired Conyers Middleton (1683–1750) to write *A Letter from Rome*; both were reprinted together (Amsterdam, 1744).

[2] Neville is referring to the much-discussed 'Letter', first published in 1675 between 'To the Reader' and the text of Neville's edition of Machiavelli's *Works*. See above, p. 15.

NOBLE VEN. How can that be, I beseech you, sir?

ENG. GENT. Sir, I will make you judge of it yourself. I will say nothing of those foolish writings that have been put forth by Mariana, Emanuel Sa,[1] and some others; about the lawfulness of destroying princes and states in case of heresy: because all the conscientious and honest papists, (of which I know there are great numbers in the world,) do not only not hold, but even abhor such cursed tenets; and do believe, that when the pope, by excommunication has cut off any prince from the communion of the church, he can go no further; nor ought to pretend a power to deprive him of his crown, or absolve his subjects from their oaths and obedience. But I shall confine myself to the present condition of our papists here. You know how dangerous it is for any kingdom or state to have a considerable, wealthy, flourishing party amongst them, whose interest it is to destroy the polity and government of the country where they live; and therefore if our papists prove this party, you will not wonder why this people are so eager to depress them. This is our case: for in the beginning of queen Elizabeth's reign, there was an alteration of religion in our country; which did sufficiently enrage the holy father at Rome, to see that this good cow would be milked no longer. He declares her an heretic and a bastard, (his sanctity not having declared null that incestuous marriage which her father had contracted before with his brother's wife, and which that king had dissolved to marry her mother) and afterwards excommunicated our queen, depriving her as much as in him lay, of the kingdom. Some of the zealots of that party, (having a greater terror for those thunder-bolts than I believe many have now,) began to conspire against her: and plots grew at length so frequent, and so dangerous, that it was necessary (as the parliaments then thought) to secure the queen, by making severe laws against a people, who did not believe themselves her majesty's subjects; but on the contrary, many of them thought themselves in conscience obliged to oppose and destroy her. And although that excommunication, as also the pretended doubtfulness of the title, both died with that renowned queen; yet a new desperate conspiracy against the king her successor and the whole parliament ensuing not long after her decease,[2] those rigorous laws have been so far from

---

[1] Juan Mariana (1536–1623) and Emanuel Sa (1530–90) were jesuits. Sa in his *Aphorisms* under 'clericus' said tyrannicide could be a duty for a clergyman! Mariana in a more famous work, *De Rege* (Toledo, 1599), clearly justified king-killing.

[2] Guy Fawkes, 5 Nov. 1605.

being repealed, that very many more (and far severer) have been since made, and are yet in force. Now these laws make so great a distinction between protestants and papists, that whereas the former are by our government and laws the freest in the world, the latter are little better than slaves; are confined to such a distance from their houses; are not to come near the court; (which being kept in the capital city, mostly deprives them from attending their necessary occasions) they are to pay two third parts of their estates annually to the king; their priests are to suffer as traitors, and they as felons for harbouring them. In fine one of us, if he do not break the municipal laws for the good government of the country, need not fear the king's power; whereas, their being what they are is a breach of the law; and does put them into the prince's hands to ruin them when he pleases; nay, he is bound by oath to do it; and when he does it not, is complained against by his people, and parliaments take it amiss. Now judge you, sir, whether it is not the interest of these people to desire and endeavour a change, whilst they remain under these discouragements; and whether they are not like to join with the prince, (whose connivance at the inexecution of those laws is the only means and hope of their preservation,) whenever he shall undertake anything for the increase of his own power, and the depressing his parliaments.

NOBLE VEN. What you say is very undeniable; but then the remedy is very easy and obvious, as well as very just and honourable, which is the taking away those cruel laws; and if that were done they would be one people with you; and would have no necessity, and by consequence no desire to aggrandize the king against the interest and liberty of their own country.

ENG. GENT. You speak very well; and one of the reasons amongst many which I have to desire a composure of all our troubles by a settled government, is that I may see these people (who are very considerable, most of them, for estates, birth and breeding) live quietly under our good laws; and increase our trade and wealth with their expenses here at home: whereas now the severity of our laws against them, makes them spend their revenues abroad, and enrich other nations with the stock of England. But as long as the state here is so unsettled as it is, our parliaments will never consent to countenance a party, who by the least favour and indulgence may make themselves able to bring in their own religion to be national, and so ruin our polity and liberties.

NOBLE VEN. I wonder why you should think that possible?

ENG. GENT. First, sir, for the reason we first gave, which is the craziness of our polity: there being nothing more certain, than that both in the natural and also the politic body any sinister accident that intervenes, during a very diseased habit, may bring a dangerous alteration to the patient. An insurrection in a decayed government, a thing otherwise very inconsiderable, has proved very fatal; as I knew a slight flesh-wound bring a lusty man to his grave in our wars, for that he being extremely infected with the French disease, could never procure the orifice to close. So although the designs both at home and abroad for altering our religion, would be very little formidable to a well-founded government; yet in such an one as we have now, it will require all our care to obviate such machinations. Another reason is the little zeal that is left amongst the ordinary protestants: which zeal uses to be a great instrument of preserving the religion established; as it was here in queen Elizabeth's time. I will add, the little credit the church of England has amongst the people; most men being almost as angry with that popery which is left amongst us (in surplices, copes, altars, cringings, bishops, ecclesiastical courts, and the whole hierarchy; besides an infinite number of useless, idle, superstitious ceremonies; and the ignorance and viciousness of the clergy in general) as they are with those dogmas that are abolished: so that there is no hopes that popery can be kept out, but by a company of poor people called fanatics, who are driven into corners as the first Christians were; and who only in truth conserve the purity of Christian religion, as it was planted by Christ and his apostles and is contained in scripture. And this makes almost all sober men believe, that the national clergy, besides all their other good qualities, have this too; that they cannot hope to make their hierarchy subsist long against the scriptures, the hatred of mankind, and the interest of this people, but by introducing the Roman religion; and getting a foreign head and supporter, which shall from time to time brave and hector the king and parliament in their favour and behalf: which yet would be of little advantage to them, if we had as firm and wise a government as you have at Venice.

Another reason, and the greatest, why the Romish religion ought to be very warily provided against at this time, is; that the lawful and undoubted heir to the crown, if his majesty should die without legitimate issue, is more than suspected to embrace that faith: which (if it should please God to call the king, before there be any remedy applied to our distracted state) would give a great opportunity by the power he would have in intervals of parliament either to introduce immediately that profession, with the help of our clergy, and other English and foreign aids; or else to make so fair a way for it, that a little time would perfect the work. And this is the more formidable, for that he is held to be a very zealous and bigoted Romanist; and therefore may be supposed to act anything to that end, although it should manifestly appear to be contrary to his own interest and quiet; so apt are those who give up their faith and the conduct of their lives to priests, (who to get to themselves empire, promise them the highest seats in heaven; if they will sacrifice their lives, fortunes, and hopes, for the exaltation of their holy mother, and preventing the damnation of an innumerable company of souls which are not yet born) to be led away with such erroneous and wild fancies. Whereas Philip the second of Spain, the house of Guise in France, and other great statesmen, have always made their own greatness their first aim; and used their zeal as an instrument of that: and, instead of being cozened by priests, have cheated them; and made them endeavour to preach them up to the empire of the world.

So I have done with the growth of popery; and must conclude that, if that should be stopped in such manner that there could not be one papist left in England, and yet our polity left in the same disorder that now afflicts it, we should not be one scruple the better for it nor the more at quiet: the growth and danger of popery not being the cause of our present distemper, but the effect of it. But as a good and settled government would not be at all the nearer, for the destruction of popery; so popery and all the dangers and inconveniences of it would not only be further off, but would wholly vanish, at the sight of such a reformation. And so we begin at the wrong end, when we begin with religion before we heal our breaches. I will borrow one similitude more, with our doctor's favour from his profession. I knew once a man given over by the physicians, of an incurable cachexy;[1] which they said proceeded from the ill quality of the whole mass of blood, from great adustion, and from an ill habit of the whole body: the patient had very often painful fits of the colic, which they said, proceeded from the sharpness of the humour which caused the disease; and, amongst the rest, had one fit which tormented him to that degree, that it was not expected he could

---

[1] 'Cachexy'—a bad state of bodily health.

out-live it; yet the doctors delivered him from it in a small time: notwithstanding, soon after the man died of his first distemper. Whereas, if their art had arrived to have cured that which was the cause of the other, the colic had vanished of itself and the patient recovered. I need make no application nor shall need to say much of the succession of the crown, (which is my next province,) but this I have said already; that it is needless to make any provision against a popish successor, if you rectify your government; and if you do not, all the care and circumspection you can use in that particular will be useless and of none effect; and will but at last (if it do not go off easily, and the next heir succeed peaceably, as is most likely, especially if the king live till the people's zeal and mettle is over) end probably in a civil war about title: and then the person deprived may come in with his sword in his hand, and bring in upon the point of it both the popish religion, and arbitrary power. Which, though I believe he will not be able to maintain long, (for the reasons before alleged,) yet that may make this generation miserable and unhappy.

1**It will certainly be agreed by all lovers of their country, that popery must be kept from returning and being national in this kingdom; as well for what concerns the honour and service of God, as the welfare and liberty of the people. And I conceive there are two ways, by which the parliament may endeavour to secure us against that danger. The first, by ordering such a change in the administration of our government, that whoever is prince can never violate the laws; and then we may be very safe against popery, (our present laws being effectual enough to keep it out, and no new ones being like to be made in parliament that may introduce it;) and this remedy will be at the same time advantageous to us, against the tyranny and encroachments of a protestant successor; so that we may call it an infallible remedy both against popery and arbitrary power. The second way is, by making a law to disable any papists (by name, or otherwise) from inheriting the crown; and this is certainly fallible, that is, may possibly not take place (as I shall show immediately:) and besides it is not improbable that an heir to this kingdom in future times, may dissemble his religion till he be seated in the throne; or possibly be perverted to the Roman faith after he is possessed of it, when it may be too late to limit his

1 **...* addition to the second edition; and following paragraph has very slightly different wording in the first edition.

prerogative in parliament: and to oppose him without that will, I fear, be judged treason.*

DOCT. But sir, would you have the parliament do nothing, as things stand, to provide (at least as much as in them lies) that whoever succeeds be a good protestant?

ENG. GENT. Yes, I think it best in the first place to offer to his majesty the true remedy; and if they find him averse to that, then to pursue the other which concerns the succession: because the people (who are their principals and give them their power) do expect something extraordinary from them at this time; and the most of them believe this last the only present means to save them from popery, which they judge (and very justly) will bring in with it a change of government. But then, I suppose, they may be encouraged to propose, in the first place, the true cure: not only because that is infallible, as has been proved; but likewise because his majesty in probability will sooner consent to any reasonable demand towards the reforming of the government and to the securing us that way, than to concur to the depriving his only brother of the crown: And possibly this (as I said before) may be the only way the parliament can hope will prove effectual: for if you please to look but an age back into our story, you will find that Henry the eighth did procure an act of parliament, which gave him power to dispose of the crown by his last will and testament;[1] and that he did accordingly make his said will, and by it devise the succession to his son Edward the sixth, in the first place, and to the heirs of his body; and for want of such, to his daughter Mary, and to the heirs of her body; and for want of which heirs, to his daughter Elizabeth (our once sovereign, of immortal, and blessed memory) and the heirs of her body; and for want of all such issue, to the right heirs of his younger sister; who was, before he made this will, married to Charles Brandon duke of Suffolk, and had issue by him. By this testament he disinherited his elder sister; who was married in Scotland: and by that means did, as much as in him lay, exclude his majesty (who now, by God's mercy, reigns over us) as also his father and grandfather. And to make the case stronger, there passed an act long after, in the reign of queen Elizabeth; that it should be treason during that queen's life, and a *praemunire* afterwards, to assert that the imperial crown of England could not be disposed of by act of parliament.[2] Yet after the

[1] 35 Hen. VIII. c. 1.   [2] 13 Elizabeth I. c. 1.

decease of that queen, there was no considerable opposition made to the peaceable reception and recognition of king James of happy memory: and those who did make a little stir about the other title, as the lord Cobham,[1] sir Walter Rawleigh, and a few others, were apprehended and condemned according to law. And notwithstanding that, since, in the reign of king Charles the first, there was a bloody civil war, in which men's minds were exasperated at a high rate, yet in all the course of it the original want of title was never objected against his late majesty. I do not urge this to aver that the parliament with the king's consent cannot do lawfully this, or any other great matter; (which would be an incurring the penalty of that law, and a solecism in the politics:) but to show, that when the passions of men are quieted, and the reasons other than they were, it happens oftentimes that those acts which concern the succession fall to the ground of themselves; and that even without the sword, which in this case was never adopted, and that therefore this remedy in our case may be likely never to take place, if it please God the king live till this nation be under other kind of circumstances.

DOCT. Sir, you say very well: but it seems to me, that the last parliament was in some kind of fault, if this be true that you say; for I remember that my lord chancellor did once during their sitting, in his majesty's name, offer them to secure their religion and liberties any way they could advise of, so they would let alone meddling with the succession; and invited them to make any proposals they thought necessary to that end.[2]

ENG. GENT. Hence these tears! If this had been all, we might have been happy at this time: but this gracious offer was, at the beginning, accompanied with such conditions that made the parliament conjecture that it was only to perplex and divide them; and did look upon it as an invention of some new romance (counsellors and those too, possibly, influenced by the French), to make them embrace the shadow for the substance; and satisfying themselves with this appearance, to do their ordinary work of giving money, and be gone and leave the business of the kingdom as they found it. For it was proposed, that

---

[1] Henry Brooke, eighth baron Cobham (d. 1619), was arrested in 1603 as a conspirator in the 'Main Plot' to place Arabella Stuart on the throne; his testimony involved Sir Walter Ralegh, though neither suffered the extreme penalty until 1618.

[2] Grey, *Debates*, VII, 158-64, 30 Apr. 1679. Neville was writing between the end of this Parliament and the meeting of the next, 21 Oct. 1680.

whatsoever security we were to receive should be both conditional, and reversionable. That is, first, we should not be put into possession of this new charter (be it what it will) till after the death of his majesty who now is: whereas such a provision is desirable, and indeed necessary for us for this only reason; that when that unfortunate hour comes, we might not be (in that confusion) unprovided of a calm, settled and orderly, as well as a legal way, to keep out popery: whereas otherwise if we be to take possession in that minute, it must either miscarry, or be gotten by a war. If it be true that possession be nine points of the law in other cases, it is in this the whole ten: and I should be very unwilling in such a distraction to have no sanctuary to fly to, but a piece of parchment kept in the pells; and to have this too, as well as other advantages, in the power and possession of him in whose prejudice it was made. This had been almost as good an expedient to keep out popery, as the bill which was thrown out that parliament; which provided, that in the reign of a king that should be a papist, the bishops should choose one another upon vacancies. Those counsellors who put my lord chancellor upon this proposal, were either very slender politicians themselves; or else thought the parliament so. If Magna Charta, and the Petition of Right, had not been to take place till after the decease of those princes who confirmed them, neither had the barons shed their blood to so good purpose; nor the members of the parliament in the third year of king Charles [1628] deserved so glorious an imprisonment, after it was ended.[1] The other condition, in this renowned proposal, is; that all provision and security which is given us to preserve our religion shall cease immediately, whenever the prince shall take a certain oath to be penned for that purpose: and I leave it to all thinking men to determine what that will avail us, when we shall have a king of that profession over us, who shall not have so much zeal for his religion, as he who is now the next successor has; but shall possibly prefer his ambition, and his desire to get out of wardship, before the scruples of his confessor; and yet may afterwards, by getting absolution for, and dispensation from such oaths and compliance, employ the power he gets himself, and the security he deprives us of, to introduce violently what worship and faith he pleases. This gracious offer had the fatality to disgust one of the best parliaments that ever sat, and the

---

[1] Among the prisoners, of course, after the third Parliament of Charles I was dismissed in 1629, was Sir John Eliot.

most loyal: so that laying it aside, they fell upon the succession (the only thing they had then left) and were soon after dissolved: leaving the kingdom in a more distracted condition than they found it. And this can no way be composed, but by mending the polity; so that whoever is king cannot (be he never so inclined to it) introduce popery, or destroy whatever religion shall be established. As you see in the example of the duchy of Hanover, whose prince, some fourteen years since, was perverted to the Roman church; went to Rome to abjure heresy, (as they call the truth;) returned home; where he lived and governed as he did before; without the least animosity of his subjects for his change, or any endeavour of his to introduce any in his government or people: and dying this last spring, left the peaceable and undisturbed rule of his subjects to the next successor, his brother the bishop of Osnaburg, who is a protestant.[1] And this because the polity of that dukedom has been conserved entire for many years, and is upon a right basis: and if our case were so, we should not only be out of danger to have our religion altered (as I said before) whoever is king, but should in other things be in a happy and flourishing condition. But I have made a long and tedious digression to answer your demands: now 'tis time you assist me to find the natural cure of all our mischiefs.

DOCT. Stay, sir; I confess myself to be wonderfully edified with your discourse hitherto, but you have said nothing yet of the duke of Monmouth.

ENG. GENT. I do not think you desire it, though you were pleased to mention such a thing; for I suppose you cannot think it possible, that this parliament (which is now speedily to meet by his majesty's gracious proclamation) can ever suffer such a thing to be so much as debated amongst them.

DOCT. Sir, you have no reason to take that for granted, when you see what books are printed; what great and honourable persons frequent him in private, and countenance him in public; what shoals of the middle sort of people have in his progress this summer met him before he came into any great town; and what acclamations and bonfires have been made in places where he lodged.

[1] John Frederick of Calenberg (Hanover) (1667–79), a convert to catholicism, was succeeded by Ernest Augustus, the youngest of four brothers, since 1662 bishop of Osnabruck, and since 1658 husband of Sophia, daughter of Elizabeth of Bohemia and granddaughter of James I. See A. W. Ward, *Great Britain and Hanover* (Oxford, 1899), pp. 20–2.

ENG. GENT. These things, I must confess, show how great a distemper the people are in; and the great reason we have to pray God of his mercy to put an end to it by a happy agreement in parliament. But certainly this proceeds only from the hatred they have to the next successor and his religion; and from the compassion they have to the duke of Monmouth (who as they suppose, has suffered banishment and disfavour at court, at his instance;) and not from any hopes, or expectations, that the parliament will countenance any pretence that can be made in his behalf to the succession.

DOCT. It may be when we have discoursed of it, I shall be of your mind; as indeed I am inclined already. But yet as nothing in war is more dangerous than to contemn an enemy; so in this argumentation that we use to secure our liberties, we must leave nothing unanswered that may stand in the way of that; especially the duke of Monmouth's claim, which is pretended to confirm and fortify them: for (say some men) if you set him up, he will presently pass all bills that shall concern the safety and interest of the people; and so we shall be at rest forever.

ENG. GENT. Well, I see I must be more tedious than I intended. First then, the reasoning of these men you speak of, does in my apprehension suppose a thing, I cannot mention without horror; which is, that this person should be admitted immediately to the possession of the crown, to do all these fine matters. For otherwise, if he must stay till the death of our sovereign who now reigns, (which I hope and pray will be many years,) possibly these delicate bills may never pass; nor he find hereafter the people in so good a humour to admit him to the reversion; which if it could be obtained (as I think it impossible politically) yet the possession must be kept by a standing army; and the next successor cannot have a better game to play, nor a better adversary to deal with, than one who leaps in over the heads of almost all the protestant princes' families abroad; (besides some papists who are greater:) and when we have been harrassed with wars and the miseries that accompany it some few years, you shall have all these fine people, who now run after him, very weary of their new prince. I would not say anything to disparage a person so highly born, and of so early merit; but this I may say, that if a lawful title should be set on foot in his favour, and a thousand Dutch hosts and such like should swear a marriage, yet no sober man that is not blinded with prejudice will believe, that our king (whom none can deny to have an excellent

165

understanding) would ever marry a woman so much his inferior as this great person's mother was; and this at a time when his affairs were very low, and he had no visible or rational hopes to be restored to the possession of his kingdoms, but by an assistance which might have been afforded him by means of some great foreign alliance.

Well, but to leave all this, do these men pretend that the duke of Monmouth shall be declared successor to the crown in parliament, with the king's concurrence, or without it? If without it, you must make a war for it; and I am sure that no cause can be stated upon such a point, that will not make the asserters and undertakers of it be condemned by all the politicians and moralists of the world, and by the casuists of all religions: and so by consequence, it is like to be a very unsuccessful war. If you would have this declared with the king's consent; either you suppose the royal assent to be given, when the king has his liberty either to grant it or not grant it, to dissolve the parliament or not dissolve it, without ruin or prejudice to his affairs: if in the first case, it is plain he will not grant it, because he cannot do it without confessing his marriage to that duke's mother, which he has already declared against in a very solemn manner, and caused it to be registered in Chancery; and which not only no good subject can choose but believe, but which cannot be doubted by any rational person: for it would be a very unnatural, and indeed a thing unheard of, that a father who had a son in lawful matrimony, and who was grown to perfection, and had signalized himself in the wars, and who was ever entirely beloved by him, should disinherit him by so solemn an asseveration (which must be a false one too) to cause his brother to succeed in his room. And whereas it is pretended by some, that his majesty's danger from his brother's counsels and designs may draw from him something of this: beside that they do not much complement the king in this; it is clear, his brother is not so popular, but that he may secure him when he pleases without hazard, if there were any ground for such an apprehension.

But we must in the next place suppose that the king's affairs were in such a posture, that he could deny the parliament nothing without very great mischief and inconvenience to himself and the kingdom: then I say, I doubt not, but the wisdom of the parliament will find out divers demands and requests to make to his majesty of greater benefit, and more necessary for the good of his people than this would be;

which draws after it not only a present unsettledness, but the probable hazard of misery and devastation for many years to come, as has been proved. So that as on the one side, the parliament could not make a more unjustifiable war than upon this account; so they could not be dissolved upon any occasion wherein the people would not show less discontent and resentment, and for which the courtiers would not hope to have a better pretext to strive in the next choice to make their arts and endeavours more successful in the election of members more suitable to their designs for the continuance of this present misgovernment: for if this parliament do misspend the peoples' mettle which is now up, in driving that nail which cannot go; they must look to have it cool, and so the ship of this commonwealth, which if they please may be now in a fair way of entering into a safe harbour, will be driven to sea again in a storm; and must hope for, and expect another favourable wind to save them: and God knows when that may come.

**DOCT.[1] But, sir, there are others, who not minding whether the parliament will consider the duke of Monmouth's concern so far as to debate it, do yet pretend that there is great reason to keep up the peoples' affections to him; and possibly to foment the opinion they have of his title to the crown: to the end, that if the king should die before such time as the government is redressed, or the duke of York disabled by law to succeed, the people might have a head; under whose command and conduct they might stand upon their guard, till they had some way secured their government and religion.

ENG. GENT. What you have started is not a thing that can safely be discoursed of, nor is it much material to our design; which is intended to speculate upon our government, and to show how it is decayed. I have industriously avoided the argument of rebellion, as I find it couched in modern politicians; because most princes hold, that all civil wars in mixed monarchies must be so; and a politician (as well as an orator) ought to be an upright man; so ought to discourse nothing, how rational soever, in these points under a peaceable monarchy which gives him protection, but what he would speak of his prince if all his counsel were present. I will tell you only that these authors hold, that nothing can be alleged to excuse the taking arms by any people in opposition to their prince from being treason, but a claim

---

[1] **...* long addition on 'exclusion' starts here in the second edition. Notice that Neville, unlike Sidney in his (unpublished) 'Discourses', dissociates himself from rebellion.

167

to a lawful jurisdiction or coordination in the government, by which they may judge of and defend their own rights; and so pretend to fight for and defend the government. For though all do acknowledge, that the good of the people is, and ought to be, the most supreme or sovereign law in the world; yet if we should make private persons, how numerous soever, judge of the welfare of the people, we should have all the risings and rebellions that should ever be made, justified by that title: as happened in France, when The League of the Public Weal took that name; which was raised by the insatiable ambition of a few noblemen, and by correspondency and confederacy with Charles, son of the duke of Burgundy, and other enemies to that crown.[1]

DOCT. But would you have our people do nothing then, if the king should be assassinated, or die of a natural death?

ENG. GENT. You may ask me a very fine question, doctor. If I say, I would have the people stir in that case, then the king and his laws take hold of me; and if I should answer, that I would have them be quiet, the people would tear me in pieces for a jesuit; or at least, believe that I had no sense of the religion, laws, and liberty of my country. In fact, I do suppose, that if the people do continue long in this heat which now possesses them; and remain in such a passion at the time of the king's death without settling matters; they may probably fall into tumults and civil war: which makes it infinitely to be desired, and prayed for by all good Englishmen, that during the quiet and peace we enjoy by the blessing of his majesty's life and happy reign, we might likewise be so wise and fortunate as to provide for the safety and prosperity of the next generation.

DOCT. But if you would not have the people in such a case take the duke of Monmouth for their head, what would you have them do?

ENG. GENT. Doctor, you ask me very fine questions! Do not you know that Machiavel, the best and most honest of all the modern politicians, has suffered sufficiently by means of priests, and other ignorant persons?[2] who do not understand his writings, and therefore impute to him the teaching subjects how they should rebel and conspire against their princes; which if he were in any kind guilty of, he would deserve all the reproaches that have been cast upon him, and ten times more; and so should I, if I ventured to obey you in this. I am very

---

[1] 'The League of the Public Weal'—*La Guerre du bien publique*, 1465-7, 1472; see Commines, no. 7 in 'Political Discourses', above, p. 66.
[2] Defended in the 'Letter', see above, p. 15.

confident, that if any man should come to you, to implore your skill in helping him to a drug that might quickly, and with the least fear of being suspected, dispatch an enemy of his, or some other, by whose death he was to be a gainer; or some young lass that had gotten a surreptitious great belly, should come to you to teach her how to destroy the fruit; I say, in this case you would scarce have had patience to hear these persons out: much less would you have been so wicked to have in the least assisted them in their designs. No more than Solon, Lycurgus, Periander, or any other of the sages could have been brought to have given their advice to any persons who should have begged it, to enable them to ruin and undermine the government of their own commonwealths.

DOCT. Sir, this reprehension would be very justly given me, if I had intended by this question to induce you to counsel me, or any other how to rebel. My meaning was to desire you (who have heretofore been very fortunate in prophesying concerning the events of our changes here) to exercise your faculty a little at this time; and tell us, what is like to be the end of these distractions we are under, in case we shall not be so happy as to put a period to them by mending our government and securing our religion and liberty in a regular way.

ENG. GENT. Doctor, I will keep the reputation of prophecy, which I have gained with you; and not hazard it with any new predictions, for fear they should miscarry.

Yet I care not, if I gratify your curiosity a little in the point about which you first began to interrogate me, by presaging to you; that in case we should have troubles and combustions here, after his majesty's decease (which God avert) we must expect a very unsuccessful end of them, if we should be so rash and unadvised as to make the great person we have been lately speaking of, our head; and that nothing can be more dangerous and pernicious to us than such a choice. I have not in this discourse the least intention to except against, much less to disparage the personal worth of the duke of Monmouth, which the world knows to be very great; but do believe that he has courage and conduct proportionable to any employment that can be conferred upon him, whether it be to manage arms or counsels: but my opinion is, that no person in his circumstance can be a proper head in this case. For the people having been already put on upon the scent of his title to the crown, will be very hardly called off; and so will force the wiser men, who may design better things, to consent that he be proclaimed king immediately: except there be some other head, who by his power, wisdom, and authority, may restrain the forwardness of the multitude, and obviate the acts of some men, whose interest and hopes may prompt them to foment the humours of the people. Now the consequences of hurrying a man to the throne so tumultuously, without the least deliberation, are very dismal: and do not only not cure the politic distemper of our country which we have talked so much of, but do infinitely augment it; and add to the disease our state labours under already (which is a consumption) a very violent fever too; I mean war at home, and from abroad, which must necessarily follow in a few years: nor is it possible to go back, when once we have made that step; for our new king will call a parliament, which being summoned by his writ, neither will nor can question his title or government, otherwise than by making addresses and by presenting bills to him, as they do to his now majesty.

NOBLE VEN. It seems to me, that there needs nothing more than that: for if he consent to all laws as shall be presented to him; you may reform your government sufficiently, or else it is your own fault.

ENG. GENT. We have showed already, and shall do more hereafter, that no laws can be executed till our government be mended: and if you mean we should make such as should mend that, (besides that it would be a better method to capitulate that, before you make choice of your prince, as wise people have done in all ages, and the cardinals do at Rome in the conclave before they choose their pope) I say besides this, it is not to be taken for granted that any bills that tend to make considerable alterations in the administration, (and such we have need of as you will see anon) would either in that case be offered, or consented to. Both prince and people being so ready to cry out upon forty-one, and to be frighted with the name of a commonwealth; even now when we think popery is at the door: which some people then will think farther off, and so not care to make so great alterations to keep it out. Besides, the great men, and favourites of the new prince, will think it hard that the king should be so bounded and limited both in power and revenue, that he shall have no means to exercise his liberality towards them; and so may use their interest and eloquence, in both houses, to dissuade them from pressing so hard upon a prince, who is a true zealous protestant, and has always headed that party; and who is justly admired, if not adored by the people: and considering too that all the power they leave him, will serve but to enable him to defend us the better from popery and arbitrary power; to prevent the latter of which most monarchies were originally instituted.

Thus we may exercise, during a parliament or two, love-tricks between the prince and his people; and imitate the honeymoon that continued for about two years after his majesty's Restoration: till the ill management of affairs, and the new grievances that shall arise, (which will be sure never to fail till our true cure be effected, notwithstanding the care of the new king and his counsellors) shall awaken the discontents of the people; and then they will curse the time, in which they made this election of a prince; and the great men, for not hindering them. Then men will be reckoning up the discontents of the peers, sometime after they had made a rash choice of Henry the seventh in the field, (who had then no title,) when they saw how he made use of the power they gave him; to lessen their greatness and to fortify himself, upon their ruins. When it comes to this, and that the governing party comes to be but a little faction; the people, who never know the true cause of their distemper, will be looking out abroad who has the lawful title; (if the next heir be not in the meantime with an army of English and strangers in the field here, as is most likely:) and look upon the prince of Orange,[1] or the next of kin, as their future saviour; in case the duke be dead in the meantime, and so the cause of all their distrust taken away. Thus most men, (not only discontented persons, but the people in general,) looked upon his majesty that now is, as their future deliverer, during our late distractions; when his condition was so weak that he had scarce wherewithal to subsist, and his enemies powerful at home and victorious abroad: which will not be, I fear, our case.

I prophesy then, (because you will have me use this word,) that if nobles or people make any such unfortunate choice as this, during the distractions we may be in upon his majesty's death, we shall not only miss our cure; or have it deferred, till another government make it; but remain in the confusion we now suffer under; and besides that, shall be sure to feel, first or last, the calamity of a civil and foreign war: and in the meantime to be in perpetual fear of it, and suffer all the burden and charge which is necessary to provide for it; besides all the other ill consequences of a standing army. To conclude, I assure you on the faith of a Christian, that I have made this discourse solely and

---

[1] The future William III, married to Mary Stuart, in 1677.

singly out of zeal and affection to the interest of my country; and not at all with the least intention to favour or promote the cause or interest of the duke of York, or to disparage the duke of Monmouth: from whom I never received the least unkindness; nor ever had the honour to be in his company: and to whom I shall ever pay respect suitable to his high birth and merit.*

NOBLE VEN. Well, sir, your reasoning in this point has extremely satisfied me; and the doctor, I suppose, was so before, as he averred; therefore pray let us go on where we left.

ENG. GENT. I cannot take so much upon me as to be dictator in the method of our cure, since either of you is a thousand times better qualified for such an office; and therefore shall henceforth desire to be an auditor.

DOCT. Pray, sir, let us not spend time in compliments, but be pleased to proceed in this business; and we doubt not but as you have hitherto wonderfully delighted us, so you will gratify us in concluding it.

ENG. GENT. I see I must obey you: but pray help me, and tell me in the first place, whether you do not both believe, that as the chief cause of all our distractions is (as has been proved) the breach of our government, so that the immediate causes are two; first, the great distrust on both sides between the king, and his people and parliament; the first fearing that his power will be so lessened by degrees, that at length it will not be able to keep the crown upon his head: and the latter seeing all things in disorder, and that the laws are not executed, (which is the second of the two causes,) fear the king intends to change the government and be arbitrary.

NOBLE VEN. I am a stranger; but (though I never reflected so much upon the original cause, as I have done since I heard you discourse of it) yet I ever thought, that those two were the causes of the unquietness of this kingdom. I mean the jealousy between the king and his people; and the inexecution of the great law of calling parliaments annually, and letting them sit, to dispatch their affairs: I understand this in the time of his majesty's grandfather and father, more than in his own reign.

ENG. GENT. Then whoever can absolutely lay these two causes asleep forever, will arrive to a perfect cure: which I conceive no way of doing, but that the king have a great deal more power, or a great deal less. And you know that what goes out of the king must go into the people, and so vice versa; insomuch that the people must have a great deal more power, or a great deal less. Now it is no question, but either of these two would rather increase their power than diminish it: so that if this cannot be made up by the wisdom of this age, we may see in the next; that both the king will endeavour to be altogether without a parliament, and the parliament to be without a king.

DOCT. I begin to smell what you would be nibbling at; the pretence which some had before his majesty's Restoration, of a commonwealth, or democracy.

ENG. GENT. No; I abhor the thoughts of wishing, much less endeavouring, any such thing, during the circumstances we are now in: that is, under oaths of obedience to a lawful king. And truly, if any Themistocles should make to me such a proposal, I should give the same judgement concerning it that Aristides did in such a case. The story is short. After the war between the Greeks and the Persians was ended, and Xerxes driven out of Greece; the whole fleet of the Grecian confederates, (except that of Athens, which was gone home) lay in a great arsenal (such as were then in use) upon the coast of Attica: during their abode there. Themistocles harrangues one day the people of Athens, (as was then the custom,) and tells them, that he had a design in his head, which would be of infinite profit and advantage to the commonwealth: but that it could not be executed without the order and authority of them; and that it did likewise require secrecy, and if it were declared there in the market-place, (where strangers as well as citizens might be present,) it could not be concealed; and therefore proposed it to their consideration what should be done in it. It was at length concluded, that Themistocles should propose it to Aristides; and if he did next morning acquaint the people that he gave his approbation to it, it should be proceeded in. Themistocles informs him, that the whole fleet of their confederates in the war against the Medes had betaken themselves to the great arsenal upon their coast, where they might be easily fired; and then the Athenians would remain absolute masters of the sea, and so give law to all Greece. When Aristides came the next day to deliver his judgement to the people, he told them that the business proposed by Themistocles, was indeed very advantageous and profitable to the Athenians; but withal, the most wicked and villainous attempt that ever was undertaken: upon which it was wholly laid aside. And the same judgement do I give, doctor, of your democracy, at this time. But to return to the place where I was; I do believe that this difference may easily be terminated very fairly; and that our house need not be pulled down, and a new one built; but may be very easily repaired, so that it may last many hundred years.

NOBLE VEN. I begin to perceive that you aim at this; that the king must give the people more power, as Henry the third, and king John did; or the parliament must give the king more, as you said they did in France in the time of Lewis the eleventh; or else that it will come in time to a war again.

ENG. GENT. You may please to know; that in all times hitherto, the parliament never demanded anything of the king, wherein the interest and government of the kingdom was concerned, (excepting acts of pardon,) but they founded their demands upon their right; not only because it might seem unreasonable for them to be earnest with him, to give them that which was his own; but also because they cannot choose but know that all powers which are fundamentally and lawfully in the crown, were placed there upon the first institution of our government, to capacitate the prince to govern and protect his people: so that for the parliament to seek to take from him such authority, were to be *felo de se*, as we call a self-homicide. But as in some distempers of the body the head suffers as well as the inferior parts, so that it is not possible for it to order, direct and provide for the whole body, as its office requires; since the wisdom and power which is placed there, is given by God to that end: in which case, though the distemper of the body may begin from the disease of some other part, or from the mass of blood, or putrefaction of other humours; yet since that noble part is so affected by it that reason and discourse fail, therefore to restore this again remedies must be applied to, and possibly humours or vapours drawn from the head itself; that so it may be able to govern and reign over the body, as it did before: or else the whole man, like a slave, must be ruled and guided from without, that is, by some keeper: so is it now with us, in our politic disease: where granting (if you please) that the distemper does not proceed from the head, but the corruption of other parts; yet in the cure, applications must be made to the head as well as to the members, if we mean poor England shall recover its former perfect health: and therefore it will be found, perhaps, essential to our being, to ask something (in the condition we now are) to which the king as yet may have a right; and which except he please to part with, the pheno-

174

mena of government cannot be salved; that is, our laws cannot be executed; nor Magna Charta itself made practicable: and so both prince and people, that is the polity of England, must die of this disease; or in this delirium, must be governed from without and fall to the lot of some foreign power.

NOBLE VEN. But, sir, (since the business is come to this dilemma) why may not the king ask more power of the parliament, as well as they of him?

ENG. GENT. No question but our present counsellors and courtiers would be nibbling at that bait again, if they had another parliament that would take pensions for their votes; but in one that is come fresh from the people, and understands their sense and grievances very well, I hardly believe they will attempt it: for both council and parliament must needs know by this time-a-day, that the cause of all our distractions coming (as has been said an hundred times) from the king's having a greater power already, than the condition of property at this present can admit without confusion and disorder, it is not like to mend matters for them to give him more; except they will deliver up to him at the same instant their possessions and right to their lands, and become naturally and politically his slaves.

NOBLE VEN. Since there must be a voluntary parting with power, I fear your cure will prove long and ineffectual: and we reconcilers, shall, (I fear,) prove like our devout Capuchin at Venice. This poor man's name was Friar Bernardino da Udine; and was esteemed a very holy man, as well as an excellent preacher: insomuch that he was appointed to preach the Lent sermons in one of our principal churches; which he performed at the beginning with so much eloquence, and applause, that the church was daily crowded three hours before the sermon was to begin. The esteem and veneration this poor friar was in, elevated his spirit a little too high to be contained within the bounds of reason: but before his delirium was perceived, he told his auditory one day; that the true devotion of that people, and the care they had to come to hear his word preached, had been so acceptable to God and to the virgin, that they had vouchsafed to inspire him with the knowledge of an expedient, which he did not doubt but would make men happy and just even in this life; and that the flesh should no longer lust against the spirit; but that he would not acquaint them with it at that present, because something was to be done on their parts to make them capable of this great blessing; which was to pray zealously for a happy success upon his endeavours, and to fast and to visit the churches, to that end: therefore he desired them to come the Wednesday following to be made acquainted with this blessed expedient. You may imagine how desirous our people were, to hear something more of this fifth monarchy. I will shorten my story, and tell you nothing of what crowding there was all night, and what quarrelling for places in the church; nor with what difficulty the 'sages', who were sent by the magistrate to keep the peace, and to make way for the preacher to get into the pulpit, did both: but up he got: and after a long preamble of desiring more prayers, and addressing himself to our senate to mediate with the pope, that a week might be set apart for a jubilee and fasting three days all over the Christian world; to storm heaven with masses, prayers, fasting and alms to prosper his designs; he began to open the matter: that the cause of all the wickedness and sin, and by consequence of all the miseries and affliction which is in the world, arising from the enmity which is between God and the devil; by which means God was often crossed in his intentions of good to mankind here and hereafter, the devil by his temptations making us incapable of the mercy and favour of our creator: therefore he had a design (with the helps before-mentioned) to mediate with almighty God, that he would pardon the devil; and receive him into his favour again after so long a time of banishment and imprisonment; and not to take all his power from him, but to leave him so much as might do good to man, and not hurt: which he doubted not but he would employ that way, after such reconciliation was made, as his faith would not let him question. You may judge, what the numerous auditory thought of this: I can only tell you, that he had a different sort of company at his return from what he had when he came; for the men left him to the boys, who with great hoops instead of acclamations brought him to the gondola, which conveyed him to the Redentore; where he lodged: and I never had the curiosity to enquire, what became of him after.[1]

DOCT. I thank you heartily for this intervention; I see you have learned something in England: for, I assure you, we have been these

[1] Is the Noble Venetian fathering his *novella* upon Friar Bernardino Occhino (1487–1564), a well-known preacher and critic of social vices of Venetians, and later a reformer who emigrated to Geneva and then Moravia? 'Sages'—*saffi* or more likely *savii*, officers sent by the council of ten who helped in matters of public order, etc. The Redentore, Church of the Redeemer, on the Fondamento San Giacomo, in the Venetian suburb of Giudecca.

twenty years turning this, and all serious discourses into ridicule. But yet your similitude is very pat: for in every parliament that has been in England these sixty years, we have had notable contests between the seed of the serpent and the seed of the woman.

ENG. GENT. Well, sir, we have had a Michael here in our age, who has driven out Lucifer, and restored the true deity to his power:[1] but where omnipotency is wanting, (which differs the Friar's case and mine,) the devil of civil war and confusion may get up again; if he be not laid by prudence and virtue, and better conjurers than any we have yet at court.

NOBLE VEN. Well, gentlemen, I hope you have pardoned me for my farce: but, to be a little more serious, pray tell me how you will induce the king to give up so much of his right as may serve your turn? Would you have the parliament make war with him again?

ENG. GENT. There cannot, nor ought to be, any change but by his majesty's free consent: for besides, that a war is to be abhorred by all men that love their country; any contest of that kind in this case (viz. to take away the least part of the king's right) could be justified by no man living. I say besides that, a civil war has miscarried in our days; which was founded (at least pretendedly) upon defence of the people's own rights: in which, although they had as clear a victory in the end, as ever any contest upon earth had, yet could they never reap the least advantage in the world by it; but went from one tyranny to another, from Barebone's parliament, to Cromwell's reign; and from that, to a committee of safety: leaving those grave men, who managed affairs at the beginning, amazed to see new men and new principles governing England: and this induced them to cooperate to bring things back, just where they were before the war. Therefore this remedy will be either none, or worse than the disease: it not being now as it was in the barons' time, when the lord who led out his men, could bring them back again when he pleased, and rule them in the meantime, being his vassals: but now there is no man of so much credit, but that one who behaves himself bravely in the war, shall out-vie him; and, possibly, be able to do what he pleases with the army and the government: and in this corrupt age, it is ten to one, he will rather do hurt than good with the power he acquires. But because you ask me how we would persuade the king to this? I answer; by the parliament's humbly remonstrating to his majesty, that it is his own interest, preservation,

[1] John Milton's *Paradise Lost* appeared in 1667.

quiet and true greatness, to put an end to the distractions of his subjects; and that it cannot be done any other way: and to desire him to enter into debate with some men authorized by them, to see if there can be any other means than what they shall offer to compose things: if they find there may, then to embrace it; otherwise, to insist upon their own proposals; and if in the end they cannot obtain those requests, which they think the only essential means to preserve their country, then to beg their dismissal; that they may not stay, and be partakers in the ruin of it.

Now, my reasons why the king will please to grant this after the thorough discussing of it, are two. First, because all great princes have ever made up matters with their subjects upon such contests, without coming to extremities. The two greatest and most valiant of our princes, were Edward the first, and his grandchild Edward the third: these had very great demands made them by parliaments, and granted them all; as you may see upon the statute-book. Edward the second, and Richard the second, on the contrary, refused all things till they were brought to extremity. There is a memorable example in the Greek story of Theopompus, king of Sparta; whose subjects finding the government in disorder for want of some persons that might be a check upon the great power of the king, proposed to him the creation of the ephors (officers who made that city so great and famous afterwards.) The king finding by their reasons, which were unanswerable, (as I think ours now are,) that the whole government of Sparta was near its ruin without such a cure; and considering that he had more to lose in that disorder than others, freely granted their desires: for which being derided by his wife, who asked him what a kind of monarchy he would leave to his son? He answered; a very good one, because it will be a very lasting one. Which brings on my second reason, for which I believe the king will grant these things; because he cannot any way mend himself, nor his condition, if he do not.

NOBLE VEN. You have very fully convinced me of two things: first, that we have no reason to expect or believe that the parliament will ever increase the king's power: and then, that the king cannot by any way found himself a new and more absolute monarchy, except he can alter the condition of property: which I think we may take for granted to be impossible. But yet, I know not why we may not suppose that (although he cannot establish to all posterity such an empire) he may, notwithstanding, change the government at the present; and calling parliaments no more, administer it by force, (as it is done in France,) for some good time.

ENG. GENT. In France it has been a long work: and although that tyranny was begun, as has been said, by petition from the states themselves not to be assembled any more; yet the kings since, in time of great distraction, have thought fit to convocate them again: as they did in the civil wars thrice, once at Orleans, and twice at Blois.[1]

I would not repeat what I have so tediously discoursed of concerning France already; but only to entreat you to remember that our nation has no such poor and numerous gentry, which draw better revenues from the king's purse, than they can from their own estates: all our country people consisting of rich nobility and gentry, of wealthy yeomen, and of poor younger brothers; who have little or nothing, and can never raise their companies, if they should get commissions, without their elder brother's assistance amongst his tenants, or else with the free consent and desire of the people; which, in this case, would hardly be afforded them. But we will suppose there be idle people enough to make an army, and that the king has money enough to arm and raise them: and I will grant too, to avoid tediousness (although I do not think it possible) that the people will at the first for fear, receive them into their houses and quarter them against law; nay, pay the money, which shall be by illegal edicts imposed upon the subjects to pay them: yet is it possible an army can continue any time to enslave their own country? Can they resist the prayers, or the curses, of their fathers, brothers, wives, mothers, sisters, and of all persons wherever they frequent? Upon this account, all the Greek tyrants were of very short continuance: who being in chief magistracy and credit in their commonwealths, by means of soldiers and satellites, usurped the sovereignty. But did ever any of them, excepting Dionysius, leave it to his son? who was driven out within less than a year after his father's death. Many armies of the natives have destroyed tyrannies: so the decemvirate was ruined at Rome, and the Tarquins expelled before that.

Our own country has been a stage, even in our time, where this tragedy has been sufficiently acted: for the army, after the war was done, fearing the monarchy should be restored again, held counsels; got agitators; and though there were often very severe executions upon

[1] The States General met at Orleans in 1560; Blois 1576, and 1589.

179   12-2

the ring-leaders, did at length by their perseverance necessitate their officers to join with them, (having many good headpieces of the party to advise them;) and so broke all treaties. And the parliament adhering to a small party of them who consented to lay aside kingly government, they afterwards drove them away too; fearing they would continue to govern by an oligarchy. I am far from approving this way they used; in which they broke all laws divine and human, political and moral: but I urge it only to show how easily an army of natives is to be deluded with the name of liberty; and brought to pull down anything, which their ring-leaders tell them tends to enslaving their country. 'Tis true, this army was afterwards cheated by their general; who without their knowledge, (much less consent,) one morning suddenly made himself tyrant of his country.[1] It is true, that their reputation (not their arms) supported him in that state for some time; but it is as certain that they did very often, and to the last, refuse to be instrumental to levy moneys, though for their own pay: and so he, against his will, was fain to call from time to time parliamentary conventions. And it is most certain, that he did, in the sickness of which he died, often complain that his army would not go a step farther with him: and, in fact, some months after his death, they did dethrone his son, and restore the remainder of the old parliament; upon promise made to them in secret, (by the demagogues of that assembly,) that a commonwealth should be speedily framed and settled.

NOBLE VEN. Sir, I am satisfied that an army raised here on a sudden, and which never saw an enemy, could not be brought to act such high things for the ruin of their own government; nor possibly, would be any way able to resist the fury and insurrection of the people: but what say you of a foreign army, raised by your king abroad, and brought over, whose officers and soldiers shall have no acquaintance or relations amongst the people here?

ENG. GENT. All forces of that kind must be either auxiliaries, or mercenaries. Auxiliaries, are such as are sent by some neighbour prince or state, with their own colours, and paid by themselves; though possibly, the prince who demands them may furnish the money. These usually return home again, when the occasion for which they were demanded is over: but whether they do or not, if they be not mixed and over-balanced with forces which depend upon the prince who calls

---

[1] Cromwell, whom Neville mentions always with resentment.

them, but that the whole weight and power lies in them; they will certainly, first or last, seize that country for their own sovereign. And as for mercenaries; they must be raised ('tis true) with the money of the prince who needs them, but by the authority and credit of some great persons who are to lead and command them: and these, in all occasions, have made their own commander prince: as F. Sforza at Milan drove out by this trick the Visconti, ancient dukes of that state; and the Mamelukes in Egypt made themselves a military commonwealth. So that the way of an army here, would either be no remedy at all; or one very much worse than the disease, to the prince himself.

NOBLE VEN. Well, sir, I begin to be of opinion, that anything the king can grant the parliament (especially such a parliament as this is, which consists of men of very great estates and so can have no interest to desire troubles) will not be so inconvenient to him, as to endeavour to break the government by force. But why may he not, for this time (by soothing them and offering them great alliances abroad for the interest of England, and balancing matters in Europe more even than they have been; and, in fine, by offering them a war with the French, to which nation they have so great a hatred;) lay them asleep, and get good store of money; and stave off this severe cure you speak of, at least for some time longer?

ENG. GENT. There has been something of this done too lately; and there is a gentleman lies in the tower, who is to answer for it.[1] But you may please to understand, that there is scarce any amongst the middle sort of people, much less within the walls of the house of commons, who do not perfectly know, that we can have no alliance with any nation in the world that will signify anything to them, or to ourselves, till our government be redressed and new modelled: and therefore, though there were an army landed in this island, yet that we must begin there; before we are fit to repulse them, or defend ourselves. And the fear and sense of this people, universally, is; that if we should have any war, either for our own concerns, or for those of our allies, whilst matters remain as they do at home, it would certainly come to this pass: that either being beaten, we should subject this kingdom to an invasion, at a time when we are in a very ill condition to repel it; or else, if we were victorious, that our courtiers and

---

[1] Thomas Osborne, earl of Danby, later duke of Leeds (1631–1712); impeached 1678; in Tower 1679–84.

counsellors ardently (or as the French cry, in a trice)[1] would employ that mettle and good fortune, to try some such conclusions at home, as we have been discoursing of. And therefore, if any war should be undertaken without parliament; you would see the people rejoice as much at any disaster our forces should receive, as they did when the Scots seized the four northern counties, in 1639; or, before that, when we were beaten at the isle of Rhee;[2] or when we had any loss in the last war with Holland. And this joy is not so unnatural as it may seem to those who do not consider the cause of it: which is the breach of our old government, and the necessity our governors are under to make some new experiments; and the fear we are in, that any prosperity may make them able to try them, either with effect, or at least with impunity. Which consideration made a court-droll say lately to his majesty, (who seemed to wonder why his subjects hated the French so much;) sir, it is because you love them, and espouse their interest; and if you would discover this truth clearly, you may please to make war with the king of France; and then you shall see, that this people will not only love them, take their parts, and wish them success: but will exceedingly rejoice, when they are victorious in sinking your ships, or defeating your forces. And this is sufficient to answer your proposal for alliances abroad, and for a war with France. Besides this (to wind all up in a word) it is not to be imagined; that so good and wise a prince as we have at this time should ever be induced, when he comes to understand perfectly his own condition, to let his own interest (granting his power to be so, which is very false) contest with the safety and preservation of his people; for which only it was given him: or that he will be any way tenacious of such prerogatives, as now by a natural revolution of political circumstances are so far from continuing useful to his governing the people, that they are the only remora and obstacle of all government, settlement, and order. For his majesty must needs know, that all forms of regulating mankind under laws were ordained, by God and man, for the happiness and security of the governed; and not for the interest and greatness of those who rule: unless where there is better nature in the case. So God governs man, for his own glory only; and men reign over beasts, for their own use and service. But where an absolute prince rules over his own servants, whom he feeds

---

[1] Text incorrect here; *in fragrante* for *flagrante* and *d'emble* for *d'emblée*.
[2] Buckingham's ill-fated venture to assist the Huguenots, 1627.

and pays, (as we have said;) or the master of a great and numerous family governs his household; they are both bound, by the law of God and nature, and by their own interest, to do them justice; and not anger or tyrannize over them, more than the necessity of preserving their empire and authority requires.

DOCT. But sir, considering the difficulty which will be found in the king, and possibly in the parliament too, to come up to so great an alteration at the first; and the danger that may happen by our remaining long in this unsettled condition, which does hourly expose us to innumerable hazards, both at home, and from abroad; why may we not begin, and lay the foundation now, by removing all his majesty's present council, by parliament? Which is no new thing; but has been often practised, in many kings' reigns.

ENG. GENT. First, the council (that is, the privy council, which you mean) is no part of our government; as we may have occasion to show hereafter: nor is the king obliged by any fundamental law, or by any act of parliament, to hearken to their advice; or so much as to ask it: and if you should make one on purpose, besides that it would not be so effectual as what we may propose, it would be full as hard to go down either with king or parliament. But besides all this, you would see some of these counsellors so nominated by parliament, perhaps, prove honest; and then they would be forced to withdraw, as some lately did; because they found, I suppose, that till the administration be altered, it is impossible that their counsels can be embraced; or anything be acted by them which may tend to the good of their country.[1] Those, who have not so great a sense of honour and integrity, will be presently corrupted by their own interest; whilst the prince is left in possession of all those baits and means to answer such men's expectations: it being most certain, that if you have a musty vessel, and by consequence dislike the beer which comes out of it, and draw it out; causing the barrel to be immediately filled with good and sound liquor: it is certain by experience, that both your new drink, and all that ever you shall put into the cask, till it be taken in pieces, and the pipes shaved and new-modelled, will be full as musty and unsavoury as the first which you found fault with.

[1] The Council was a favourite target of would-be reformers who wished nothing between the King and his old Council or Parliament. When Neville wrote, Charles had just tried the experiment suggested by Sir William Temple of a council of thirty, but it had lasted only a short time.

NOBLE VEN. Now sir, I think we are at an end of our questions: and I for my part am convinced, that as the king cannot better himself any way by falling out with his people at this time; so that his goodness and wisdom is such, that he will rather choose to imitate the most glorious and generous of his predecessors; as Edward the first, and Edward the third; than those who were of less worth, and more unfortunate; as Edward the second, and Richard the second. And therefore we are now ready to hear what you would think fit to ask of so excellent a prince.

ENG. GENT. I never undertook to be so presumptuous: there is a parliament to sit speedily,[1] and certainly they are the fittest every way to search into such matters; and to anticipate their wisdom would be unreasonable, and might give them just offence. But because all this tittle-tattle may not go for nothing, I shall presume to give you my thoughts how the cure must be wrought, without descending to particulars. The cause immediate (as we have said) of our disease, is the inexecution of our laws: and it is most true, that when that is altered for the better, and that all our laws are duly executed, we are in health. For as we can never have the entire benefit of them, till our government is upon a right basis; so whenever we enjoy this happiness, to have the full benefit of those constitutions which were made by our ancestors for our safe and orderly living, our government is upon a right basis: therefore we must enquire into the cause, why our laws are not executed; and when you have found and taken away that cause, all is well. The cause can be no other than this, that the king is told, and does believe, that most of these great charters or rights of the people, of which we now chiefly treat, are against his majesty's interest; though this be very false (as has been said) yet we will not dispute it at this time, but take it for granted: so that the king having the supreme execution of the laws in his hand, cannot be reasonably supposed to be willing to execute them whenever he can choose whether he will do it or no; it being natural for every man not to do anything against his own interest when he can help it. Now when you have thought well what it should be that gives the king a liberty to choose whether any part of the law shall be current or no; you will find, that it is the great power the king enjoys in the government: when the parliament has discovered this, they will no doubt demand of his majesty an abatement of his royal pre-

[1] 20 Oct. 1680.

184

rogative in those matters only which concern our enjoyment of our all, that is our lives, liberties and estates; and leave his royal power entire and untouched, in all the other branches of it. When this is done, we shall be as if some great hero had performed the adventure of dissolving the enchantment, we have been under so many years; and all our statutes from the highest to the lowest, from Magna Charta to that for burying in woollen,[1] will be current: and we shall neither fear the bringing in popery, nor arbitrary power in the intervals of parliament; neither will there be any dissensions in them; all causes of factions between the country and court party being entirely abolished; so that the people shall have no reason to distrust their prince, nor he them.

DOCT. You make us a fine golden age: but after all this, will you not be pleased to show us a small prospect of this Canaan, or country of rest? Will you not vouchsafe to particularize a little, what powers there are in the king, which you would have discontinued? Would you have such prerogatives abolished, or placed elsewhere?

ENG. GENT. There can be no government, if they be abolished. But I will not be like a man who refuses to sing amongst his friends at their entreaty, because he has an ill voice; I will rather suffer my self to be laughed at by you in delivering my small judgement in this matter: but still with this protestation, that I do believe than an infinity of men better qualified than myself for such sublime matters, and much more the house of commons, who represent the wisdom as well as the power of this kingdom, may find out a far better way than my poor parts and capacity can suggest. The powers then which now being in the crown do hinder the execution of our laws, and prevent by consequence our happiness and settlement, are four. First, the absolute power of making war and peace, treaties and alliances with all nations in the world; by which means, by ignorant counsellors, or wicked ministers, many of our former kings have made confederations and wars, very contrary and destructive to the interest of England: and by the unfortunate management of them, have often put the king in great hazard of invasion. Besides that, as long as there is a distinction made between the court party and that of the country, there will ever be a jealousy in the people; that those wicked counsellors, (who may think they can be safe no other way,) will make alliances with powerful princes, in which there may be a secret article by which those princes shall stipulate to

[1] 18 and 19 Car. II. c. 4.

185

assist them with forces upon a short warning to curb the parliament, and possibly to change the government. And this apprehension in the people will be the less unreasonable; because Oliver Cromwell, (the great pattern of some of our courtiers,) is notoriously known to have inserted an article in his treaty with cardinal Mazarin, during this king of France's minority, that he should be assisted with ten thousand men from France upon occasion, to preserve and defend him in his usurped government, against his majesty that now is; or the people of England; or in fine, his own army; whose revolt he often feared.[1]

The second great prerogative the king enjoys, is the sole disposal and ordering of the militia by sea and land, raising forces, garrisoning and fortifying places, setting out ships of war, so far as he can do all this without putting taxations upon the people; and this not only in the intervals of parliament, but even during their session; so that they cannot raise the train-bands of the country or city to guard themselves, or secure the peace of the kingdom. The third point is; that it is in his majesty's power to nominate and appoint as he pleases, and for what time he thinks fit, all the officers of the kingdom that are of trust or profit, both civil, military, and ecclesiastical, (as they will be called,) except where there is patronage. These two last powers may furnish a prince who will hearken to ill-designing counsellors, with the means either of invading the government by force, or by his judges and other creatures undermining it by fraud. Especially by enjoying the fourth advantage; which is the laying out and employing, as he pleases, all the public revenues of the crown or kingdom, and that without having any regard (except he thinks fit) to the necessity of the navy, or any other thing that concerns the safety of the public. So that all these four great powers, as things now stand, may be administered at any time, as well to destroy and ruin the good order and government of the state; as to preserve and support it, as they ought to do.

NOBLE VEN. But if you divest the king of these powers, will you have the parliament sit always to govern these matters?

ENG. GENT. Sir, I would not divest the king of them; much less would I have the parliament assume them, or perpetuate their sitting. They are a body more fitted to make laws, and punish the breakers of

---

[1] Cromwell signed a treaty with Mazarin in 1657 which had secret articles, none, however, of precisely this import: see W. C. Abbott, *Writings and Speeches* (4 vols. Harvard, 1937–47), IV, 914–19.

them, than to execute them. I would have them therefore petition his majesty by way of bill, that he will please to exercise these four great *magnalia* of government, with the consent of four several councils to be appointed for that end, and not otherwise; that is, with the consent of the major part of them, if any of them dissent. In all which councils, his majesty, (or who he pleases to appoint) shall preside. The councils to be named in parliament; first all the number, and every year afterwards a third part: so each year a third part shall go out, and a recruit of an equal number come in; and in three years they shall be all new: and no person to come into that council, or any other of the four, till he have kept out of any of them full three years, being as long as he was in: and this I learnt from your *Quarantias* at Venice.[1] And the use is excellent: for being in such a circulation, and sure to have their intervals of power; they will neither grow so insolent as to brave their king, nor will the prince have any occasion to corrupt them; although he had the means to do it, which in this new model he cannot have. These men in their several councils should have no other instructions, but to dispose of all things and act in their several charges, for the interest and glory of England; and shall be answerable to parliament, from time to time, for any malicious or advised misdemeanour. Only that council which manages the public revenue, shall (besides a very copious and honourable revenue which shall be left to his majesty's disposal for his own entertainment, as belongs to the splendour and majesty of the government) have instructions to serve his majesty (if he pleases to command them, and not otherwise) in the regulating and ordering his economy and household: and if they shall see it necessary, for extraordinary occasions of treating foreign princes and ambassadors, or presenting them, (and the like ostentation of greatness) to consent with his majesty moderately to charge the revenue to that end.

I verily believe that this expedient is much more effectual, than either the justiciar of Aragon was, or the ephors of Sparta: who being to check the king almost in every thing, without having any share in his counsels or understanding them, could not choose but make a sullen posture of affairs:[2] whereas these both seem, and really are, the king's

---

[1] Note principle of rotation. *Quarantia*—court of the forty judges of criminal cases.
[2] Admiration is expressed here and below, when the Doctor recurs to the subject, for the Spartan ephors, the justiciars of Aragon, guardians of liberty against all encroachments, suggestive of a supreme court as in the United States. Englishmen of the seventeenth century thought of parliament as such a guardian.

ministers; only obliged by parliament to act faithfully and honestly: to which, even without that, all other counsellors are bound by oath. As for the other council, now called the privy council, the king may still please to continue to nominate them at his pleasure; so they act nothing in any matters properly within the jurisdiction of these four councils; but meddle with the affairs of merchants, plantations, charters, and other matters to which the regal power extends.[1] And provided that his majesty call none of the persons employed in these other four councils, during their being so; nor that this council do any way intermeddle with any affairs, criminal or civil, which are to be decided by law; and do belong to the jurisdictions of other courts or magistrates: they being no established judicatory, or congregation, which either our government or laws do take notice of: (as was said before) but persons congregated by the king, as his friends and faithful subjects, to give him their opinion in the execution of his regal office. As for example, the king does exercise, at this time, a negative voice as to bills presented to him by the parliament; which he claims by right: no man ever said that the privy council had a negative voice; yet former kings did not only ask their advice as to the passing or not passing of such bills; but often decided the matter by their votes: which, although it be a high presumption in them, when they venture to give him counsel contrary to what is given him by his greatest council, yet never any of them have been questioned for it; being looked upon as private men who speak according to the best of their cunning, and such as have no public capacity at all. But if this be not so, and that this council have some foundation in law, and some public capacity; I wish in this new settlement it may be made otherwise: and that his majesty please to take their counsel in private, but summon no persons to appear before them; much less give them authority to send for in custody, or imprison any subject; which may as well be done by the judges and magistrates: who, if secrecy be required, may as well be sworn to secrecy as these gentlemen; and (I believe) can keep counsel as well, and give it too.

NOBLE VEN. But would you have none to manage state-affairs? None imprisoned for secret conspiracies, and kept till they can be fully discovered? You have made an act here lately, about imprisonments; that every person shall have his habeas corpus, I think you call it: so

[1] Neville, it will be noted, allows the King a free hand with imperial and mercantile concerns.

that no man, for what occasion soever, can lie in prison above a night, but the cause must be revealed, though there be great cause for the concealing it.

ENG. GENT. This act[1] you mention, (and a great many more which we have to the same purpose, that is against illegal imprisonments) shows, that for a long time the power over men's persons has been exercised (under his majesty) by such as were likely, rather to employ it ill than well: that is, would rather imprison ten men for honourable actions; (such as standing for the people's rights in parliament, refusing to pay illegal taxes, and the like) than one for projecting and inventing illegal monopolies; or any other kind of oppressing the people. This made, first Magna Charta, then the Petition of Right, and divers other acts besides this last, take that power quite away; and make the law and the judges the only disposers of the liberties of our persons. And it may be, when the parliament shall see the fruit of this alteration we are now discoursing of, and that state-affairs are in better hands, they may think fit to provide that a return or warrant of imprisonment from one of these four councils, (which I suppose will have a power of commitment given them as to persons appearing delinquents before them) wherein it shall be expressed; that if the public is like to suffer or be defrauded, if the matter be immediately divulged; I say in this case, the parliament may please to make it lawful for the judge to delay the bailing of him for some small time: because it is not to be judged, that these counsellors, so chosen, and so instructed, and to continue so small a time, will use this power ill; especially being accountable for any abusing of it to the next parliament: and I suppose the parliament, amongst other provisions in this behalf, will require that there shall be a register kept of all the votes of these several councils, with the names as well of those who consented, as of such who dissented. And as to the former part of your question, whether I would have none to manage state-affairs? I think there are very few state-affairs, that do not concern either peace and war, and treaties abroad; the management of the armies, militia, and the county force at home; the management of all the public moneys, and the election of all officers whatsoever. The other parts of state-affairs, which are making and repealing of laws, punishing high crimes against the state, with levying and proportioning all manner of impositions upon the people, this is reserved to the

[1] Habeas Corpus, 31 Car. II. c. 2.

189

parliament itself: and the execution of all laws, to the judges and magistrates. And I can think of no other affairs of state than these.

DOCT. Do you intend that the council for choosing officers shall elect them of the king's household, that is his menial servants?

ENG. GENT. No; that were unreasonable. Except any of them have any jurisdiction in the kingdom; or any place or pre-eminence in parliament annexed to such office; but in these things which concern the powers and jurisdictions of these several councils, (wherein the protection of liberty, as Machiavel calls it, is now to be placed) I shall not presume to say anything; but assure yourself, if ever it come to that, it will be very well digested in parliament: they being very good at contriving such matters, and making them practicable; as well as at performing all other matters, that concern the interest and greatness of the kingdom.

DOCT. I have thought, that the ephors of Sparta were an admirable magistracy; not only for the interest of the people, but likewise for the preservation of the authority of the kings, and of their lives too. For Plutarch observes, that the cities of Messene and Argos had the same government with Lacedaemon; and yet for want of erecting such an authority as was in the ephors, they were not only perpetually in broils amongst themselves, and for that reason ever beaten by their enemies; (whereas the Spartans were always victorious;) but even their kings were the most miserable of men: being often called in question judicially, and so lost their lives; and many of them murdered by insurrections of the people. And at last, in both these cities, the kings were driven out; their families extirpated; the territory new divided; and the government turned into a democracy. And I ever thought that this expedient you propose (for I have heard you discourse of it often before now), would prove a more safe and a more noble reformation, than the institution of the ephors was: and that a prince who is a lover of his country; who is gracious, wise and just, (such a one as it has pleased God to send us at this time;) shall be ten times more absolute when this regulation is made, than ever he was or could be before: and that whatsoever he proposes in any of these councils will be received as a law, nay as an oracle: and, on the other side, ill and weak princes shall have no possibility of corrupting men; or doing either themselves, or their people, any kind of harm or mischief. But have you done now?

ENG. GENT. No, sir; when this provision is made for the execution of the laws, which I think very effectual, (not to say infallible,) although it is not to be doubted, but that there will be from time to time many excellent laws enacted; yet two I would have passed immediately. The one, concerning the whole regulation of the elections to parliament: which we need very much; and no doubt but it will be well done.[1] That part of it which is necessary to go hand in hand with our settlement, and which indeed must be part of it, is: that a parliament be elected every year at a certain day, and that without any writ or summons; the people meeting of course at the time appointed in the usual place; (as they do in parishes at the church-house to choose officers;) and that the sheriffs be there ready to preside and to certify the election. And that the parliament so chosen shall meet at the time appointed; and sit and adjourn, as their business is more or less urgent; but still setting yet a time for their coming together again. And if there shall be a necessity (by reason of invasion, or some other cause) for their assembling sooner; then the king to call the counsellors of these four councils all together, and with the consent of the major part of them, intimate their meeting sooner. But when the day comes for the annual meeting of another parliament, they must be understood to be dissolved in law, without any other ceremony; and the new one to take their place.

DOCT. I would have this considered too, and provided for; that no election should be made of any person who had not the majority of the electors present to vote for him: so the writ orders it; and so reason dictates. For else how can he be said to represent the county, if not a fifth part have consented to his choice? As happens sometimes; and may do oftener: for where seven or eight stand for one vacant place, (as I have known in our last Long Parliament,)[2] the votes being set in columns, he who has had most votes has not exceeded four hundred, of above two thousand who were present.

NOBLE VEN. This is a strange way! I thought you had put every man by himself, as we do in our government, and as I understood they do in the house of commons, when there is any nomination; and then, if he has not the major part, he is rejected.

ENG. GENT. This is very material; and indeed essential: but I make no doubt, but if this project should come in play in parliament, this

---

[1] Corruption was thought to be growing and Commonwealthmen long advocated reform of election methods, annual parliaments, the ballot, and other devices to prevent it.
[2] 'Last Long Parliament', that is, 1661–79.

and all other particulars (which would be both needless and tedious to discourse of here) will be well and effectually provided for. The next act I would have passed, should be concerning the house of peers: that as I take it for granted, that there will be a clause in the bill concerning elections, that no new boroughs shall be enabled to send members to parliament except they shall be capacitated thereunto by an act; so it being of the same necessity as to the liberty of parliament, that the peers (who do and must enjoy both a negative and deliberative voice in all parliamentary transactions, except what concern levying of money originally) be exempted from depending absolutely upon the prince; and that therefore it be declared by act, for the future, that no peer shall be made but by act of parliament, and then that it be hereditary in his male line.[1]

NOBLE VEN. I am not yet fully satisfied how you can order your matters, concerning this house of peers: nor do I see, how the contests between the house of commons and them can be so laid asleep, but that they will arise again. Besides, the house of commons must necessarily be extremely concerned to find the house of peers, (which consists of private persons, though very great and honourable ones,) in an instant, dash all that they have been so long hammering for the good of all the people of England, whom they represent. Were it not better, now you are upon so great alterations, to make an annual elective senate; or at least one wherein the members should be but for life, and not hereditary?[2]

ENG. GENT. By no means, sir; the less change the better: and in this case, the metaphysical maxim is more true than in any, viz. nothing should be multiplied unnecessarily: for great alterations fright men, and puzzle them; and there is no need of it at all in this case. I have told you before, that there is a necessity of a senate; and how short this government would be without it; and how confused in the meantime. The Roman senate was hereditary amongst the *patricii*; except the censor left any of them out of the roll during his magistracy, for some very great and scandalous offence: and in that case too there was an appeal to the people, as in all other causes; witness the case of Lucius Quinctius, and many others.[3] To show that there can be no need of such a change here as you speak of, you may please to consider;

---

[1] Note the appointment of peers by parliament.
[2] When appointed, peers are to be hereditary: cf. Machiavelli, *Discourses*, I, 25.
[3] Cf. Moyle, below, p. 236, and Plutarch, 'Marcus Cato'.

that all differences between the several parts of any government, come upon the account of interest. Now when this settlement is made, the house of peers and the house of commons can have no interest to dissent: for as to all things of private interest, (that is, the rights of peers, both during the sitting of parliaments, and in the intervals,) is left to their own house to judge of; as it is to the house of commons, to judge of their own privileges. And as for the contest of the peers' jurisdiction as to appeals from courts of equity; (besides that I would have that settled in the act which should pass concerning the lords' house,) I believe it will never happen more, when the government is upon a right foundation; it having been hitherto fomented by two different parties: the court-party sometimes blowing up that difference to break the session, lest some good bills for the people should pass; or that the king, by rejecting them, might discontent his people. To avoid which dilemma, there needed no more, but to procure some person to prosecute his appeal before the lords. Some honest patriots afterwards possibly might use the same policy which they learnt from the courtiers, to quash some bill very destructive in which they were out-voted in the commons house; otherwise it is so far from the interest of the commons to hinder appeals from courts of equity, that there is none amongst them but know we are almost destroyed for want of it. And when they have considered well, and that some such reformation as this shall take place; they will find that it can never be placed in a more honourable and unbiased judicatory than this: and I could wish, that even in the intermission of parliamentary sessions, the whole peerage of England, (as many of them as can conveniently be in town) may sit in their judicial capacities, and hear appeals in equity; as well as judge upon writs of error.

Now as to your other objection, (which is indeed of great weight,) that the house of commons must needs take it ill, that the lords should frustrate their endeavours for the people's good by their negative; if you consider one thing, the force of this objection will vanish: which is, that when this new constitution shall be admitted, the lords cannot have any interest or temptation to differ with the commons in anything wherein the public good is concerned; but are obliged by all the ties in the world to run the same course and fortune with the commons; their interest being exactly the same: so that if there be any dissenting upon bills between the two houses, when each of them shall think their own expedient conduces most to the advantage of the public, this difference will ever be decided by right reason at conferences; and the lords may as well convince the commons, as be convinced by them: and these contests are and ever will be of admirable use and benefit to the commonwealth. The reason why it is otherwise now, and that the house of peers is made use of to hinder many bills from passing, that are supposed to be for the ease of the people, is; that the great counsellors and officers which sit in that house do suggest, (whether true or false,) that it is against his majesty's will and interest that such an act should pass; whereupon it has found obstruction. But hereafter, if our expedient take place, it cannot be so; first, because our king himself cannot have any designs going (as was proved before) which shall make it his advantage to hinder any good intended his people, whose prosperity then will be his own; and then, because in a short time the peers, being made by act of parliament, will consist of the best men of England both for parts and estates; and those who are already made, if any of them have small estates, the king, (if he had the interest,) would not have the means to corrupt them: the public moneys, and the great offices being to be dispensed in another manner than formerly: so their lordships will have no motive in the world to steer their votes and counsels, but their own honour and conscience, and the preservation and prosperity of their country. So that it would be both needless and unjust to pretend any change of this kind. Besides, this alteration in the administration of our government being proposed to be done by the unanimous consent of king, lords, and commons, and not otherwise, it would be very preposterous to believe, that the peers would depose themselves of their hereditary rights; and betake themselves to the hopes of being elected. It is true, they have lost the power they had over the commons; but that has not been taken from them by any law, no more than it was given them by any, but is fallen by the course of nature; as has been shown at large. But though they cannot lead the commons by their tenures as formerly, yet there is no reason or colour that they should lose their coordination; which I am sure they have by law, and by the fundamental constitution of the government: and which is so far from being prejudicial to a lasting settlement, (as was said) that it infinitely contributes to it; and prevents the confusion which would destroy it. If I should have proposed anything in this discourse, which should have entrenched upon the king's hereditary right; or that should have hindered the majesty and greatness of these kingdoms from being represented by his royal person; I should have made your story of the capuchin friar very applicable to me.

NOBLE VEN. I see you have not forgiven me that novel yet: but pray give me leave to ask you one question. Why do you make the election of great officers, to be by a small secret council? That had been more proper for a numerous assembly; as it is in most commonwealths.

ENG. GENT. It is so in democracies, and was so in Sparta; and is done by your great council in Venice: but we are not making such a kind of government, but rectifying an ancient monarchy; and giving the prince some help in the administration of that great branch of his regality: besides it is sufficient, that our parliament chooses these councils; (that is always understood, the lords and commons, with the king's consent.)[1] Besides, it is possible that if such a regulation as this come in debate amongst them, the parliament will reserve to itself the approbation of the great officers; as chancellor, judges, general officers of an army, and the like; and that such shall not have a settlement in those charges, till they are accordingly allowed of; but may in the meantime exercise them. As to particulars, I shall always refer you to what the parliament will judge fit to order in the case: but if you have anything to object, or to show in general, that some such regulation as this cannot be effectual towards the putting our distracted country into better order; I shall think myself obliged to answer you: if you can have patience to hear me, and are not weary already; as you may very well be.

NOBLE VEN. I shall certainly never be weary of such discourse; however I shall give you no further trouble in this matter: for I am very fully satisfied, that such reformation, (if it could be compassed;) would not only unite all parties; but make you very flourishing at home, and very great abroad. But have you any hopes that such a thing will ever come into debate? What do the parliament-men say to it?

ENG. GENT. I never had any discourse to this purpose, either with any lord, or member of the commons house; otherwise than as possibly some of these notions might fall in, at ordinary conversation: for I do not intend to entrench upon the office of God, to teach our senators wisdom. I have known some men so full of their own notions, that

---

[1] Parliamentary control of the executive would be established and so there would not be a separation of powers, in one sense, but persons so nominated would not presumably themselves sit in either House thereafter.

they went up and down, sputtering them in every man's face they met. Some went to great men during our late troubles; nay, to the king himself; to offer their expedients from revelation. Two men I was acquainted with, of which one had an invention to reconcile differences in religion; the other, had a project for a bank of lands to lie as a security for sums of money lent; both these were persons of great parts and fancy; but yet so troublesome at all times, and in all companies, that I have often been forced to repeat an excellent proverb of your country: 'God deliver me from a man that has but one business!'[1] And I assure you there is no man's reputation that I envy less, than I do that of such persons; and therefore you may please to believe, that I have not imitated them in scattering these notions; nor can I prophesy, whether any such apprehensions as these will ever come into the heads of those men, who are our true physicians.

But yet to answer your question, and give you my conjecture; I believe that we are not ripe yet for any great reform. Not only because we are a very debauched people; I do not only mean that we are given to whoring, drinking, gaming and idleness; but chiefly that we have a politic debauch, which is a neglect of all things that concern the public welfare, and a setting up our own private interest against it: I say, this is not all; for then the polity of no country could be redressed: for every commonwealth that is out of order, has ever all these debauches we speak of, as consequences of their loose state.

But there are two other considerations which induce me to fear that our cure is not yet near. The first is; because most of the wise and grave men of this kingdom are very silent, and will not open their budget upon any terms: and although they dislike the present condition we are in as much as any men, and see the precipice it leads us to, yet will never open their mouths to prescribe a cure; but being asked what they would advise, give a shrug, like your countrymen. There was a very considerable gentleman[2] as most in England, both for birth, parts, and estate; who being a member of the parliament that was called in 1640, continued all the war with them: and by his wisdom and elo-

---

[1] Possibly the two projectors were Nicholas Philpot, *Reasons and proposals* (for a land registry) (1671), and the author of *The Grounds of Unity in religion*, by a Gent. of the Middle Temple (1679).

[2] The great man was William Pierrepont (1607–78), whose daughters married, respectively, the earl of Ogle, the duke of Newcastle, the earl of Clare and the marquis of Halifax, and whose son (this item added to the second edition) married a daughter of Sir John Evelyn.

quence (which were both very great) promoted very much their affairs. When the factions began between the presbyters and independents, he joined cordially with the latter: so far as to give his affirmative to the vote of no addresses: that is, to an order made in the house of commons, to send no more messages to the king, nor to receive any from him. Afterwards, when an assault was made upon the house by the army, and divers of the members taken violently away and secluded; he disliking it, though he were none of them, voluntarily absented himself; and continued retired (being exceedingly averse to a democratical government, which was then declared for,) till Cromwell's usurpation: and being infinitely courted by him, absolutely refused to accept of any employment under him; or to give him the least counsel. When Cromwell was dead; and a parliament called by his son, or rather by the army; the chief officers of which did, from the beginning, whisper into the ears of the leading members, that if they could make an honest government, they should be stood by (as the word then was) by the army: this gentleman, at that time, neither would be elected into that parliament, nor give the least advice to any other person that was; but kept himself still upon the reserve. Insomuch that it was generally believed, that although he had ever been opposite to the late king's coming to the government again, though upon propositions; yet he might hanker after the restoration of his majesty that now is. But the apprehension appeared groundless when it came to the pinch: for being consulted as an oracle by the then general Monk, whether he should restore the monarchy again or no; he would make no answer, nor give him the least advice: and, in fact, has ever since kept himself from public business. Although, upon the banishment of my lord of Clarendon, he was visited by one of the greatest persons in England; and one in as much esteem with his majesty as any whatsoever; and desired to accept of some great employment near the king: which he absolutely refusing, the same person, not a stranger to him, but well known by him, begged of him to give his advice how his majesty (who desired nothing more than to unite all his people together, and repair the breaches which the civil war had caused, now my lord Clarendon was gone who by his counsels kept those wounds open) might perform that honourable and gracious work: but still this gentleman made his excuses. And, in short, neither then, nor at any time before or after, (excepting when he sat in the Long Parliament of the year '40;) neither during the distracted times, nor since his majesty's return, when they seemed more reposed; would ever be brought, either by any private intimate friend, or by any person in public employment, to give the least judgement of our affairs; or the least counsel to mend them: though he was not shy of declaring his dislike of matters as they went. And yet this gentleman was not only by repute and esteem a wise man, but was really so; as it appeared by his management of business, and drawing declarations, when he was contented to act; as also by his exceeding prudent managing of his own fortune, which was very great; and his honourable living and providing for his family: his daughters having been all married to the best men in England; and his eldest son to the most accomplished lady in the world. I dare assure you, there are above an hundred such men in England; though not altogether of that eminency.

NOBLE VEN. Methinks these persons are altogether as bad an extreme as the loquacious men you spoke of before. I remember when I went to school, our master, amongst other commonplaces in the commendation of silence, would tell us of a Latin saying; that a fool while he held his peace did not differ from a wise man: but truly I think we may as truly say, that a wise man whilst he is silent does not differ from a fool: for how great soever his wisdom is, it can neither get him credit, nor otherwise advantage himself, his friend, nor his country. But let me not divert you from your other point.

ENG. GENT. The next reason I have to make me fear, that such an expedient as we have been talking of will not be proposed suddenly; is the great distrust the parliament has of men. Which will make most members shy of venturing at such matters, which being very new, at the first motion are not perfectly understood; at least to such as have not been versed in authors who have written of the politics; and therefore the mover may be suspected of having been set on by the court party to puzzle them; and so to divert, by offering new expedients, some smart mettlesome debates they may be upon concerning the succession to the crown, or other high matters. For it is the nature of all popular councils (even the wisest that ever were, witness the people of Rome and Athens, which Machiavel so much extols) in turbulent times, to like discourses that heighten their passions and blow up their indignation; better than those that endeavour to rectify their judgements, and tend to provide for their safety. And the truth is, our

198

parliament is very much to be excused, or rather justified, in this distrust they have of persons; since there has been of late so many and so successful attempts used by the late great ministers, to debauch the most eminent members of the commons house, by pensions and offices:[1] and therefore it would wonderfully conduce to the good of the commonwealth, and to the composing our disordered state; if there were men of so high and unquestionable a reputation, that they were above all suspicion and distrust, and so might venture upon bold, that is (in this case) moderate counsels, for the saving of their country. Such men there were in the parliament of 1640; at least twenty or thirty:[2] who having stood their ground in seven parliaments before, which in the two last kings' reigns had been dissolved abruptly and in wrath; and having resisted the fear of imprisonment and great fines for their love to England, as well as the temptation of money and offices to betray it; both offered by the wicked counsellors of that age, tending both to the ruin of our just rights and the detriment of their master's affairs: I say, having constantly and with great magnanimity and honour made proof of their integrity, they had acquired so great a reputation, that not only the parliament, but even almost the whole people stuck to them; and were swayed by them in actions of a much higher nature than any are now discoursed of; without fear of being deserted, or as we say, left in the lurch; as the people of France often are by their grandees, when they raise little civil wars to get great places; which as soon as they are offered, they lay down their arms, and leave their followers to be hanged.

But although these two reasons of the silence of some wise men, and the want of reputation in others, does give us but a sad prospect of our land of promise; yet we have one consideration, which does encourage us to hope better things ere long: and that is the infallible certainty that we cannot long continue as we are; and that we can never meliorate, but by some such principles as we have been here all this while discoursing of: and that without such helps and succours as may be drawn from thence, we must go from one distraction to another, till we come into a civil war; and in the close of it be certainly a prey to the king of France, who (on which side it matters not) will be a gamester

[1] A familiar theme: cf. A. Marvell (reputed author), *A Seasonable Argument* (1677).
[2] Neville's statement about twenty M.P.s of the Long Parliament of 1640–60 having served in seven previous parliaments is substantially accurate. See Mary F. Keeler, *The Long Parliament* (Philadelphia, 1954), p. 16, n. 76; five had sat in eight, sixteen in seven and twenty-four in six, the first two categories adding up to twenty-one. All were knights, and about one-third royalists.

and sweep stakes at last; the world not being now equally balanced between two princes alike powerful, as it was during our last civil war: and if as well this danger, as the other means to prevent it, be understood in time, (as no doubt it will;) we shall be the happiest and the greatest nation in the world in a little time; and in the meantime, enjoy the best and most just easy government of any people upon earth. If you ask me, whether I could have offered anything that I thought better than this; I will answer you as Solon did a philosopher, who asked him whether he could not have made a better government for Athens? Yes; but that his was the best, that the people would or could receive. And now I believe you will bear me witness; that I have not treated you as a wise man would have done, in silence: but it is time to put an end to this tittle-tattle, which has nauseated you for three days together.

NOBLE VEN. I hope you think better of our judgements than so; but I believe you may very well be weary.

DOCT. I am sure the parish priests are often thanked for their pains, when they have neither taken half so much as you have, nor profited their auditory the hundredth part so much.

ENG. GENT. The answer to thank you for your pains, is always, thank you, sir, for your patience; and so I do, very humbly, both of you.—

NOBLE VEN. Pray, sir, when do you leave the town?

ENG. GENT. Not till you leave the kingdom. I intend to see you, if please God, aboard the yacht at Gravesend.

NOBLE VEN. I should be ashamed to put you to that trouble.

ENG. GENT. I should be much more troubled, if I should not do it; in the meantime I take my leave of you for this time, and hope to wait on you again tomorrow. What, doctor, you stay to consult about the convalescence? Adieu to you both.

DOCT. Farewell, sir.

Nullum numen abest, si sit prudentia.
[If prudence be present, no divine power is absent.]

FINIS

DEMOCRACY VINDICATED.

AN ESSAY

ON THE

CONSTITUTION & GOVERNMENT

OF THE

Roman State;

FROM THE POSTHUMOUS WORKS OF

WALTER MOYLE;

WITH A PREFACE AND NOTES,

BY JOHN THELWALL,

Lecturer on Classical History.

Norwich:

PRINTED AND SOLD BY J. MARCH, COCKEY-LANE,

LONDON:—Sold by J. Smith, Portsmouth-Street, Lincoln's Inn Fields, and to be had of the Booksellers in Town and Country.

1796.

Contents

Preface to the French translation, 1801   *page* 205

Part One: *Foundation and Fall of the*   207
Monarchy, Establishment of the Aristocracy,
Creation of the Republic

Part Two: *Declension and Fall of the Republic*   242

Preface to the French Translation, 1801

[This 'avertissement' by the publisher is almost certainly by Bertrand Barère.]

D'Alembert said of the work of Montesquieu on the Romans, that it could be called, 'Roman history for the use of philosophers and statesmen'. This title would be equally appropriate for the work of Walter Moyle, which we publish today.

It is a thing worth noticing, that the English, a nation whose ancestors were overthrown by the Romans, are the first who have written philosophical reflexions, and given to Europe profound ideas about the Roman Empire. Thus the defeated have become the judges of the conquerors. Gibbon has presented historically the causes of the rise and decadence of this empire. Ferguson has treated the same subject. Edward Wortley Montagu has published his thoughts upon the rise and fall of the Roman Republic. Hooke has produced critical disquisitions on the history and government of ancient Rome.

But most of these works, which may be thought of as the philosophy of Roman history, are posterior to the work which we translate today, under the modest title given it by its author Walter Moyle, *Essay upon the Government of Rome*.

At that time, none of those excellent works cited, had appeared; and the immortal treatise *On the Causes of the Grandeur and the Decadence of the Romans* had not yet illuminated Europe.

This valuable work by Montesquieu, the most perfect of those which have come from his vigorous pen, did not, it is true, appear until 1734; and this which we give to the public was printed in London in 1726, that is, eight years before the work of Montesquieu.

The genius of the author of *The Spirit of the Laws* was formed to discover in itself all that came out of it. But, despite the riches of these resources, several beautiful pages of his *Spirit of the Laws* may be found in Tacitus and Plutarch. Why could it not have found in the English work, the chief ideas which inspired the treatise about *The Causes of the Grandeur and Decadence of the Romans?* . . . Before writing on the Romans and *The Spirit of the Laws*, Montesquieu travelled in England, and gathered all those ideas which he needed to complete those masterpieces, by which he has enlightened France. It is no mean encomium for a work to have inspired a genius as great and profound as that of Montesquieu, and this praise is merited by the *Essay* Walter Moyle published in London in 1726. Voltaire, in writing that *The Persian Letters* were imitations of Siamois de Dufresny, did nothing to detract from the worth of the ingenious creator of the letters of Usbek and Rica. We are equally free from any attempt to belittle the great fame of the author of *The Causes of the Grandeur and Decadence of the Romans*, in publishing a work translated from English, which prepared or inspired the profound thought of this worthy admirer of a great people. We seek only to enrich political literature with a volume useful to statesmen and philosophers, and, in the Roman manner, we crown the fountain head.

Part One[1]

Romulus at the head of a numerous colony from Alba,[2] was the first founder of the Roman State. This colony, was in the original state of nature free, and independent of any dominion whatsoever, and only chose Romulus for their leader, till their new city was built, and they were at leisure to consider what form of government they should resolve upon.

Monarchy was the ancient government of Alba, and continued down for many ages in a lineal succession of princes, famous for their justice and moderation at home, and their conquests abroad. The love of their ancient constitution, (so natural to mankind) together with the ease and plenty they enjoyed under former reigns, (which they imagined to be owing to the civil orders and institutions of the state, and not to the virtue and emulation of their particular kings) were considerations strong enough to incline the people in favour of monarchy, which they made choice of by universal consent, and elected Romulus for their first king: who, immediately after his advancement, erected a frame of government, upon such admirable orders, both civil, military and religious, that, if no alteration had been made in the fundamental laws by himself, or his successors, it would have been the most noble, as well as most lasting constitution of limited monarchy that ever was in the world.

His first care was to possess the people with the notion of his divine appointment over them: before he attempted the crown, the gods were consulted in the usual forms; and all the tokens of divine approbation appeared: which left no room for pretenders to dispute his title, nor to the people to repeal their choice. This begot a reverence and a

[1] Thelwall's text, though not his paragraphing, is followed here, with his translations of Latin passages cited by Moyle; he omitted annotations and references to authorities used, and these are listed in appendix III below, pp. 262–3. One or two of Thelwall's own notes, when they have seemed interesting, are included below. Names of persons will be identified in the index, and also the Roman laws referred to by Moyle. A good brief summary of Roman history may be found conveniently in the *Oxford Classical Dictionary* (Oxford, 1949); A. H. McDonald, *Republican Rome* (London, 1966), is most helpful.

[2] Alba Longa, south-east of Rome, founded about 1152 B.C. and the reputed birthplace of Romulus. Thelwall notes a distinction between monarchical and regal government, the latter including limited and elective monarchies; the former properly, he wrote, belonging to the hereditary and despotic states.

veneration for his person, added weight and authority to his laws, and strength and reputation to his government.

The belief of this divine designation once infused into the minds of the people, he proceeded to lay the foundation of his government, and began with securing the possession of the regal power by a wise institution of an hereditary order of nobility, composed out of the richest and the noblest of his new colony. Out of this order were chosen all the council and magistracies of the commonwealth; all officers, civil and military; and out of these he formed the great council of state, called the senate. A faction, doubtless devoted to the king, by whose favour it was appointed, says Livy: and indeed, this distinction of honour and power, these mighty privileges and immunities, created a necessary dependence of the nobility upon the crown, and engaged them entirely in the support of monarchy, under whose protection they enjoyed these advantages, to the exclusion of the rest of the people. And in all ages the nobility has been the guard of sovereign power in limited monarchies, and always opposed any innovations in favour of popular government; for fear of introducing an equality, inconsistent with their privileges.[1]

But Romulus, wisely considering that this division of the people into two orders would make different parties and factions in the state, which in time would dissolve the government, unless they were united by some common interest, resolved, since he could not make an equality, at least to create a dependence of the commons upon the nobility, by introducing the custom of patronage; which was, allotting such patrons out of the nobility to the commons, who were obliged to defend them in the possession of their rights and properties: to advise them in all matters of weight, and to protect them against all violence and oppression; while the client on his part was obliged to pay all deference and esteem to his patron, and to serve him with his life and fortune in any extremity. This mutual intercourse of good offices begot a confidence and good correspondence between the nobility and commons, without those jealousies and animosities which are the infallible consequences of two parties, between whom there is no common bond of union.[2]

---

[1] Moyle indicates the connexion of divine right, a privileged nobility, and increased royal power. Compare above paragraph with Neville's similar connexion of aristocracy and kingly prerogative.

[2] Though Moyle, like Machiavelli, preferred a 'factious liberty' to a 'settled tyranny', he, like most contemporaries and many eighteenth-century writers—among them E. W. Montagu—attributed many of the troubles of Rome, at certain stages, to party strife.

Having provided for the support of the monarchy, his next care was to secure his own person from the dangers of any sudden tumult, or popular insurrection, by establishing a guard, composed of the bravest youth of the nobility, who constantly attended his person, and were the executioners of all his orders in the city, and fought by his side in the field.

To defray the necessary expenses of the court, he reserved to himself a good share out of the general division of the land to the people, which he appropriated to the maintenance of the civil list, and to support a splendour becoming his dignity. For the ordinary revenue of the kings of Rome lay in their crown lands; and the extraordinary charges of war and other contingencies, were supported by levying taxes upon the people.

Though he shared the legislative in common with people and senate, and had no power to pass any law without concurrence of both orders, yet he had the sole right of proposing to the people in their assemblies by virtue of his prerogative, which amounted to a full negative voice in all their determinations; neither the people nor senate have the liberty of proposing, debating or enacting laws, till they were first moved from the throne.

Besides this advantage of having the largest share of the legislative power of the commonwealth, he had all the executive power of the state lodged in his hands. He had the supreme power of administration of justice in all causes, civil and criminal, unless in those of little consideration, which he referred to the senate; but in all others he was sovereign judge in the last resort, without any further appeal to the people: and in time of war he had the absolute command of all the forces of the state.

Thus I have run briefly through the civil orders upon which this great lawgiver founded his dominion, viz. the opinion of a divine appointment; the dependence of the nobility upon his interest, and the dependence of their clients upon them; his standing body of guards; his great revenue in lands; the sole power of the executive, and part of the legislative; and last of all, the administration of justice, and the command of the armies, which were the great branches of the royal prerogative.[1]

The next thing I shall proceed on, is the religious institution of Rome; which, whether we consider the simplicity of its precepts, and

[1] Again, compare with Neville on prerogative.

their mighty influence upon the morals of the people, or their admirable application to all the ends of civil society, and particularly the support of the monarchy, will appear to be the wisest and the most politic system of religion, that ever any lawgiver founded.

Romulus drew only the rough draft of religion, which was finished and brought to perfection by the great genius of Numa; who from a private man, and a foreigner, was courted to accept of the crown, purely upon the renown of his piety and justice. The principles from which he derived authority and belief to his religion, were, first the reputation of sincerity, which is the universal ground of persuasion; his innocent practice upon the credulity of a barbarous people, by pretending to a supernatural revelation of his laws; and lastly the operation of miracles. This has been the current practice of all the great legislators of antiquity, who thought the opinion of a divine mission and authority, absolutely necessary to procure belief to all their doctrines, and a blind and abandoned submission to all their laws.

Upon this bottom Numa[1] erected the scheme of his religion; in which he avoided all the follies and absurdities of other legislators. He did not enjoin the belief of contradictions and impossibilities, which take off from the reputation of the lawgiver, and discredit his religion; nor did he introduce any opinions unworthy of the gods and inconsistent with the divine nature; nor did he require the belief of many articles of faith, which create schisms and heresies in the church, and end in the ruin of religion. For if schisms and heresies were traced up to their original causes, it would be found that they all sprung chiefly from the multiplying articles of faith, and narrowing the bottom of religion, by clogging it with creeds and catechisms, and endless niceties about the essence, properties and attributes of God. The common principles of religion all mankind agree in; and the belief of these doctrines a lawgiver may venture to enjoin; but he must go no further if he means to preserve an uniformity in religion. For the injunction of positive laws, how much soever they contradict the inclinations of mankind, rarely produce any schisms; so much easier it is for men to practise against their passions, than to believe against

Numa Pompilius, c. 715–673 B.C., the second of the kings of Rome, was traditionally the founder of the religious system described by Moyle at much greater length than other historians of the early history of the city. Moyle was anti-clerical, and was aspersing the English church of his time, which he considered too rich, too powerful and too intolerant. Compare with Neville, above, pp. 115–19.

their understandings. But Numa, by a wise conduct, prevented all factions and divisions in the church, by the institution of only two articles of faith: 1st, That the Gods were the authors of all good to mankind. 2nd, That to obtain this good, the Gods were to be worshipped; in which worship, the chief of all was to be innocent, good and just. These were the two fundamental articles of the Roman religion, which Zaleucus seems to have copied in the institution of his commonwealth.[1]

As for the first, though in compliance to the popular opinion, and in a vulgar way, the great men of antiquity spoke of the godhead in the plural number; yet upon all solemn occasions, when they mentioned the godhead with any gravity and emphasis, it was by the name of the best and greatest God. Though the unity of the godhead be as demonstrable as its existence, and though this principle was embraced not only by many private men and sects of philosophers, but by whole nations of antiquity; yet flattery to the memories of their benefactors, the interest of priests, the ignorance of mankind, and many other causes had introduced polytheism into the national religion of the greatest part of the world.

Whatever sentiments Numa had of the godhead, 'tis plain he complied with the current divinity of the times, and established a plurality of gods in his system; perhaps from this consideration, that the absolute and perfect unity of the godhead, was a notion too refined to gain reception in an age universally overrun with polytheism; when even Moses himself, with all his divine inspiration, and the irresistible force of his miracles, found much difficulty to master the popular prejudice against it. But though this perfect unity of the godhead was a doctrine less known to the world, yet the existence of a God, and the providence of some superior powers, are acknowledged by all civilized nations.

The second article is but a natural consequence of the first: and thus we see Numa's system of religion took in all the common opinions of mankind. As for the particular forms of divine worship, he instituted a ritual, which directed the priests in the solemn ceremonies and services of religion, without denying a toleration of other forms; of which more hereafter.

The doctrine of the immortality of the soul, though it was no part

[1] Zaleucus of Locri in Greece, c. 660 B.C., a celebrated legislator who produced what may have been the first written code.

of the religion of the Romans, but seems left rather as a problem of philosophy than an article of divinity, yet was always cherished and encouraged by the commonwealth, as an opinion of great use and service to the state. Had it been an established doctrine, Veturia would not have talked so doubtfully of it in her speech to Coriolanus; nor Caesar have openly derided it in the face of the whole senate. I am inclined to believe, it was first transplanted from Greece to Italy by Pythagoras, and from thence derived to the Romans; however it might first have been introduced, we find it was received as a thing plausible; though in the same rank and upon the same level with those fables and other religious histories and traditions which the poets sang. And Polybius blames some who made it their business to dispossess the vulgar of that opinion. Numa likewise interwove his moral precepts with his religious doctrine; for the great principle of his morality, justice, which in a manner comprehends all other moral virtues, was grounded upon this persuasion, 'That the gods were the most excellent nature, and the great examples of highest virtue; that they administered every thing justly, and had a due care and providence over the whole; and that they never bestowed their favours upon unjust men'. From this root sprung that noble branch of their morals, the love of their country;[1] which afterwards grew to be the fundamental article of their ethics, and the standard of all virtue and vice. This principle was passionately pursued by all the great Romans; at this, the inexorable Coriolanus relented; for this, the Decii and Curtii devoted themselves; to this principle Brutus sacrificed his son; this was improved and cultivated by the force of education, and confirmed by more generous examples than any age or nation can boast of.

Nor did he sour his religion with needless severities and affected austerities, by imposing doctrines of penance, abstinence, and mortification, which serve only to cross the innocent appetites of mankind, without making them better or wiser.

Besides the influence of his religion upon the duties of private life, he likewise made it a part of the Roman policy and subservient to all

---

[1] Thelwall comments: 'Patriotism, or the love of our country is after all but a narrow sectarian principle: the source very often, it must be confessed, of very splendid actions, but the parent at the same time of much illiberality and injustice, of contentions, massacres, and devastations. The true actuating principle of virtue is the love of the human race; the benevolent sentiment which enfolds the world in one large embrace, and sanctifies the universal equality of rights.'

the great ends of government and society. All the elections of their magistrates, and all their public resolutions, were ratified by the solemn approbation of their gods, consulted by their college of diviners; than which nothing could be a greater reach of policy, to teach the people obedience to their magistrates and subjection to their laws. This was likewise a mighty incentive to valour and resolution to their armies upon any desperate service, and won them many victories; for prophecies by the assurance they give of success, are oftentimes the causes of the events that they foretell.

Numa, by the wide bottom of his religion, prevented all heresies in fundamentals; and in the particular forms of divine worship he allowed a general liberty of conscience. This generous principle of tolerating all religions in the commonwealth, was that above all others which fitted his system to the chief design of the government; for the rise and progress of the Roman greatness were wholly owing to the mighty confluence of people from all parts of the world, (with customs and ceremonies very different from the Romans) who would never have settled there, with an allowance of the free exercise of their particular religions. It is true, the Romans were very cautious of introducing any new rites into their national religion; and there are frequent instances in their histories of their forbidding the magistrates to make any innovations in the public worship. But this order did not extend to regulate the opinions or devotions of private men, as appears by the decree of the senate, enacted upon the suppression of the Bacchanalia: that any one who asked leave of the senate might celebrate the mysteries in private, though they dissolved the public assemblies of the Bacchanalia, as a seminary of all debauchery, and dangerous to the state.

This wise institution of an universal liberty in religion, seems to be owing to this single cause, viz. 'That the government of the national religion was lodged in the senate and people'. It is true, under the government of the kings, the priests had a very large jurisdiction, being the public directors of all the divine rights, with an unlimited power of judging and determining all religious disputes whatsoever, without being accountable to any superior authority: but their mighty power declined after the subversion of the monarchy; and after that, the sole power of religion devolved upon the civil magistrate, as may be easily made appear by the Roman historians. First, all neglects of the national religion, and the introduction of foreign rites and ceremonies, were punished and prohibited by the senate, the priests never interposing their authority: but the execution of all the religious orders of the senate were committed to the aediles and praetors, who were civil magistrates; and all toleration of mysteries and ceremonies, contrary to the established religion, were granted by the senate. All innovations in the national worship, such as adoption of new gods, and the institutions of new forms and ceremonies in religion, were appointed by the authority of the senate. Nor had the priests any right to consult the great oracles of their divine worship, the sibylline verses, in which they placed the infallibility of their religion, unless by the express command of the senate. Nor did the senate make any scruple of acting against the authority of the high priest, who was the supreme governor of the hierarchy.[1]

It is evident likewise that the whole order of the high-priests were subject to the jurisdiction of the tribunes of the people, for Cicero tells Claudius, the tribune, that by the virtue of his tribuneship he could compel them to obey his orders. Cicero likewise declares the supreme power of religion to be lodged in the people; for when Claudius had consecrated his house, and one of the high priests assisted at the solemnity, the people in their assembly pronounced the consecration void. In the people's hands, says Tully, the supreme power of all things is placed. And when the further consideration of that affair was referred to the college of the high-priests by the orders of the senate, not that the thing admitted of any doubt after the determination of the people, their sentence was not valid till it was reported to the senate, and ratified by their authority.

By what paces and methods the civil power wrested the government of religion out of the hands of the priests, is difficult to determine, in the silence of all the ancient writers. But probably the usurping the right of electing the high priest, after the expulsion of the kings, was the leading step to the invasion of all their other privileges.

The government of religion being in the hands of the state, was a necessary cause of liberty of conscience; for there is scarce any instance in history of a persecution raised by a free government. Persecutions are generally made to gratify the pride, the ambition, or the interests of the clergy; which a state, that has the command of the national conscience, will never indulge at the expense of the public good.

[1] Moyle exaggerates the role of the senate.

A free government is designed for the liberty of the whole society, which persecution is inconsistent with; and it is against all the rules of policy to persecute opinions not destructive to humane society; for a necessary consequence of such a practice, is the narrowing of the bottom of the community, by weakening the strength and force of the commonwealth, which consists in the number of the people, who in all appearance will, when thus disturbed, retire to an easier government; nor can this fail to break the firm unity of the nation, which these severe arts of government are inconsistent with. But persecutions are generally encouraged only by tyrants and priests. By tyrants, either from a false bigotry or misguided zeal for religion; or from a boundless vanity and pride of forcing all their subjects to comply with their opinions as well as commands; or from a barbarous policy of thinning the people, that they may with the greater ease oppress the rest; or from an apprehension that revolutions in religion may be attended with revolutions in state; or from the hopes of gaining a further support to their tyranny by engaging the clergy, whose interest it will eternally be, to make war upon all contrary religions. This last consideration has produced most of the modern persecutions. Priests and tyrants having joined their interest to enslave the world, and share the booty between them. Persecutions are made by priests from a dread that changes in national religion may end in the ruin of all their privileges and revenues; which being originally bestowed upon them from an opinion of their divine mission, and the reverence to the religion committed to their charge, whenever the religion is abolished, must of course return to the state, or be transferred to the heads of the prevailing sect. This was the fate of the revenues of the heathen priesthood, (which were all seized upon by Theodosius the Great, in the final dissolution of their religion) and the same also was the fate of the Romish clergy at the time of the Reformation.[1]

As the religion of the Romans was a part of their policy, so their clergy likewise was a part of their laity, and interwoven into the general interest of the state; not a separate independent body from the rest of the community, nor any considerable balance of the civil government; but settled upon such an institution, as they could have neither interest nor power to act against the public good. A constitution which the

---

[1] The thesis that intolerance on the part of the clergy was motivated by their fear of losing privileges and wealth was common to Moyle's circle and throughout the eighteenth century.

modern policy has overlooked out of ignorance or neglected out of design; as appears from the unlimited power of the modern priesthood, who have usurped a supremacy, or at least an independency on the civil power over half of Europe, and (where their jurisdiction is more restrained) by virtue of their great possessions and endowments, look the civil government in the face, and have raised such convulsions in the later ages, as were unknown to the ancient world.

But the Roman priests had no interest to set up any particular by ends in opposition to the national good; for their stake in the civil government was infinitely greater than their dependence upon the church. They were by their original constitution all chosen out of the nobility, and afterwards out of the richest and greatest men of the commonwealth: and consequently had such an interest in the civil state, as they would not sacrifice to their particular order. They were likewise promiscuously admitted to all the great offices and dignities of the commonwealth, which they set a much higher value upon, than any of their ecclesiastical charges; as appears from the resentment the nobility showed upon the admission of the commons to the great magistracies of the Republic. The *Salii* and *Flamines* are never void of command and authority, but when they offer sacrifices for the people. That was the sense of the nobility upon the passing of that law. And there are instances in the Roman story, of men who have been compelled against their inclination to accept the priesthood; so far were the dignities of the church from being equal to those of the state. These considerations must necessarily make the clergy true to the interests of the whole community, because their own advantages were involved in the national good. Thus the Romans, wisely prevented the two only fatal effects which the religious orders of the state can have upon the civil government. The first is, from the nature and institution of the religion itself, which from the multitude of doctrines and articles of faith, may divide the people into schisms and heresies in the church, which generally end in parties and factions in the state, and they always in the dissolution of the government. The other is, making the clergy a separate independent body from the laity, with ends and designs interfering with the public interests of the civil society; which is erecting one empire on another, and directly opposite to all the maxims of ancient policy. Nor had the Roman priesthood power to set up for themselves, or to give laws to the civil magistrate, or to usurp any extraordinary jurisdictions, or to make any considerable figure in the balance of the civil government.

Power is of two kinds, imaginary or real. Imaginary power is authority founded upon opinion: real power is authority founded upon dominion and property. But the Roman clergy had little of the first, and none of the last, till the ruin of the commonwealth.

Authority built upon opinion is usually derived to the clergy, from a persuasion in the people of their divine mission and designation; or from a reverence to their mystic ceremonies and institutions; or for their pretended empire over the consciences of mankind. As for the first, they had no more title to claim such a supernatural warrant to their authority, than all the civil officers of the state, whose elections as well as theirs were all confirmed by divine approbation. They were likewise chosen in the assemblies of the people, and were frequently degraded upon very slight occasions, and oftentimes by the authority of the civil power: which is a proof that they had no extraordinary virtue, or privilege inherent to their character: the priests of the first order (all but the augurs) not being exempt from the penalty of deprivation. Their empire over the consciences of mankind, is exercised either by the infliction of spiritual censures, which they pretend to be seconded by divine displeasure, or by the absolution of crimes, by virtue of certain lustrations and expiatory sacrifices: and all the precedents that I can meet with of the first kind amount to no more than an exclusion of impious and irreligious persons from the solemn sacrifices; a sentence which had little authority with men of their character. Their power of absolution extended no farther than to pardon crimes of inadvertency, or some neglects in the outward form of religious worship: but great offences and notorious immoralities could be atoned by no expiation whatsoever. Omissions of external ceremonies, says Tully, were done away by the sprinkling of water, or length of time: but those of a blacker hue could never be blotted out, either by length of years, or the greatest efforts. And whenever the priests pretended to a power of expiating immoralities, the Romans were too wise and too virtuous to admit of such an infamous refuge. Witness the famous instance of Regulus, who having taken a solemn oath to return to Carthage, in case the Romans refused the conditions offered by the Carthaginians, when the high priests, by virtue of their authority offered to absolve him from the guilt of perjury, he rejected the notion with indignation;

which he never would have done, had he imagined that any power upon earth could dissolve so sacred an obligation or any expiation atone for such a crime.

The mystic ceremonies and institutions of the Grecians, which procured such a veneration and reverence to the Grecian clergy, were grounded upon a superstitious apprehension amongst the weaker sort of people, 'That many advantages in life, and certain benefits in a state hereafter depended on their admission to participate in those mysterious rites and institutions'. Which trade, however advantageous it may seem to have been to the priesthood of that time, was not however of that profit and honour, as to raise them to any consideration or note above other professions, so as to be an order of men making any figure, or bearing any sway in the states or commonwealth we read of. These mysteries had no part in the religious institutions of the Romans, for Dionysius expressly says they had no occult mysteries, in the very corruption of the commonwealth. From hence it is evident that the Roman church wanted these natural sources, by which authority is derived to the characters and persons of the clergy, and by which arts, others have so successfully mastered the opinions and consciences of mankind, and consequently influenced their actions, and commanded their fortunes.

Authority founded on dominion, results to the clergy, either from a right of supremacy over the church, or from a legal jurisdiction and coercive power over the actions, the lives, and the conduct of the laity. But I have already proved, that the high priest was so far from having the government of the church, that his authority under the popular state amounted to little more than a power of representation, or advice to the senate in all religious controversies that lay before the consideration of the senate. Besides the arguments already urged, the dependence of the Roman church upon the civil power, appears from the appeals made by the clergy to the people, upon disputes arising between the priests of different orders. Their subjection to the tribunes appears from their being compelled by their authority to pay their share to the general taxes, in spite of their pretended immunities; and their exemption from all wars, which they enjoyed by the donation of Romulus, was repealed by a civil law. Appius the censor likewise transferred the priesthood of Hercules, entailed upon the Potitian family by Hercules himself, to the public servants of the state. Thus the people by their authority obliged the high priest, in spite of all his protestations against it, to consecrate the temple of Concord. Domitius the tribune translated the right of electing the priests to the people, although by the constitution of Numa, that power was vested in the college of the high priests themselves.

As for the coercive power of the church, Dionysius says that the high priests had power to fine such of the clergy and laity as disobeyed their orders. But this privilege of the clergy, originally instituted by Numa, was abolished immediately after the expulsion of the kings, by the Valerian Law,[1] which gave liberty to any citizen that was fined or condemned by the sentence of any magistrate, to appeal to the judgement of the people: and there are instances in the Roman story of the people's reversing fines imposed by the high priests. From these numerous instances it is plain that the Roman church was subject to the civil power: and that the state had power to make what alterations they pleased in the ecclesiastic constitution. I have insisted larger upon this subject, because Dionysius seems to give the college of the high priests such an unlimited jurisdiction; but it is evident that that passage must be understood of their authority during the monarchy only.

The consideration I shall next enter upon, is the authority of the priests founded on property and possessions, which is the only standing foundation of dominion; for power grounded upon opinion is seldom long-lived, unless backed by temporal greatness and solid force.

The ordinary revenues of the priesthood in all ages, have consisted either in the voluntary oblations of the people, or in endowments of lands, and possessions, or in certain shares of the gains and labour of the people.

That the profits of the Roman priests were very inconsiderable, is evident from the opinion the nobility had of ecclesiastical dignities, which they always held inferior to the posts of the civil government; and instead of pursuing and canvassing were often compelled to accept them: which is a proof that they could get little benefit or advantage by them; and there can be no reasons assigned why the employments of the church should have any extraordinary maintenance, when all the civil magistrates had none. Their clergy were all men of quality and riches, and were content with the bare honour of their dignities, and had a temporal fortune to support their expenses: and the reason why

[1] Laws giving rights to the plebians.

their priests were originally composed of the nobility, was, lest the sacred authority of their religion, by the poverty of its professors, should be prostituted to mercenary, ungenerous ends. This is plain from Tully, who says there was an ancient law, that such a number of the young noblemen should be instructed in the Tuscan arts of divination; lest so great an art should lose the authority and dignity of religion, and be brought so low as to be considered a recompense, or reward, on account of the low state of them who were engaged therein. And Dionysius seems to reckon the salaries of the augurs, after the ruin of the commonwealth among the corruptions of their religion. But the diviners had the greatest power and authority, of all the religious orders; and if they had no revenues, it is improbable the rest had any: and Augustus after the subversion of the commonwealth, and Tiberius were forced to settle large appointments upon the clergy, to give authority and reputation to the order. The Vestal Virgins, it is true, by their original constitution, had public allowance settled on them by the state. But I cannot collect from any of the ancient writers, that any considerable revenue, salary, or perquisites belonged to any of the other orders, till the time of Augustus.

First, they were not supported by the voluntary oblations of the people. The Romans in their religious institutions took particular care that religion should not be a rent-charge on the people: from that principle arose the frugality of their sacrifices, and the meanness of their offerings, and presents to the gods. This order likewise extended to regulate the bounties and charities of private men to the clergy, for fear the superstition of the common people should ruin their families.

Cicero in the model of his commonwealth (which he owns to have transcribed out of the ancient laws and constitutions of Rome) forbids all these kinds of voluntary offerings, unless to the priests of Cybele, lest they gut their houses of their contents. And there are frequent instances in Livy of forbidding, under severe penalties, all those, who under different pretences raised contributions upon the people, by working on their superstition; and such as exercised this unlawful gain, were called by the opprobrious name of *aeruscatores*.[1] It is true, there were some mendicant orders, who had a privilege of driving this trade, as the priests of Cybele and Isis; but these were of a foreign growth, and not of a Roman institution, and were had in contempt by

---

[1] Aulus Gellius uses this: it means tricksters or itinerant beggars living by their wits.

the wisest and best of the Romans, as no Roman was ever a priest of that order. We likewise often read of voluntary oblations of the people; but those were applied (not to the maintenance of their priests), but to the celebration of their religious games, or the solemn feasts and entertainment of their gods. And in general we find that all those kinds of offerings were discouraged by the state: I will not own them, says Cicero, who enrich themselves on such occasions. Nor were the incomes of the church appropriated to the revenues of the priests, but entered into the treasury, and issued out in order to be applied to the adornment and decoration of their temples, or to the expenses of their solemn plays and sacrifices; it being originally exacted from fines and forfeitures in cases criminal and civil.

The second branch of the usual revenues of the church consists in donations of lands and possessions. Romulus in the first division of the lands of Rome, reserved a considerable share to be applied to the expenses of the sacrifices and other religious duties, (but these lands were afterwards divided in common to the people by Tullus Hostilius, upon his accession to the throne; and the charges of the public sacrifices defrayed out of his paternal estate) but it does not appear that these lands which were excepted out of the general dividend by Romulus, were ever appropriated to the private revenues of the clergy, but to the building of temples, and the solemn services and sacrifices of their religion. There is frequent mention made in the Roman story of lands and territories consecrated to particular gods. But it is manifest from the authority of the best writers, that those lands could be applied to no human purpose whatsoever; much less converted to the gains and profits of any particular body of men; they lay fallow and uncultivated, and it was esteemed the highest irreligion and sacrilege to turn them to the common use of other lands. Thus the Romans, when Tarquin had plowed up the field of Mars, which had been anciently dedicated to that god; though they divided all the rest of Tarquin's goods, yet threw the corn of that field into the river; not daring, from a religious apprehension, to make use of the products of a consecrated soil.

My next consideration is the revenues of the priest, which arise from the payment of certain portions out of the gains and labour of the people, which are commonly made to consist of the tenths of their incomes. I shall first examine whether there lay any obligation upon the Romans from their religion or the laws of the land, of paying such a proportion out of their fortunes and incomes. Secondly, I shall examine the reasons upon which this obligation was founded. And lastly, to what uses it was applied.

Had there been any obligations upon the Romans to pay their tenths, it must have extended indifferently to all, which it plainly did not; for why should the decimations made by Sulla, Crassus and Lucullus, be reckoned so extraordinary if the rest of the people had made the same offering? Why should so many authors barely affirm that there were frequent consecrations of the tenths? Why should not one of any authority make mention of a standing law, which enforced the payment of tithes to the whole community? Nothing is more frequently mentioned than the payment of tithes by the ancient writers: yet not one mentions it as a custom of universal obligation, but only practised upon some extraordinary occasions: nor would so superstitious a people as the Romans have banished Camillus for vowing the tenths of the spoil of Veii to Apollo, if the payment of tithes had been an article of their religion, or an institution of their state. For though there were other causes that concurred to his banishment, yet this above all other inflamed the animosity of the people against him, imposing tithes upon the citizens; so averse were the people to all these kind of offerings. And Camillus probably forced the people to contribute the tenths of all the spoils to Apollo, for the same politic consideration that Cyrus did upon the like occasion, for fear the people should grow rich and ungovernable. It is true, Aurelius Victor (a modern author of little authority) says, that originally tithes were paid to kings, but by institution of Hercules were afterwards paid to the gods. And even this passage concludes strongly against those who assert the divine right of tithes from the antiquity and universality of their application to divine uses, since they were anciently offered up to kings by the confession of Victor.

As for the consecration of tithes to the gods by Hercules, if we should allow the authority of Victor it only extended to Evander and his successors, and never was a law in force among the Romans; for all the conquered provinces paid the tenths of the annual products of their harvests to the state, and not to the gods; and the tenths of the spoils of war were sometimes bestowed on a single person, who had particularly distinguished himself in the action.

The usual reason for making these oblations to the gods, and more particularly to Hercules, was sometimes from an opinion that a consecration of such a portion of their goods, would make their lives easy and happy; sometimes from politic considerations of the envy and jealousy which great riches are always attended with, and which they wisely avoided by such a decimation of their fortunes. But I never met with any historian who assigns the maintenance of the clergy to be the reason of these oblations. All the ancient writers unanimously agree in the application of these offerings to the public feasts and entertainments of the people: feasts were given in the public squares in the honour of Orestes out of the tithes, says Cicero. Thus Sulla made a mighty entertainment to the people from the oblation of his tithes to Hercules; as likewise Lucullus. And Varro in Macrobius, says that the old Romans every tenth day feasted the people from the expenses of these offerings. And they were so far from being appropriated to the priests of Hercules, that of two families, who had the priesthood by descent, the one was excluded from those solemn banquets; the other, by the persuasion of Appius, transferred their hereditary honour to the care of public servants: which they never would have so tamely submitted to, had they enjoyed such a mighty income, as the oblation of the tenths of Hercules.

It may seem strange to our age, where the appearance of godliness is such a great gain, that the Roman clergy should serve their gods for nought; but there will be no reason to wonder, if they consider that none of their civil officers had any pensions, and that even their private soldiers fought the battles of the state without pay, for some hundreds of years after the foundation of the city. Romans took particular care never to trust the state in mercenary hands, and seldom listed any of the poorer ranks of citizens in their armies, but upon great extremities.[1] And the commons, as Dionysius expressly says, were excluded from the priesthood in regard of their poverty; which would have been no reason, had there been any profits or revenues belonging to their order. After the subversion of the commonwealth, the emperors (for priestcraft and tyranny go hand in hand) settled large stipends, salaries and endowments upon the clergy, and established lands for the maintenance of the Vestal Virgins. And indeed in all ages it has been a current maxim of arbitrary princes, to engage the authority of the church to support

---

[1] Compare Machiavelli, *The Prince*, chapters XII, XIII; *Discourses*, I, xxi, and the various tracts of 1697-8 against standing armies.

their tyranny: witness the mighty power and jurisdiction of the clergy, under the eastern tyrannies, and their subjection to all popular governments, both ancient and modern, that ever were founded in the world. My next consideration shall be to examine how Numa applied the authority of the church to defend the grandeur of the monarchy. The people, by their original constitution, had a negative vote in the choice of their magistrates, in the passing of all laws, and in the resolution of peace and war. The elections of the magistrates before the institution of the Assembly of the People[1] by Servius, lay almost wholly in the power of the people, who out-voted the nobility by their numbers. But Numa, by an artful policy, curbed this mighty privilege of the commons: for he instituted a college of augurs, or diviners, who were to consult the gods upon the creation of their officers; and without the concurrence and authority of this college, all the public resolutions of the people were void: so that the augurs were a kind of fourth estate; and, being chosen out of the nobility, were the creatures and dependents of the kings, and interposed their authority to vacate the election of any magistrates disliked by the king, without throwing the odium upon the regal power. The supreme power of the result,[2] in the enacting of all laws, was likewise vested in the commons: which Numa destroyed by the same policy. 'Tis true, by the ancient constitution of Rome, the kings had the sole right of proposing laws to the people, and consequently had no need of the augurs to put a negative upon any law. But Numa was too wise to hazard the affection of the people, by refusing to propose any popular laws, and rather chose to make use of the authority of the augurs upon a dead-lift, than expose his prerogative to the hatred of the people. Though it appears from Pliny, that Numa had parted with that branch of the regal power, the sole right of proposing to the people; for he makes mention of a *lex posthumia* (Posthumous law), (and all laws were denominated from their proposers) enacted in the time of Numa: a concession which Numa very dextrously destroyed by the authority of his college of diviners. By the same artifice he invaded the third branch of the people's power, the right of determining of peace and war. But in his nature being averse to war, and turning the streams of his counsels to the peaceful arts of government, he took

---

[1] *Comitia Centuriata*, an assembly of the people voting by centuries, military units, not by individual vote as, according to Moyle, the Romans did before Servius, *c.* 578–535 B.C.
[2] 'Result' [obsolete]—decision of an assembly.

224

particular care to secure the possession of his right to the crown; in order to which design, he added to the unlimited jurisdiction of the augurs an institution of a College of Heralds at Arms, composed of the nobility, whose province was to judge and determine of the rights of war and peace, and were, in other words, the public casuists of the state: with such an unbounded authority, that though the three states and the augurs had concurred upon declaring war, yet the heralds, by virtue of their office, had power to reverse their resolutions, unless the causes of the war appeared to them to be just and honourable. This order was founded upon the same principle with the former. That if the people had resolved upon war, against his inclination, he might still have a reserve to apply to in order to prevent it.

That these were the considerations upon which Numa founded the institution of the augurs, is apparent from the authority of Cicero; who says expressly, may the augurs be kept for the use of the commons, and for other great services of the common people: and in another place, that their favourable delays might hinder many useless meetings. Besides the power of dissolving the assemblies of the people, and annulling their votes and decrees, the monarchy derived other advantages from the creation of these two orders: for by making the consent and approbation of the gods (consulted by their diviners) necessary to the success of all their public councils and undertakings; and the nobility claiming this right of enquiring into the will of heaven, by virtue of a pretended sanctity inherent to their characters; the commons were excluded the great magistracies of the state, under a pretence that they had not the *auspicia*; that is, that they had not such an imaginary holiness as was necessary to engage the gods to give manifest tokens of their approbation or dislike upon their election, or upon any expedition to be undertaken by a plebian magistrate. This politic device of the nobility lasted for some ages after the expulsion of the kings, till the commons grew wiser, and discovered the juggle. But of the declension of these two orders, I shall treat hereafter, when I come to examine the causes of the dissolution of the aristocracy of Rome.[1]

These politic orders were the great springs and wheels upon which this mighty fabric turned: but as all natural bodies are born with seeds of dissolution in their own frame, so these great artificial bodies,

[1] What follows gives Moyle's explanation of historical progression. Note the commendation of elective monarchies, for which whiggish historians of the seventeenth century often express nostalgia.

commonwealths, are founded with such original flaws in their first constitution, as, in some periods of time, corrupt and dissolve them.

The guard of the Roman monarchy was the clergy and the nobility, whose interests were closely interwoven with those of the royalty; which is the only balance in nature, that a limited constitution of monarchy can be founded on. This was wisely thought on by Romulus; but he took some false measures, which were the leading steps to change the form of government from monarchic to popular; the most considerable of which were, the making the monarchy elective; allowing such a share of property to the commons; increasing the number of people by naturalizing all foreigners,[1] and trusting arms in their hands.

The first defect in the constitution of the monarchy was the making it elective. It is true, elective monarchies are for the interest and advantage of the people, but are not calculated to support the authority and grandeur of the crown. The people by the favour of elective empires, avoid all the weak reigns of minors and women, successions of dissolute and degenerate princes, and contests about disputed titles and pretensions, which make such convulsions in hereditary governments. And the crown being conferred upon virtue and merit, not on the rash result of fortune and descent, must produce a more illustrious succession of princes. Witness the mild and happy reigns of the kings of Rome, who came to the crown by the free choice and consent of the people, all renowned for justice, virtue and the honest arts of government: whilst of all the Roman emperors that inherited the monarchy by succession and descent, two only had the reputation of virtuous and moderate princes.

For a proof of this assertion, that elective monarchy is less dangerous to the liberties of the people, I need only observe, there is not one instance in ancient or modern story of an absolute elective monarchy, except that of Rome under the emperors, and that of Egypt under the Mamelukes, which were both military governments, and the popedom which is an ecclesiastic one; and 'tis generally observed that elective empires end in commonwealths, and hereditary ones in tyrannies and arbitrary governments. These are the happy effects of elective mon-

---

[1] The Roman kings are praised for allowing citizens arms and for their supposed encouragement of population. Moyle had written about citizen armies, and had voted for a general naturalization bill when in parliament; an act was passed in 1708 but repealed in 1711 because of some disillusionment brought about by the problems raised by the immigration of the 'poor Palatines' into England.

archies with regard to the liberties of the subjects: but they want force and vigour from their inward constitution, to preserve the authority of the regal rights, much more to increase and enlarge the prerogative of the crown.

Men advanced from a private fortune to this great station, retain their first impressions of freedom, which the condition of a private life taught them under the dominion of their predecessors which incline them to protect those rights and privileges as sovereigns, which they contended for as subjects. And a wise people seldom make choice of a man to command them, the experience of whose private life has not warranted the moderation of his reign; and none are so likely to make good governors, as they who in their private capacities have observed the different tempers and inclinations of the people, upon the different conduct and genius of princes: the true vein and current of a nation being generally concealed from kings by crowds of designing ministers, and adulation of servile flatterers. These considerations may probably sway with some princes, not to invade the liberties and laws of the nation: but most elective kings are deterred from such an attempt, by the difficulty of the undertaking: they rarely have strength to put in force such resolutions.

Hereditary princes, whose authority has been established by a long succession of their ancestors, strengthened with leagues and alliances abroad, supported by mighty dependencies at home, of those who share with them in the government, or push on their fortunes at the expense of the public, cultivated by the same course of measures and counsels, and made sacred by the force of custom and the habit of obeying, may aspire with all these helps to absolute dominion with some probable grounds of success. But elective monarchs are destitute of all these great springs of power and authority; and rarely succeed in such an attempt without a lucky hit or an extraordinary concurrence of accidents and causes; but generally lose ground, and decline every succession, by reason of the authority of the people, who being vested with the right of disposing the crown, force every new prince they advance, to prune his prerogative; and increase their privileges to a degree inconsistent with the sovereign power. Nor can the nobility (the best guards of monarchy) in such a constitution be so wholly devoted to the king; for they must engage the votes and interests of the people, by all the arts of popularity, if ever they expect to have their pretensions to the crown upon a vacancy, seconded by the favour and concurrence of the multitude.

Besides these limitations and bounds of elective monarchs, they have a nearer interest not to invade the liberties of their country, which is the good of their families; for the crown not descending to the next of blood, they are certain that as much as they add to the grandeur of the monarchy, so much they add to the slavery of their posterity, who are to be private men. And should an elective prince form a design of making the crown hereditary he will certainly be opposed by the commonalty, whose right of election is violated, and by the nobility, whose hopes of succeeding are destroyed. From these considerations I am inclined to think, that this constitution of the Roman monarchy was a fault in the first concoction, and was the original of the succeeding laws in favour of the people. But whether it was first designed by Romulus, or instituted by the Romans after his death, is uncertain; though I am apt to believe that Romulus having no children, as in his life time he gave liberty to Alba, which descended to him by the death of his grandfather Numitor; so after his death he designed at least to have left the election of their kings to the people, without appointing any successor of his own nomination. Whoever was the author of this institution, it is certain, that it was the great moving cause of all their following concessions and privileges to the people.

Romulus, their first king, to reward the good affections of his new subjects, made an equal distribution among the people of the territory belonging to Rome, except of the crown and church lands; and as he grew greater, divided all the conquered lands among the multitude, (a custom followed by most of the succeeding kings.) This donation was a false step never to be reconciled to the true interest of sovereign power, from that eternal principle, that equality of possession makes equality of power: and whenever the balance of property sways to the people, the monarchy naturally resolves into a popular government.

The third fault was the making a limited monarchy, a government for increase in order to which the numbers of the people must be enlarged, and the sword put in their hands; for conquests abroad must be gained by the vigour of a brave militia at home; and a brave militia must be formed of men spirited by freedom, plenty, and property. Conquests abroad must be preserved by force of numbers of people; and numbers of people can be gained only by naturalization of foreigners, who never will be tempted from their native seats, unless allured by the ease and liberty of the government. Thus the generous ambition of extending their empire, made the kings of Rome sacrifice the rights of the monarchy to the liberties of the people; for without freedom and property they found it impossible to compose a brave or a numerous militia, both which are the genuine roots of a commonwealth: for a people that have property in possession, and swords in their hands, rarely submit to the dominion of one. Independence being the interest of the many, and monarchy but of the few; by how much greater the number of the people is, by so much stronger is the guard of liberty.

These were the natural seeds of the generation of the Roman commonwealth, concurring with many other accidental causes, such as the example of most of the neighbouring states of Greece and Italy, who were generally republics. For changes of government are often derived by imitation into the humours and customs of a nation; and the Jews chose a monarchy, because the people round them were all under that constitution: and the late revolutions in England were in some manner owing to the example of Holland, and other foreign commonwealths. Another cause, was, their king's leaving no issue behind him, (at least of age and abilities to command) who by the numbers of his father's dependants and retainers, might have pretended to the crown, and made it hereditary. And last of all, the moderation and virtue of their kings (which was owing to the constitution of elective monarchy) who all successively vied in emulation who should be the greatest benefactors to the people.

In this place it will not be improper to take a short survey by what paces and steps this great revolution, from a kingly government to an aristocracy, was brought about in Rome. Romulus made the first institution of dividing the public and conquered lands among the people, and afterwards made Alba a free state; which set the Romans a longing for a commonwealth, (as Plutarch observes) which they established upon his death, but had not strength to continue, from their own divisions and the unsettled posture of their own affairs; which made way for the promotion of Numa, who divided the public lands of the city among the citizens who had no lots, and committed a great oversight in dividing the chief priesthood from the kingly power, it having been vested before in Romulus, and afterwards by the policy of the Roman emperors inseparably annexed to the crown. Numa likewise disbanded his guards. Hostilius divided all the church and crown lands among the people and instituted or confirmed their rights of hearing all appeals which was making them sovereign judges in the last resort.

And though Ancus left things in the same state he found them, and Tarquin made some steps to recover the grandeur of the monarchy by the addition of one hundred new senators (he enlarged the dignity of the senate by adding members thereto, says Florus) and adorned the imperial dignity with the ensigns of royalty, and the outward forms of greatness; yet he debased the majesty of his character by submitting his title to the people, and pleading his cause before them; which was owning the supreme authority to be lodged in them.

But Servius being advanced to the throne by the favour of the commons, against the will of the nobility, gave the finishing stroke to the ruin of the monarchy, by dispossessing the patricians of all the public lands they had engrossed,[1] and distributing them to the people; by paying the debts of the commons; by erecting courts of judicature independent of the crown; and by the institution of such laws as established an equality between the two orders, in the decision of civil controversies, and in their contributions to the public charges. It is true, he strengthened the patrician interest by introducing an inequality of suffrages in their favour. But he quickly repented his conduct, and applied himself so entirely to the good of the people, that the nobility were alarmed at it; and in conjunction with the new pretender Tarquin, formed a design to dethrone him. And when (by his great authority with the commons) they miscarried in an open attempt of deposing him, they cut him off by a barbarous assassination, in the midst of that glorious design he had formed of introducing an equal commonwealth. Thus Tullius plainly inclined the balance of power and property from the nobility to the commons.

After his death, Tarquin usurped the throne in a lawless manner, without the usual forms of election and consecration, to the dislike of the nobility, and an utter abhorrence and detestation of the commons, for the barbarous murder of their great patron and benefactor Servius. And the whole course of his reign was answerable to his beginning; he invaded the senate and people, and exercised his tyrannies with all the inhumanity and barbarity imaginable, without engaging any party to support him, or making use of one order to destroy the other, that

[1] See above, p. 224, n. 1. Thelwall appends a long note to this passage denying that the Roman laws were laws of 'levelling and plunder', and declaring that they were merely an attempt to defend the equal right of the people to land.

he might with more ease oppress all. His foreign guards, instead of protecting him from the popular fury, served only to inflame the general abhorrence of his tyrannies, without being an over-balance to the people. But his arbitrary government being settled upon no solid foundation, could be of no long standing: the senate wanting nothing but a favourable conjuncture, and the commons nothing but a warm leader, to break out into open rebellion. The rape of Lucretia inflamed the general discontents, and raised such a storm, as ended in the expulsion of Tarquin and his family, and the dissolution of the monarchy.

Thus I have traced this great revolution from its original, in its remotest and most distant causes, down to the last period of the monarchy under Tarquin. The natural causes of it were the mighty concessions and privileges conferred on the commons by the bounty of their kings, and such a share of property as over-balanced the possessions of the kings and the nobility together, which begets an independence; after which there can be no cause in nature assigned for obedience and subjection. So that the balance of dominion being vested in the commons, the monarchy of course must die a natural death. And to finish the revolution, the nobility disobliged by Tarquin, closing with the people: and the army (the last refuge of tyranny) being composed of men of property, and by consequence conspiring with the national interest, Tarquin had no reserve to appeal to, but lost his crown without striking a blow: and the monarchy resolved into an aristocracy; and that into a democracy; and that too relapsed into a monarchy, as the balance of lands varied from one order to another.

These periods and revolutions of empires are the natural transmigrations of dominion, from one form of government to another: and make the common circle in the generation and corruption of all states. The succession of these changes Polybius knew from experience, but not from their true natural causes: for he plainly derives these alterations from moral reasons; such as vices and corruptions, the oppression and tyranny of their governors, which made the people impatient of the yoke, and fond of new forms; and not from the change of the only true ground and foundation of power, property.[1] To confute

---

[1] Moyle and many other English writers abandoned the Polybian theory of cycles in history, and maintained that changes were brought about by disturbances in the 'balance'. Thelwall commented that the French Revolution, then in progress, might introduce a new variety of political theorists, believing in the diffusion of political knowledge and thus, of course, the extension of political rights.

this great man, I only appeal to the examples of the famous monarchies of Rome (under the emperors) and of Turkey; which being founded on the balance of land, after so many successions of effeminate and tyrannical princes, stood firm; and the people, provoked often by their oppressions, rebelled against the monarch, but never against the monarchy: for while the root of power continues, the government will last, though the branches are lopped off. But the first Roman empire not being founded on this steady balance, the people, who were in possession of it, wanted nothing but oppression to make them exert their power, and nothing but a tyrant to set them free. Thus it appears that land is the true centre of power, and that the balance of dominion changes with the balance of property; as the needle in the compass shifts its points just as the great magnet in the earth changes its place. This is an eternal truth, and confirmed by the experience of all ages and governments; and so fully demonstrated by the great Harrington in his *Oceana*, that it is as difficult to find out new arguments for it, as to resist the cogency of the old.

But to return from my digression, in the next place I shall examine what methods the Romans took to hinder the restoration of Tarquin, and preserve their liberties.

Their first step was their solemn abjuration of the regal title and office, made by the whole body of the Roman people, in the name of themselves and their posterity; a precedent which they copied from the Greek commonwealths, who after the expulsion of their tyrants, entered into solemn oaths and engagements to defend their liberty. This was a wise council of the Romans, and in the greatest distress of their affairs, made them suffer the last extremities rather than hearken to any overtures of restoring their tyrants: so sacred and binding was the obligation of an oath to that great and virtuous people. Secondly, an act of general indemnity and oblivion, which took in all those who joined with Tarquin, more from an apprehension and dread of punishment from the state, or having favoured the illegal usurpations of the tyranny, than from any personal affection or engagement to his cause. The severe punishment of the consul's sons, and the rest of the nobility, who had conspired to restore the Tarquins: for however monarchies or tyrannies may subsist, commonwealths can never stand without a rigorous execution of that great sanction of their laws, rewards and punishments. And last of all, the restoration of the popular laws of

Servius, and the institution of new ones together with the distribution of the goods of Tarquin among the people, and the division of all his lands to the commons; which with all the forfeitures and confiscations under such a tyrannical reign, must amount to a mighty revenue. This made the breach between the crown and the people irreparable, by involving the whole community in one common guilt: and widened the popular balance, by multiplying the property of the state into so many hands; which gave the people such a degree of power as made the return of Tarquin, by any inward convulsion, impossible: for it is ridiculous to imagine, that any free, brave, independent people, could have the least shadow of interest to subject their reasons, lives and liberties to the arbitrary commands and resolutions of a private will, instead of being ruled by laws of their own making, magistrates of their own creation, and a form of government of their own choosing.

These popular concessions of the nobility, effectually excluded Tarquin and the monarchy: but were the leading causes of the destruction of their new aristocracy, which shall be the subject of my next consideration.

I have often wondered that the Romans, instead of settling a democracy after the expulsion of their kings, should make choice of an aristocracy; considering that the revolution was brought about by the people and not by the nobility, who had been utterly ruined by the tyranny of Tarquin, and were in no condition to make head against his arbitrary conduct: much less by their numbers, and their authority, to influence such a mighty turn of affairs. Their share in the revolution was no more than breaking the ice, and inflaming the people to take up arms; but without their concurrence they had infallibly perished in the attempt. All that can be said in vindication of the people, is, that they were unused to command; and from the habit of obeying, willingly submitted to any constitution which the nobility imposed on them; or else for want of a demagogue to form a popular model, or from ignorance of union, were not sensible to their true force and strength; or else their terror and apprehension from abroad of Tarquin and his return, made them assent to the dominion of the senate, rather than hazard all by an unseasonable division at home. But whatever the considerations were, it is plain they lodged the sovereign power in the senate and the two consuls, who were vested with all the royal authority: But when the storm of Tarquin blew over, and their apprehensions of foreign invasions ceased, they grew quickly sensible of their error, in surrendering the government into so few hands; and in short time turned their new masters out of their seats, and by degrees moulded the government into a more popular model.[1]

The aristocracy was founded upon the shattered balance of the monarchy and composed of the nobility, unequal either by their numbers, possessions or authority, to the riches and greatness of the commons, who had been growing many ages, by the lenity and indulgence of the former reigns, and the new concession of the senate, after the expulsion of the last kings (which I have already mentioned:) so that the government stood on no solid foundation of real power, and only depended upon an imaginary balance of authority, derived from the institution of these two laws.

First, the exclusion of the commons from all places of command, under a pretence that they were not qualified for the right of divination, which was necessary to the obtaining all the great magistracies. And secondly, the institution of the dictatorian power, which was an expedient contrived by the nobility to destroy the right of appeals, confirmed to the people by the Valerian Law; which this magistracy absolutely subverted, and got an unlimited jurisdiction in all criminal and civil cases, in the last resort, without any appeal to the people. But these laws being founded against the true balance of the commonwealth, wanted force and strength to support the dominion of the patricians; nor had the patricians authority and power to support these laws against the irresistible greatness of their rivals, the commons, who would obey no longer than the counsels and resolutions of the senate were directed to the public good of the whole community. For when the commons saw pretences of one kind, and actions of another; when they beheld the senate to be governed by their private factions and interests, violating their own laws and liberties, exercising power with all the inhumanity and barbarity imaginable, handling their debtors without mercy, and imprisoning them for not paying money taken up at unreasonable interest, the debtors (not the seventh part of the people) in conjunction with part of the senate, and the whole order of the commons, kindled such a flame as ended in the dissolution of the aristocracy, and the settlement of an equal commonwealth. The causes from

[1] Moyle may here be alluding to the English Revolution of 1688, and to the hopes of his own circle for further perfecting of the constitutional settlement and for greater protection of liberty.

234

which this revolution was derived, shall be the subject of my next consideration.

A man who would take a survey of the original principles of this second change of government, must take wing from a rising ground, and mount up to those remoter and more distant causes which insensibly and by degrees influenced this mighty revolution, viz. The decay of the power and authority of the patricians, under so many successions of kings; their visible declension under Servius; and the almost utter ruin of the order, under the tyranny of Tarquin: and the proportionable growth and increase of the commons by the addition of so many privileges and immunities to their order; their great possessions, the plenty of their fortunes, their independence of the nobility; of all which, power and dominion is but the natural result.

These two former causes I have discoursed of at large; the more immediate cause, was the dissolution of the monarchy by the joint counsels and united interests of the whole body of the people; this made them reasoners in matters of politics and government, and impatient of any insolence and oppression: this taught them a refuge to appeal to from the tyranny of any other governors, and made them disdain any other subjection, than to the empire of the laws: the filling up of the vacant places in the senate with commoners, who must of course be more warmly concerned for the interests of the people than hereditary nobles. The right of electing the senate conferred on them by Brutus, after the expulsion of the kings: which the people continued in possession of till the first creation of the censors. This gave the people an advantage of choosing more popular members into the senate, and was perhaps the reason which engaged such a strong party in the senate to oppose the unjust encroachments of the patricians, and to favour the just pretensions of the people.

These were the natural causes of the final period of this government, with which some other accidents concurred: as, 1. The conjuncture of a foreign war; which the senate being unable to manage, in such a distracted state, they consented more easily to the demands of the commons. 2. The invincible courage and matchless virtue of the old Romans, and their disdain of servitude, from the force of custom, or the impressions of education. All these causes conspired to make the aristocracy an easy triumph to the people. Thus the weak constitution of this government, not founded on the true centre of dominion, land, nor on any standing foundation of authority or reverence, nor riveted in the esteem and affections of the people; and being attacked by the strong passion, general interest, and joint forces of the people, mouldered away of course, and pined of a lingering consumption, till it was totally swallowed up by the prevailing faction, and the nobility were moulded into the mass of the people.

In the next place, I shall examine upon what laws and orders the popular frame of government was erected, and by what policies and institutions secured from a relapse into any of the old forms.

The first blow given to the aristocracy, was the recision of the debts to the commons, which weakened the interest of the nobility, by taking off the great dependence of the inferior rank of the people upon them. The second was the erection of the tribunes and other plebeian magistrates, for the security and protection of the commons, with a sacred authority and negative vote upon all the proceedings of the senate. The institution of this magistracy of the people, besides all the other advantages derived from it to the commons, united the whole body of the people under the general conduct of leaders and demagogues of their own order, made their counsels steady, and their resolutions unanimous; and took off that impression of single fear, which the commons had of the patricians, from the ignorance of union; was a certain refuge to appeal to, for the redress of all their grievances; and taught them to make regular advances and approaches to the destruction of the aristocracy.

The third was the power of proposing and debating laws, which the commons assumed by virtue of their new magistrates, whom they advanced at last to a power of enacting laws, with the authority of the senate. The fourth was the usurping a right to try the nobility for crimes committed against the state; which was a security wisely provided for by the people, to soften the absolute power of the dictator, who by this law was accountable to the people, after the resignation of his office, for severities exercised against them in the time of his jurisdiction. This likewise confirmed the old law of appeals to the people from the magistrates, which had been dextrously destroyed by the nobility by introducing the dictatorian power. The fifth was regaining an equality of suffrages in the elections of their own magistrates, and in the enacting of their laws; a right which they formerly enjoyed in the *Comitia Curiata*, but which they lost in the *Comitia Centuriata*, introduced by Servius Tullius, and recovered again in the trial of Coriolanus by the *Comitia Tributa*. The sixth was the obtaining a standing body of laws, collected from the wise institutions of the Grecian commonwealths. This system of laws prescribed the bounds of right and wrong, and regulated the proceedings of their courts of judicature; whereas formerly all controversies between man and man were decided by the arbitrary will of the consul, without any known forms or established methods of judging.

Seventhly, the excluding the diviners from interposing their authority and jurisdiction in the debates and resolutions of any popular assemblies: for whereas by their ancient constitution, no election of any magistrate, nor any public determination was valid, till ratified by their approbation, under this pretence they opposed all the just rights and pretensions of the people. To destroy therefore the negative vote of the diviners, the tribunes contrived an expedient to institute a new form of assembling, which they called the *Comitia Tributa*, wherein the augurs were not allowed to consult the gods; and by consequence the people were left absolute masters of their own proceedings and resolutions. Eighthly, the Agrarian Law; which though the people never perfectly obtained, yet they got large shares of the conquered lands into their possession, either by allotments to the citizens at home, or by planting colonies in the enemies' territories abroad; which confirmed and kept up the popular balance against the encroachments of the nobility. Ninthly, the mighty growth and increase of the numbers of the people, occasioned by laws prohibiting the barbarous practice of exposing their children; by manumitting their slaves, and enrolling them in the list of their free citizens: by the institution of such laws as compelled every Roman citizen to marry at such a determinate age, under severe penalties: And lastly, by the promiscuous naturalization of all foreigners.[1]

To the growth of the multitude of the people may be attributed the growth of their power; for the numbers of the people are the true guards of liberty, and always opposite in interest, and an over-match in power to an aspiring faction. This accession of strength to the

---

[1] The *Comitia Tributa* did not elect chief magistrates as Moyle suggests under 'seventhly'. Moyle also exaggerates the Roman naturalization policy under 'ninthly'. For an excellent account of assemblies, see Lily Ross Taylor, *Roman Voting Assemblies* (Ann Arbor, 1966), *passim*; a most useful table of *Comitia Curiata, Centuriata, Tributa*, 218–49 B.C., is inserted there between pp. 4 and 5.

commons, together with their warlike temper, inflamed by perpetual victory abroad, spirited them with a generous sense of freedom and made them disdain subjection to the dominion of the few. Tenthly, the repealing the law, which forbade a common intercourse of marriages between the patricians and plebeians: which rooted out that fatal distinction between the two orders, which had kindled so many flames, and raised such storms in the state: but which being now repealed, established the whole community on an equal foot of liberty: for as Livy very well observes, all the various distinctions by which the different orders and degrees were distinguished are totally done away with by liberty and equality. This promiscuous communion of marriages increased both orders, not only in alliance but interest; and by degrees formed them into one body: for whereas formerly the nobility, by virtue of an imaginary excellency peculiar to their families, challenged the sole right of divination, and consequently engrossed all the great posts of command; this law introduced such a mixture and confusion of blood as cut off that pretence and made way for the easy reception of the eleventh law, which gave the commons a right to be elected into the civil government of the state to be consuls, dictators, priests, and in course of time to be equally admitted to all the great dignities and offices of the commonwealth.[1]

The nobility being thus moulded into the mass of the people, and both orders entitled to a common right of enjoying the same privileges and dignities, the next care of the people was to secure the present settlement, by making timely provision, that no single man, or order of men, by their riches, possessions, or authority, should so over-balance the rest of the community, as to aspire to absolute dominion. In order to which, they made these following institutions: First, the Licinian Law, which limited the possessions of all private men to five hundred acres of land; which established the great balance of the commonwealth, and would have rendered it immortal, had the law been effectually put in execution. Secondly, the Cincian Law, which prohibited the payment of fees and pensions to all patrons and advocates: whereas before the enacting of this law, the people were tributary to the great men and the senators, who were the only lawyers of the state: the people, says

---

[1] Moyle has here shown the steps by which the Roman Republic achieved near perfection and is relying, *inter alia*, on Livy VI, c. 42, where the historian gives a lively account of the struggle and reconciliation between plebeian and patrician. In the next paragraphs he describes those good laws which secured, for the time being, the state.

Livy, already began to be taxed by the senate. Thirdly, the Flaminian Law, which enjoined that no senator should possess any ship of considerable burden; which hindered them from enriching themselves by the gain of foreign trade and commerce.

Fourthly, the institution of the *leges usurariae*, or the laws restraining usury within moderate bounds. The Romans had found by experience the mischievous consequences of high interest for money, and wisely sunk it, first to one per cent, and then reduced it one half lower, and at last utterly abolished all usury. These laws (as Livy remarks) were no ways pleasing to the great ones: for the senators, by the advantages they had of commanding the armies and other opportunities, were the monied men who exercised this unlawful trade, and consequently engaged a dependence of the commons upon them, which the passing of this law destroyed; and likewise established the national balance entirely on land, which the people had the largest share of. Fifthly, the institution of the *leges annales*, or the laws of determining the age requisite for enjoying all the great magistracies of the commonwealth. This law cut off the early ambition of young men, and was one way to prevent the same persons from being often in the same dignities. Sixthly, the laws against canvassing and soliciting for places, which destroyed the freedom of elections (of which a commonwealth ought to be tender) and laid open all the great honours to bribery and corruption, instead of virtue and merit; which is always fatal to the liberties of a free state, as Lucan finely remarks:

> The sordid wretch who strives a vote to gain,
> By curs'd corruption, or by bribery,
> A harmless people loads with endless pain,
> And banishes sweet freedom far away.

Seventhly, the laws in force against the continuation of magistracy; for nothing sooner dissolves a commonwealth than the continuance of authority too long in the same hands. It likewise subverts that successive change of magistracy, which is the fundamental constitution of all equal governments, where the whole community ought to have their turns of commanding and obeying: the change of the magistracy is the preservation of liberty, says Livy. Eighthly, the laws against accumulation of magistracy, directed to the same ends with the former, lest the possession of too much authority should tempt the magistracy to invade the liberties of the nation. Plurality of offices also destroys the

239

free rotation of dignities; and is, as Livy truly says, that a free city is not by any pretence, to suffer such proceedings—against all right and equity a dangerous precedent, and never to be encouraged and endured by a free government.

Ninthly, the limitations of those offices in time, which were unlimited in power, as the censors and dictators, and the limitation of those offices in power, which were unlimited in time; as the whole order of the clergy, whose jurisdiction was abridged under the popular government (as I have proved at large) and little distinction of value and authority left them after the publication of the laws, rituals, and calendars, the custody of which they were anciently entrusted with. This law was founded upon very good reasons; for, as Livy says, what greatly conduces to preserve liberty is the limiting of those offices in time which are unlimited in power, and the limiting of those offices in power which are unlimited in time. Tenthly, the making the fundamental branches of their constitution, as the abolition of the kingly office, and the institution of the magistracy of the tribunes, sacred and unalterable, and confirmed by the most solemn oaths and engagements of the whole body of the people, in the name of themselves and their posterity. Nor could any of the first rate of magistrates be admitted to act, till they had sworn to support and maintain those and all other laws of the commonwealth.

Eleventhly, the *leges tabellariae*, or the institution of voting by the ballot, which was an expedient found out to preserve the freedom of elections, which were awed and influenced by the greatness and authority of the senators. The people oppressed by the authority and power of the great ones, have insisted upon the institution of voting by ballot. This single law reprieved the fate of the commonwealth for an age, after all the other popular laws were abolished by disuse, or openly invaded or broken in upon by the great men. It was the guardian of liberty, and the only barrier which hindered the aristocracy from subverting the popular government, by engrossing all the magistracies of the state, which they could have commanded by their interests and dependencies among the people, if a way had not been contrived to conceal the suffrages of the commons, and screen them from the resentments of their patrons. And in such a case, where the people are left to their own liberty, they will make choice not of those whom they fear, but of those whom they esteem and love, for their own engagement to the national interest. Nor was the ballot only restrained to the election of magistrates, but at last was indifferently applied to all the public resolutions and determinations of the assemblies of the people.

Upon the balance of these orders and institutions stood the mighty fabric, immortal from all inward diseases, and invincible by any foreign attacks, had the same conduct and steadiness of counsels been directed to the execution of these laws,[1] as were applied to the first founding of them. But the original causes and principles of the corruption and dissolution of this admirable government, shall be the subject of another discourse.

[1] For these laws, see index under title. Moyle exaggerates the effects of some—for example, those against usury. As they appear here, the Roman laws comprise most of the suggestions made by the Commonwealthmen—some limitation of property, the prevention of corruption, the regulation of officers, placemen or 'courtiers' by age requirements, rotation, the ballot; restriction of electioneering, calling to account by accusation or impeachment, etc.

Part Two

In the former part of this discourse I have attempted to take a short survey of the civil and ecclesiastical constitution of the Roman commonwealth, together with the various changes and revolutions of their government, deduced from their true and natural causes, down to the last great reformation of their government, and the foundation of a more equal commonwealth; and in the conclusion of the whole, I have endeavoured to give a brief account of the chief laws and institutions which so equally balanced this last establishment, by such a wise and proportioned distribution of power among the several orders, councils and magistrates, as rendered it so many ages secure and unshaken by foreign force or domestic rage.

The subject of this following part is the declension and decay of the Roman government, with a free enquiry into the original causes and principles, which, by insensibly corrupting their ancient laws, discipline, and manners, reduced it in conclusion to an absolute monarchy. But before I enter upon this argument, it may not be improper to remove some popular calumnies, which have been raised in particular against the Roman commonwealth, and against all free governments whatsoever, by the advocates for tyranny. They object, that after the recovery of their liberty, the Romans immediately fell into confusion and disorder; that we find nothing in the histories of those times but tumults and seditions between the two contending parties, no stability in their councils, nor steadiness in their resolutions, but all governed by popular fury and faction: to which they oppose the quiet and tranquillity of the kingly government; and upon these grounds found all the objections they make, in order to decry the popular frames of government. But that the weakness of these objections may more fully appear, I shall advance these following observations. Firstly, the kingly government was not free from seditions. Secondly, that under the kingly government there was no sufficient security provided for the liberties of the people. Thirdly, that the kingly government was incapable of making conquests. Fourthly, that the popular seditions under the commonwealth never came to blood. Fifthly, that they reformed and

242

perfected the Roman government. Sixthly, that there were no seditions after the commonwealth became more equal. Seventhly, and that during this last period the Romans conquered the world.

Nothing can appear more manifest than the first proposition, that the kingly government was not free from seditions: for by what other name can we call so many plots and conspiracies, and the assassination of no less than four kings out of seven, and the expulsion of a fifth? If it be objected, that these were only accidental disorders raised by the ambition or discontents of a few private persons; it must still be allowed, that although they were more particular in their causes, they were more universal in their effects than the violence of any popular commotions: for what can the rage and folly of a multitude commit equal to such a desperate attempt, as dissolves the government at a blow, and exposes all to anarchy and confusion; not to mention the dangerous factions which exercised the reigns of Tarquin and Servius, and which ended in the murder of these excellent princes? What seditions were raised upon the very first interregnum, and other vacancies of the throne? A defect essential to the very nature of elective monarchy, where the supreme command must of course be more strongly contended for than the annual and successive honours of a republic.

Secondly, nor was there a sufficient security provided for the liberties of the people under the kingly governments, for want of a due balance to keep the constitution steady. The regal authority was indeed limited by laws; but laws are dead letters, and can make no resistance to the arbitrary will of a prince, unless there is such a force in the government as is strong enough to support them. The guard of liberty in most regulated monarchies, has been placed in some popular magistrates, who carefully watched all innovations upon the constitution, and had authority to question the kings themselves for any arbitrary or illegal proceedings: of this nature were the ephors at Sparta, and the justiciar at Aragon. In other mixed governments, the guard of liberty was entrusted to frequent assemblies of the people in person, or by their representatives, who had a right to enquire into the management of their rulers, and had power sufficient to face and defeat the strongest league that could be formed for the subversion of their liberties. This constitution chiefly prevailed in the gothic governments established in Europe. The wisdom of other nations limited the regal power, by placing the sword in the hands of the subject; which was the best security of all, and was the ancient constitution of England, while the power of the militia belonged to the nobility and gentry, in a manner independent of the crown.

These institutions were the great fences of liberty in the most celebrated mixed governments, both ancient and modern, which were all wanting under the kingly government of Rome. Popular magistrates they had none, till the tyranny of the senate, after the expulsion of the kings, had brought them to have recourse to that remedy. Assemblies indeed they had, but the kings only having the right of convening them, and nothing being to be propounded or debated in them, but with the royal approbation, it is no wonder they proved no stronger defences against the encroachments of the last kings. The kings had likewise the absolute command of the whole military power of the state. I easily foresee a plausible objection that may be urged. How it came to pass then that the Romans, instead of falling into absolute slavery, got ground upon the monarchy, till they entirely abolished it. To which I answer, that Romulus, about the latter end of his reign, had made himself absolute; but the government being conferred on Numa, a just and virtuous prince, he disbanded the guards, which were the chief power of his predecessor, and governed with great moderation. This example was pursued by the rest, who all generously increased the privileges of the people; whether out of fear or virtue, I will not determine; for it is manifest it was not owing to the constitution, which could not preserve them from Tarquin, who followed other maxims. But although there was no counterpoise in the laws to balance the regal authority, yet the liberty seems to have been in a great measure supported by the mere weight of the people, whose property was the noblest root of liberty; which being at first planted by Romulus, and cherished by the succeeding princes, and being attended with that valour and spirit which is the effect of ease and plenty, made it a dangerous adventure; especially for kings who did not inherit by succession, and three of whom were strangers, to attempt upon their liberties.

But errors in the superstructures may endanger the fabric, be the foundation ever so well laid, as the Romans found to their cost under Tarquin; who claiming by succession, assumed the government without the consent of the people; and being backed at first by the patrician interest, and by the keeping up foreign guards and having armed himself with a power superior to all laws, turned the government into an absolute tyranny; and had he reigned long enough to have impoverished or corrupted the people, liberty, in all likelihood, would never have been restored; but foolishly disobliging the patricians, and putting arms into the hands of his oppressed and courageous subjects, he left an example to all future tyrants, that an army of freeholders will always turn their swords against their oppressors, whenever an opportunity presents itself.

Thirdly, that the kingly government was incapable of making conquests, there needs no other argument to demonstrate, than that so many warlike and victorious princes could not extend their territories above fifteen miles beyond the walls of Rome. The little progress the Romans made under the monarchy, may be chiefly ascribed to these following reasons. Their military discipline was not established till the reign of Servius Tullius, their last king except one; nor was it then brought to perfection, but received continual improvements from the experience of after ages. Their armies received no pay, were incapable of making long expeditions. We find in their histories but one colony planted in their conquered countries, from the time of Romulus to the reign of Tarquinius Superbus: an omission which made all their victories ineffectual; colonies being the only way by which an infant state can propagate her empire, and which Romulus wisely perceived. The maxims which the following kings seemed to pursue, was increasing the numbers of their people, by transplanting the inhabitants of the cities they had conquered into Rome, and incorporating them into the commonwealth. This institution, it is confessed, was of excellent use, but much inferior in all respects to colonies, as I shall endeavour to show in the following part of this discourse. The kings did not fall into the wise measures of communicating the rights of the city to the bordering states; which was a cheap and easy way of enlarging their territories, and practised with good success by the commonwealth. Most of the wars, which the kings made, were defensive; and we commonly find, that after they had vanquished their enemies, they were content with an honourable satisfaction for the injuries committed; sometimes with a bare submission, and often with vain titles of honour bestowed on them by the conquered countries, in token of their dependence, which signified little to hold them under a real subjection: these conquests never failing to revolt upon the death of the king, either presuming on the unactive genius of the successor, or pretending they lay under no obligation to perform these conditions with the prince who came after. Rome, in its infancy, was encompassed round with warlike and numerous nations, living at their ease under free and independent governments, who contended bravely for their liberties, and held the Roman fortune long in play: under which constitution nations are very difficultly mastered by monarchies, and seldom thoroughly subdued, but by commonwealths of greater virtue and liberty than their own.

Fourthly, that the seditions of the Roman commonwealth never came to blood, is apparent from the authority of all their histories. 'Tis true, there was much clamour and violence in these popular tumults, but their utmost fury ended in a voluntary retreat from the city, says Livy. I would not be understood of those seditions which happened in the corruption of the republic, which were headed by mercenary tribunes, to promote the ambitious designs of some aspiring citizens; of which more hereafter.

Fifthly, that the seditions of Rome perfected their government. Seditions do not proceed from the nature of commonwealths in general; for many republics have been entirely free from them, as Sparta, Venice, etc., but from defects in particular constitutions. Aristocracies, where the body of the people are excluded from the administration, are most subject to these disorders; as is remarkable in the little governments of Italy, which being all aristocratical, were seldom free from commotions. The reformation of governments, which are so unequal in their constitutions, must be attended with popular tumults and violence; while the nobility contend for their hereditary honours and privileges, and the commons strive to reduce the government to an equality. From this cause arose all the seditions of Rome; which, though for the present, creating some little disorders in the state, introduced excellent orders into the government, and were succeeded by lasting quiet and tranquillity: so that upon the whole, these seditions were of excellent use to the commonwealth. Although seditious practices were in general hurtful, yet some may be said to have their good effects; for it is certain, that, unless the nobility had disagreed and quarrelled among themselves, kings never would have been driven out of the city, nor tribunes created, neither would the consular dignity have been diminished by the law of the commons, nor would the permission of appealing, which is nothing less than the bulwark of the city and support of their liberties, ever have been granted to the Roman people; as was truly and judiciously observed by Crassus in his defence of Norbanus.

I have insisted the less upon these two preceding articles, because little can be added to the remarks which Harrington and Machiavel have already made on the same subject. I shall therefore conclude this chapter with these two remarks: 1. That notwithstanding all that has been objected against the popular commotions under commonwealths, monarchies are more subject to seditions, which always come to blood, and never reform the government, unless they chance to dissolve it; which is easily proved by comparing the reigns of the twelve Caesars with that space of time during which Rome was seditious, both periods containing near the same compass of time. 2. That the tranquillity of those monarchies, which happen to be free from seditions, is an argument that the subjects are so impoverished, debased or diminished, by the arbitrary violence and oppression of their masters, that they have neither the will, the courage, nor the ability to shake off their chains: which is the present condition of most of the monarchies in Europe. And who is there that would not prefer a factious liberty before such a settled tyranny?

Sixthly, that Rome was free from seditions, after the government became more equal. The senate, after the expulsion of the kings, tyrannizing over the commons, compelled them, for their own preservation, to create new magistrates out of their own order, called tribunes; under whose conduct they gradually diminished the power of the aristocracy, till at last they utterly extinguished it, and established the whole body of the people upon an equal foundation of liberty. This gradual reformation seems to have been completed at the creation of the first plebeian consul, three hundred eighty-six years from the foundation of the city. The introduction of equality into the government may be best placed at this juncture, when the highest station in the commonwealth was communicated to the basis and extent of liberty; and which, as the same author observes, after long and violent contentions, begot an universal concord and union. After this time, the nobility made little opposition to any popular laws: seeing they were accustomed to be overcome by such kind of contentious litigations, as Livy remarks. Nor did there happen any domestic disorder, in near two hundred and forty years, which deserves the name of sedition, except a light tumult of debtors and bankrupts, who retired in a rage to Mount Janiculus; but which is omitted by several historians in the catalogue of the Roman seditions.[1] I am not ignorant that other writers make this sedition more considerable, but all authors agree that it was composed without bloodshed by Hortensius the dictator, and that it ended in the revival of an excellent but antiquated law. From this tumult, which happened in the four hundred sixty-seventh year of the city, to the seditions of Gracchus in the six hundred and twentieth year of the city, Rome enjoyed a profound quiet and prosperity, not interrupted by the least domestic dissension: an example of lasting tranquillity, that can be paralleled in no monarchy whatsoever. This interval of time was the most happy and most glorious period of the Roman commonwealth, and gave rise to that valour and industry which extended their conquests over the world. And this leads me to the last proposition I advanced.

Seventhly, that the Romans, during the equality of the commonwealth, subdued the universe. I have already assigned the most probable reasons which interrupted the progress of the Roman conquests under the monarchy. After the expulsion of the kings, the patricians assumed the government, and fell naturally into the defensive maxims, which all aristocracies do or ought to pursue. 'Tis evident, from the whole tenor of their histories that they aimed only at the quiet and preservations of their government, that the wars they at first undertook were just and necessary, either to repel or revenge a foreign invasion; but fortune, which so often seconded the virtue of Rome, would not suffer the mighty genius of that people to languish in obscurity, and found means to interrupt the establishment of those slothful measures, by foreign wars or domestic discord; both which, by a strange fatality, equally conspired to the rise and growth of Roman greatness.

After the banishment of the kings, the Roman people made a wonderful progress in all kinds of virtue; and the indulgence of the senate in the first years of their administration, had so raised their spirits, that the following oppressions of the nobility, instead of melting and quelling them, served only to inflame their minds, who were content with liberty before, to contend for honour and dominion with their proud and imperious masters. To divert these dangerous contentions at home, the nobility entered into wars abroad, not with designs of conquest,

---

[1] In spite of Moyle, there were disorders: e.g. 287, 157, 133 B.C.

but either to prevent or punish a domestic sedition; choosing rather to be vanquished in the field by their enemies, than to have hard laws imposed on them in the city by the victorious tribunes.

Colonies, the best way of securing their acquisitions, were very seldom and very unwillingly planted; sometimes to appease a popular tumult, at other times to prevent divisions of land nearer home, or else to encourage the commons to take up arms more cheerfully, to resist a dangerous invasion which threatened them from abroad. Such were the designs and policy of that government; and 'tis no wonder in such a divided state and such distracted counsels, if the progress of the Roman arms were in a manner at a stand. But this advantage they reaped from their foreign wars and civil dissensions, the one preserved the courage and discipline of their armies, and the other reformed the constitution of their government. But conquest and dominion were reserved to complete the felicity of a free and impartial commonwealth, the establishment of which I place at the three hundred eighty-sixth year of the city, when the consulship was laid open to the commons, and the Licinian law enacted, which was the chief strength of the popular constitution of government.

After this reformation of the commonwealth, their affairs quickly assumed another face: that virtue and ambition which had been so long oppressed by the faction and dominion of the few, had a free scope to exert itself, and a wide field to range in: hence fresh conquests, says Livy; at this time they began to aspire to the dominion of Italy: and although they were weakened by the revolt of their old allies the Latins, and attacked about the same time by the Samnites, the most warlike, and the Tuscans,[1] the richest and most populous nation of Italy; yet their unwearied virtue and industry overcame all these difficulties, and in less than a hundred years reduced all Italy under their obedience, which had held them at bay for so many ages before. Pyrrhus was an easy triumph; and the Carthaginians, who disputed the empire of the world with them in three long and bloody wars with various successes, being at length borne down by the mere weight of their constitution, as Polybius observes; and Philip, with Antiochus and Perseus, being an unequal match for their arms, they remained, in conclusion, the absolute masters of the universe. This amazing

[1] The Tuscans in about 367 B.C. were neither a nation nor the richest and most populous tribe in Italy.

249

progress of their conquests may be chiefly assigned to these following reasons: that their domestic factions being extinguished, left them at liberty to pursue their foreign conquests. That the counsels of popular assemblies are more bold and courageous than the resolutions of senates and princes. There is a certain natural vigour that animates the debates of a multitude, and has oftentimes a mixture of rashness in it; a defect, 'tis confessed, but flowing from a noble principle. To what other cause can be assigned the vast hopes and ambitious designs of the states of Athens, Carthage and other governments, where the people bore the greatest sway, but to an excess of courage, flowing from liberty and equality which raised the same spirit and disposition in the Romans; but regulated by wiser orders, strengthened by better discipline, and founded on a larger bottom? And to this, that fame, ambition and avarice, the common inducements to all great undertakings of this nature, reign very strongly in popular assemblies, where the spoils or the honour are to be divided among a multitude; which is more hard to satisfy, than the private glory or profits of a prince or a senate. To this may be joined the virtue and emulation of their particular magistrates and commanders, with which a commonwealth will always abound, where the supreme dignities are annual and successive, and are the never-failing reward of the highest desert and abilities.

These were the principal causes that gave rise to those counsels, which led them to all their succeeding greatness. For whereas the wars under the aristocracy were chiefly defensive, and carried on with more fury than perseverance, the conquests of Veii being the only considerable acquisition made in a hundred and forty years; under the popular government, the avarice of the people, the courage of the soldiers, and the emulation of the generals, made the Romans commonly the aggressors. Wars were undertaken upon slighter grounds, pursued with more obstinacy, and concluded with greater advantage; this remarkably appears in the first Punic war, which was voted and resolved on by the people, in conjunction with their consuls, against the express authority and approbation of the senate, and was the first foreign expedition they ever undertook. To which may be added, the advantageous situation of Rome for the conquest of Italy, and of Italy for the conquest of the world; and that the governments of Italy were less warlike in proportion to their distance from Rome, and less obstinate lovers and defenders of their liberty. Nor was the justice and

PART TWO

magnanimity of the Romans to their conquered nations, a small inducement to foreign nations to submit to their government; which was rather the patronage than empire of the world.

Besides these general and more remote considerations, I shall assign some particular causes, which concurred more immediately to the growth and preservation of the Roman conquests.

The perfection of their military discipline, which I shall handle so far forth as it bears any relation to the constitution of the civil government.

The vast increase of their people, after the equality of the government; their excellent way of maintaining their conquests by colonies at first, by equal leagues afterwards, and at last by unequal leagues and provincial governments.[1]

The people multiplied very fast under the kingly government; their stock was very much diminished under the beginnings of the aristocracy, and increased prodigiously after the commonwealth became equal: for from the general survey in the year 410, not long after the last change of their government, to the year 435, we find an increase of 90,000 inhabitants. How the growth of their numbers conduced to the enlargement of their empire, will appear by the next article of colonies.

Colonies[2] were of excellent use to the commonwealth: 1. To enlarge

[1] Moyle lists a number of surveys of citizens, omitted here.

[2] Moyle was much more explicit about the usefulness of colonies than many of his contemporaries, though Trenchard and Davenant would have agreed with him and his idea of imperial trusteeship. He is concerned less with their government than with Neville, and more with the advantages colonial expansion brings. Thelwall reacts with what would now be called a thesis of anti-colonialism.

'The ancient system of colonization was very different in many particulars from the modern. Among the Grecian states the object of planting colonies seems generally to have been the disposal of their superfluous population which, in consequence of the goodness of their institutions, and the freedom and equality of their laws, frequently multiplied beyond the convenience of the respective countries. Few modern governments have any necessity for colonies on this account [this is in 1796, before the population bulge was seriously felt]. It is to be remarked that these colonies were rather preserved in friendship and alliance, than in dependence upon the parent state. Rome seems to have had another object in addition to this—namely, the extension of her dominion and the security of the conquered countries, by amalgamating the conquerors and conquered into one people. The system of enslaving different and detached countries by what is called commercial colonization (that is to say, murdering one-half of the people, and reducing the other half to bondage, that the victor may monopolize the plunder of the country) was left to modern invention. It is to be observed, however, that in process of time the colonial or provincial governments of Rome degenerated into a system of plunder as detestable as those of certain modern nations, and produced the same lamentable effects upon the internal

251

their empire. 2. To defend their borders against a revolt of their allies. 3. To multiply their people. 4. To transplant their poor citizens. 5. To prevent seditions. 6. To reward their veterans. To which may be added, the preserving the popular balance by such large divisions of land to the commons, and the infusing the Roman manners and discipline into the conquered provinces, says Tacitus. The first institutions of colonies was owing to the wisdom of Romulus, who planted seven: but his example was ill pursued by his successors, there being only one more planted between his reign and that of Tarquin the Proud, who planted two more. The aristocracy, as they made little progress in their conquests, so by consequence sent forth very few colonies, not above ten or twelve in compass of a hundred and forty years. Under the popular government, when liberty and equality had removed all the obstacles which controlled the conquering genius of that mighty people, they extended their colonies and their victories over all Italy; having from the year 336, to the second Punic war, planted forty; and from thence to the sedition of Gracchus twenty more, with much greater numbers of citizens, larger proportions of acres, and at much greater distances from Rome than formerly. The institution of planting colonies was of greater benefit to the public, than transplanting the inhabitants of the conquered cities to Rome: a method that served only to increase the numbers of their citizens, which the other did more effectually by providing a larger subsistence for them; not to repeat the other advantages of colonies, which were all wanting in this institution.

The prodigious increase of their inhabitants enabled the Romans to plant such a barrier of colonies on the frontiers, as more effectually maintained all their conquests, than treble the number of garrisons could have done; which being composed of regular forces, kept up in constant discipline and pay, would have consumed their people, created a vast charge, and certainly destroyed their liberties: whereas their colonies still retained their reverence for their mother city, and were the only support of the Roman state, when they were sunk by so many losses in the second Punic war.

Rome, as Harrington judiciously observes, in her rise proceeded by

liberty of the country. That is to say, the governors and adventurers plundered the respective colonies in both instances with the same atrocious rapacity, and in both instances, employed the wealth with which they returned to the mother country, in debauching its morals, corrupting its legislators, and undermining its liberties and happiness' —Thelwall no doubt had many a 'nabob' in mind as he wrote.

colonies: for the acquisition of an infant government must be retained in subjection by an actual force, till the terror and reputation of their arms can procure a submission and obedience to their bare authority. Rome in growth proceeded by leagues, either equal, as the alliance with the Latins and other nations, on whom the rights of the city were bestowed; which was an excellent policy to propagate their empire, and rarely practised by the preceding governments: or unequal, as the Italian right, which was a donation of the city without suffrage, or by provincial governments; But for this last article, I shall refer the reader to Sigonius, who has handled it with great judgement and accuracy, and shall content myself with making two observations. 1. That the subjects of the Romans lived under the mildest administration, and the gentlest yoke in the world; which engaged them in a willing obedience and voluntary submission to a nation of greater virtues than their own, without those frequent tumults and rebellions with which oppression and tyranny are always attended. 2. That the Roman policy secured their conquests with so much ease, and so effectually, that there is hardly any example to be found in all their histories that they ever surrendered one spot of ground, of which they had once got the dominion.

But 'tis time to return from this long digression, and resume the subject of my discourse.

The reasons of the corruption and ruin of the Roman commonwealth, may be reduced to these general heads. The negligent execution of the laws and orders on which the popular government was founded. Some original defects in the first constitution of the government. And lastly, to some succeeding laws and institutions in favour of an aristocratical government, or of an absolute monarchy.

The ill execution of the laws and orders on which the popular government was founded, proceeded from these two causes. 1. That the government was not often enough reduced to its first principles. 2. From the alteration of their way of living. Cicero, and from him Machiavel, and other modern writers of politics lay down for a certain maxim, that commonwealths cannot subsist, unless they are frequently renewed by their magistrates, either by reviving the reverence and terror of the laws, or by restoring the ancient virtue and discipline or by a thorough reformation of those corruptions and disorders, which length of time, a loose administration, and the depravity of human nature will introduce into the soundest and firmest constitutions of government. This Machiavel styles resuming the commonwealth and reducing it to its first principles, of which there are many memorable instances in the rise of the popular government.

These renovations of the Roman commonwealth were effected either by their ordinary magistrates; as the tribunes, to whom the guard of liberty, or the censors, to whom the inspection of their discipline, manners, and suffrages was committed: or else by extraordinary ones, as the dictators, who were commonly created upon some great and sudden emergency, either to resist a foreign war, or to correct some domestic disorder. Under the vigilance and conduct of these magistrates, for some ages after the institution of the popular government, the administration was steady and regular; those laws which were the great fences of liberty were strictly obeyed, or severely executed, as the Licinian and usury laws, etc. and others whose authority was decaying were revived and re-enacted, as the law of appeals to the people, which was thrice renewed: another, that a vote of the commons without the concurrence of the senate, should have the force and authority of a law, was as often revived. It would be endless to enumerate examples of this kind during the purity of the commonwealth, by which the constitution was so often strengthened and reinforced. To this rigour and severity succeeded a loose and negligent administration; the vigour and influence of their laws was abolished by disuse; and the best constitution in the world, not being renewed or revived, departed from the principles on which it was first founded, and was entirely subverted.

This fatal management seems to owe its rise to the following occasions. 1. The mistaken liberty which the people assumed of dispensing with the most fundamental laws of their constitution, as the yearly elections, and the laws against continuation of magistracy, with many others which ought to have been sacred and unalterable.

The supreme power of a nation, 'tis confessed, can be bounded or limited by no precedent law; but in such cases it would have well become the wisdom of the people to have laid a voluntary restraint on their own authority, and have had recourse to the dictatorian power, or any other expedient, rather than to expose and weaken the great bulwarks of their constitution, by assuming such a dispensing power; which, although at first it was exercised upon good grounds, (as all evil precedents have good beginnings) yet in process of time, had a dangerous influence on the commonwealth. For this popular levity of dispensing with their most solemn orders and institutions, framed by the united wisdom and experience of so many ages, diminished by degrees the reverence and reputation of the laws; and led them naturally to conclude that those laws which at some junctures were judged inconvenient, were at all times unnecessary: and although there was an outward appearance of liberty in the maxim on which this proceeding was founded, to wit, that the last resolution of the people was the undoubted law of the commonwealth; yet nothing can be more certain, than that no constitution can subsist, where the whole frame of the laws may be shaken or suspended by the sudden temporary counsels of a multitude, and where the laws are governed by the people, instead of the people being governed by the laws. In after-times the exercise of this power was assumed, and in a manner engrossed by the senate, till the people, after they had miscarried in an attempt to restore it to their own assemblies, were content to divide it with the senate, under certain restraints and limitations.

But the commonwealth gained little advantage by this alteration; the power being equally pernicious, in whatever hands it was placed. In former times, it is confessed, it was rather dangerous in example than fact; but in the corrupt ages of the government, it gave a rise to that fatal neglect in the observance of all the laws, so essential to their constitution; and made way for the seven consulships of Marius, the early and multiplied honours of Pompey, and the long continuation of Caesar's command in Gaul; which are on all hands allowed to have been the direct and immediate causes of the ruin of the commonwealth.

2. Another reason was the omission or alteration of the custom of accusing. The laws can never be maintained in force in a nation, where it is held dishonourable to accuse: for which reason, all wise commonwealths have cherished and encouraged by rewards and marks of honour and distinction, accusations of all public offenders. At Rome, in particular, accusers were held in great esteem; such men being reputed the defenders of the laws, and the guardians of the constitution. Their greatest men commonly entered the world with the prosecution of some delinquent: nor did the highest persons in the state, as Scipio, Cato, and others, think it a disparagement, after all their honours, to undertake this province.

The laws had their due weight and authority, whilst they were defended by such excellent patrons; but in after-times, and in a more degenerate age, they were abandoned by their champions. Accusations were generally declined by the men of rank and dignity, and seldom or never undertaken unless by mean and mercenary informers, or raw and unskilful youths; so that the laws in a manner were left unguarded and defenceless; and what an effect this must have upon the constitution I leave every man to judge, and the event sufficiently declared. 'Tis true, Cicero,[1] and others, began to revive the old custom of accusing: but 'twas then too late, the corruption of the commonwealth being too big for the laws, and obstinate to all remedies. Nor was the authority of many of their laws armed with such sanctions and penalties as were necessary to imprint that awe and terror on the minds of the people, which alone can dispose them to obedience. The famous law of appeals was guarded by no other sanction than a bare declaration, that the breach of it should be esteemed a wicked action: nor were their other laws, except some few of their fundamental ones, backed with severer punishments.[2] The ordinary vigour of their laws extended only to ignomity or pecuniary mulcts: death being seldom inflicted unless in cases of high treason, parricide, or crimes of an extraordinary nature. Banishment in itself was no penalty, but a refuge to avoid the punishment of the laws; disfranchisement or deprivation of liberty, were penalties, if we may believe Cicero, above the reach of the supreme power of the commonwealth to inflict; even pecuniary mulcts were anciently limited to some determined sums, not to be exceeded. But succeeding ages, in a manner, abolished all the power of the laws, by exempting their citizens from all corporal punishments, and allowing the highest offenders to evade the sentence of the law, by retiring into voluntary exile. The moderation of the Roman laws was the worst part of their constitution;[3] and in some junctures, as the attempt of Saturninus, Catiline, etc., would have endangered the very being of commonwealth, if the senate and magistrates had not exerted an illegal, but necessary power, for the preservation of the whole. But withal, it gives one a strange idea of the excellence of the Roman discipline and

[1] Cicero did not revive the custom of accusing.
[2] At this point Moyle really begins the examination of the decline of the republic. For renewal or resumption, see Machiavelli, Discourses, III, 1; and compare Andrew Marvell, Works, ed. A. B. Grossart (4 vols. London, 1872–5), III, 381.
[3] Thelwall was surprised by Moyle's complaint about the moderation of Roman law. He disliked the sanguinary and coercive laws of his own time. But Moyle was not alone in wishing that the Bill of Rights, for example, had been less permissive.

manners, which flourished for so many ages, by a mere sense of honour and fear of ignominy, with so little dread or apprehension of severer punishments.

That the commonwealth was not oftener reduced to its first principles, chiefly arose from the reasons I have alleged: to which may be justly added certain defects and errors in the nature and power of those magistrates, to whose charge the preservation of the laws was committed, as the tribunes and censors.

In the institution of the tribunitian power, there was this original defect, that the number of the tribunes was too great; they were at first five, but their number was afterwards increased to ten, which the people weakly imagined to be an accession of strength and honour to the magistracy: but the senate wisely perceived, that the increase of their number would be a diminution of their power, as it proved in the event; for every single tribune, by virtue of his office, being armed with a power of putting a full stop to all proceedings whatsoever, as well as of the people as of the senate, they seldom found it a difficult matter, out of so great a number, to engage one corrupt tribune to hinder the result of all the popular counsels, and defeat the designs of the other nine, however unanimous soever for the public advantage.

Of this kind it would be endless to produce testimonies; so many examples occurring in the Roman histories of mercenary tribunes forbidding the passing of new popular laws, or the revival and execution of old ones. But this defect was succeeded by a worse, I mean the Atinian Law, which permitted senators to be chosen tribunes.[1] This law destroyed all the good effects of the tribunitian power, and perverted the ends of its institution: for the tribunes were at first created to be a check on the senate, and for that reason composed of men of a different order and interest, senators being expressly excluded from that office, and the two employments judged inconsistent; the ancient policy thinking it absurd to imagine that a senator in such a station would ever act for the advantage of the commons, against the interest of his own order. These were apparent defects in the powers and qualifications of the tribunes; the first rendering them in a manner useless and ineffectual, and the second dangerous and pernicious; and the ill-effects of both on the whole constitution of the Roman government,

---

[1] Moyle mistakes the effect of the Atinian Law; senators were not allowed to be chosen tribunes.

are obvious at first view to every man who considers the excellent use of the tribunitian power, whilst it continued on its ancient establishment.

The office of the censors was one of the noblest institutions of the commonwealth; their ordinary jurisdiction extended to the regulation of private expenses, the enacting of sumptuary laws, the farming the revenues, and the reformation of dangerous abuses and disorders in the popular assemblies; of which last we have many examples. But their chief province was to direct and preserve the public discipline and manners, to preside at the tribunal of fame, to reward the brave and virtuous with marks of honour and distinction, and to brand the degenerate and corrupt with dishonour and ignominy.

This institution was of admirable use in maintaining the morals and virtue of the people; and at the same time highly contributed to support the vigour of the laws, and to preserve or restore the constitution to its first principles: for it is a certain maxim, that as good laws make good men, so good men defend good laws, and are both a mutual defence to each other. But there was this essential defect in the frame of this office, that there were two censors instead of one; for all great commands are better managed by a single person than by many, especially such as require the utmost rigour and severity in their execution. For power divided between many, naturally produces discord; of which we have many remarkable examples in the censorships of Scipio and Mummius, Livius and Claudius, Crassus and Domitius, and many others, who all by their discord and dissension destroyed the good effects of their magistracy, which depended solely on their concord and unanimity; both enjoying an equal authority, and either of them having power to vacate the degrees of his colleague. But in succeeding ages this magistracy was intermitted for many years. It is true, it was some time after revived, but with such limitations in its power and authority, as disabled the censors from resisting that torrent of corruption which first overthrew the discipline, and afterwards the liberties of Rome.

Another reason which seems to have very much contributed to the steady support of the constitution upon its original principles was, that, after the rise of the popular government, there arose every age, men of such superior virtue and merit, as by their example gave an influence and authority to the laws, who made a resolute stand against all innova-

258

tions upon the great fences of their liberties, and either maintained or revived their ancient constitution. But in after-times the commonwealth was destitute of such supports. Not but that Rome, in its lowest decays, produced very extraordinary men; but they were such men, whose great qualities served only to arm their ambition against the freedom of their country.

It is an observation of Machiavel, that great dangers and violent extremities often rectify and recover a constitution of government tending towards corruption; of which he gives an excellent example in the sacking of Rome by the Gauls; to which may be added the Straits of Caudium, the battle of Cannae, and many other losses in the beginning and progress of the commonwealth: all which roused and revived their ancient virtue and discipline, and proved a remedy instead of a ruin. But in after ages, the continual success of their arms, and the profound security they enjoyed by the conquest of Carthage, and of all their foreign enemies, let loose the reins of their administration, introduced a depravity and corruption of manners, and, in conclusion, destroyed the commonwealth.[1]

[1] Machiavelli, *Discourses*, III, 1.

Appendixes

(I) ENGLISH CHRONOLOGY

1620–40 The last parliaments of James I, and the first three assembled by his son, were very critical of royal policy in church and state. Not long after granting the Petition of Right, Charles I ruled without parliament for eleven years, until the arming of Scotland, in protest against proposed alteration of their liturgy, forced a meeting.

1640–60 A short parliament was succeeded by the famous Long Parliament which obliged the King to consent to its sitting until willing to dissolve itself. Civil war began in 1642, halting in England just before the trial and execution of Charles I in 1649 and the proclamation of the Commonwealth. Only a 'Rump' of the Long Parliament remained after the departure of the cavaliers and Pride's Purge of 1648, and this was rudely dispersed by Cromwell in 1653. After the Protector's death and his son's failure to maintain authority, the Rump returned and, after various vicissitudes, was obliged by General Moncke to accept the secluded members, a prelude to its dissolution in March 1660.

1660–81 The Convention then elected restored Charles II. On its dispersal, the Cavalier, Pensioner or Long Parliament of Charles II sat until 1678, becoming, in its final sessions, obsessed with fears of a Popish Plot. Three more Parliaments in 1679, 1680 and 1681 were chiefly concerned with the suggested exclusion of Charles's heir, his catholic brother James.

1681–1702 With the end of the Oxford Parliament in 1681, conspiracies, of which the most famous was the 'Rye House Plot', disturbed the country, although order was restored by 1684. James II was able to put down the armed rebellion led by Monmouth in 1685. However, his many attempts thereafter to tamper with the laws against catholics led to an invitation to his son-in-law William to come and preserve protestantism, and thus to the Revolution of 1688. The Revolution was secured by the Bill of Rights, a Toleration Act, an act limiting the duration of parliament to three years and a Treason Act permitting counsel for the accused. The Act of Settlement of 1701 provided for the succession of William's sister-in-law, Anne, and, on her death, of the protestant house of Hanover.

1702–21 Anne's reign was marked by renewed war with France, still the protector of the exiled Stuarts, by revived Tory sentiment, leading to the trial of Dr Sacheverell for a sermon supposedly inimical to the Revolution, and by the Treaty of Utrecht. In spite of some uncertainty about public reaction, George I peacefully ascended the throne in 1714 and survived without great difficulty a Jacobite rising in the following year. By 1721 his dynasty and the Whig Ascendancy had survived another Jacobite scare and a severe financial crisis, and the long ministry of Sir Robert Walpole had begun.

(II) ROMAN CHRONOLOGY

753 B.C. Traditional date of the foundation of Rome by Romulus; rule of the Etruscan kings.

509 B.C. Traditional date of the foundation of the republic, following the rape of Lucretia, the heroic sacrifice of L. Junius Brutus; Valerian law about rights of appeal supposed to have been enacted.

496–396 B.C. Between the defeat of the Latins by A. Postumius at Lake Regillus and the successful attack on Veii by Camillus; struggles between patricians and plebeians, gradually modified by enactment of laws like Valerio–Horation and Canuleian. To this period belong the famous stories of Coriolanus and Cincinnatus.

390–287 B.C. Between the sack of Rome by Brennus the Gaul and the enactment of the Hortensian law; plebeian position improved; laws relieving debtors, and perhaps limiting the amount of public land one person could hold; wars with Latins and Samnites led to extension of area ruled by Rome. 312 B.C.: Appian Way constructed; newly subdued provinces and towns received varying degrees of citizenship.

280–202 B.C. Between the defeat of the Romans by Pyrrhus of Epirus at Heraclea and the defeat of Carthage at Zama by Scipio Africanus; wars outside Italy as well as wars carried into Italy by the Carthaginians under Hannibal, who won great victories at Trasimene and Cannae; Rome triumphed in the end, establishing provincial governments in Sicily, Corsica, Spain and, after the Macedonian wars with Philip and Antiochus III of Syria, further east into Asia Minor.

200–133 B.C. Between the triumph over Carthage, destroyed in 146 B.C., and the assassination of Ti. Sempronius Gracchus in 133 B.C.; Roman supremacy in Greece and Africa established and her power extended. Gracchus followed by his younger brother Gaius, also assassinated, attempted reform, curbing the inequalities of landholding in imitation of the Agrarian law of 367 B.C.

121–31 B.C. Between the death of Gaius Gracchus and the defeat of his foes at Actium by Caesar's nephew, Octavian, who assumed imperial power as Augustus; wars with the Cimbri, with Mithridates, as well as civil and social wars and conspiracies, led to the decline of old republican institutions and eventually to the establishment of the empire.

(III) AUTHORS CITED BY MOYLE

Ammianus Marcellinus, *c.* A.D. 330–after A.D. 390
Ampelius, Lucius, second or possibly third century A.D.
Appian, second century A.D.
Apuleius, born *c.* A.D. 123
Asconius Pedianus, Quintus, 9 B.C.–A.D. 76
Augustine, A.D. 354–430
Aurelius Victor, *fl.* A.D. 360

Cicero ('Tully'), 106–43 B.C.

Dio, Cassius, second and early third century A.D.
Diodorus Siculus, first century B.C.
Diogenes Laertius, third century A.D.
Dionysius of Halicarnassus, *fl.* 30–8 B.C.

Eusebius, A.D. 260–340
Eutropius, *fl.* A.D. 363

Fenestella, 52 B.C.–A.D. 19, or possibly 35 B.C.–A.D. 36
Festus, Sextus Pompeius, second century A.D.
Florus, *fl.* A.D. 122
Frontinus, *c.* A.D. 30–104

Gellius, Aulus, *c.* A.D. 123–*c.* 165

Harrington, J., 1611–77
Herodotus, *c.* 485 B.C.–after 430 B.C.
Hotoman (Francis), 1524–90
Hyginus (*Fables*), probably second century A.D.

Juvenal, *fl.* A.D. 100

Livy, 59 B.C.–A.D. 17
Lucan, A.D. 39–65
Lucian, *c.* A.D. 120–after 180
Lucretius, probably 94–55 B.C.

Machiavelli, N., 1469–1527
Macrobius, *fl.* A.D. 400
Messalla Corvinus, 64 B.C.–A.D. 8

Nepos, *c.* 99–*c.* 24 B.C.

Orosius, *fl.* A.D. 417
Ovid, 43 B.C.–A.D. 17

Phaedrus, *c.* 15 B.C.–*c.* A.D. 50
Plautus, born not later than 251 B.C., died 184 B.C.
Pliny the Elder, A.D. 23/4–79
Pliny the Younger, A.D. 61 or 62–114
Plutarch, *c.* A.D. 46–after 120
Polybius, *c.* 203–*c.* 120 B.C.

Sallust, 86–*c.* 34 B.C.
Servius, fourth century A.D.
Sigonius, 1520–84
Spartianus, Aelius, fourth century A.D.
Suetonius, *c.* A.D. 69–*c.* 140
Symmachus, *c.* A.D. 340–*c.* 402

Tacitus, born *c.* A.D. 55, died after A.D. 115

Valerius Maximus, first century A.D.
Varro, 116–27 B.C.
Velleius Paterculus, *c.* 19 B.C.–after A.D. 31
Vopiscus, Flavius, fourth century A.D.

Xenophon, *c.* 430–*c.* 354 B.C.

Zosimus, *fl.* A.D. 425

(IV) WORKS ON ROMAN HISTORY

[often cited in the eighteenth century]

Nicholas Machiavelli (1469–1527), *Discourses*, *c.* 1517; Eng. tr. Neville, 1675.

L. Eachard (1670–1730), *The Roman History—to Augustus* (London, 1695), 8 editions.

Charles de Saint-Évremond (1610–1703), 'Reflections upon the Different Genius of the Roman People at Different Times of the Republic', Eng. tr. in *Works* (2 vols. London, 1700), I, 1–100, and 'Observations upon Sallust and Tacitus', I, 101–10.

J. Swift, *A Discourse on the Contests and Dissension in Athens and Rome* (London, 1701).

Abbé R. A. deVertot (1655–1735), *Revolutions of the Roman Republic* (Eng. tr. 2 vols. London, 1720), reprinted in 1738, with addition of remarks on Roman Senate.

W. Moyle (1672–1721), *Works* (2 vols. London, 1726), I, 147, *An Essay* (*c.* 1699).

Charles Secondat de Montesquieu, *Reflexions on the Causes of the Grandeur and Declension of the Romans* (Eng. tr. London, 1734).

Charles Rollin (1661–1741), *Roman History* (2 vols. tr. London, 1739).

Louis de Beaufort (d. 1795), *Dissertation upon the uncertainties of the Roman History during the first five hundred Years* (Fr. 1738, Eng. tr. 1740).

Thomas Chapman (1717–80), *Essay on the Roman Senate* (London, 1750).

Conyers Middleton (1683–1750), 'A Treatise on the Roman Senate' (1735); printed in *Works* (3 vols. London, 1742), III, 374–471.

J. B. L. Crévier, *History of the Roman Emperors* (6 vols. 1750).

Gabriel Bonnet de Mably (1709–85), *Observations on the Romans* (Geneva, 1751).

Nathaniel Hooke (d. 1763), *Observations upon Vertot, Middleton, Chapman on the Roman Senate* (London, 1758).

Edward Wortley Montagu (1713–76), *Ancient Republicks* (London, 1759).

Edward Gibbon (1737–94), *The Decline and Fall* (first three vols. London, 1776–81).

Adam Ferguson (1723–1816), *Progress and Termination of the Roman Republic* (3 vols. London, 1782).

Translations, with or without commentary, too numerous to list here; but perhaps most popular in the eighteenth century were *Tacitus*, Thomas Gordon (d. 1750) (1728), and *Sallust* (1744), by the same hand; and *Dionysius* (fragmentary only), from Edward Spelman (d. 1767).

I have found useful Edward Grimston's *Polybius* (1634), Clement Edmond's 'Observations upon *Caesar's Commentaries*' (1655), and *The Roman History of Titus Livius* (London, 1686).

Index

[This index attempts only to point out, and where necessary identify, persons and places in the text, and to indicate some references to subjects discussed there.]

Aaronical priesthood, 117
Abingdon, Berks., 6
Abraham, 86
absolutism, see monarchy
accusation or impeachment, 29, 33, 45, 255–6
Achaean League, 104
Adam, 86
Adams, John, 1735–1826, 42, 56
adaptation, see change, renewal
Adriatic sea, 93
aediles, plebeian officials, 214
Aesculapius, 71, 73
Aetolians, 104
Africa, 103
Agis IV, king of Sparta, c. 262–241 B.C., 100
Aglionby, William, fl. 1666, 66
Agrarian Law, 30, 48–9, 96–9, 132, 237–8, 257; see also Licinian Laws
Alba Longa, 207, 228–9
Albemarle, George Monck, duke of, restorer of Charles II, 11
Aleppo, 111
Alexander the Great, 356–323 B.C., 104, 143
Amelotte de la Houssaye, Abraham Nicolas, 65
anarchy, 101, 102
Ancus Marcius, fourth king of Rome, c. 642–617 B.C., 230
annales, leges, 239
anti-Christ, 116, 118
anti-clericalism, 7, 15, 17, 30, 33, 49–50, 115–19, 154–8, 168; see also diviners, Numa, religion
Antiochus the Great, 241–187 B.C., 249
Antoninus Pius, emperor, A.D. 138–61, 91
Apollo, 91, 96, 222
Apostles' Creed, 36
Appius Claudius Caecus, consul, 307 and 296 B.C., censor, 312 B.C., 218, 223
Arabians, 108
Aragon, 55, 141–3, 187, 243; see also Justiciar
Argos, 190

An Argument shewing that a Standing Army..., 28–9
Aristides, d. c. 468 B.C., 173
aristocracy or optimacy, 88, 91, 93, 100–1, 106–7, 133, 225, 229, 232–6; dissolution, 238–40; prevented by ballot from subverting republic, 240
Aristotle, c. 384–322 B.C., 51, 83, 88–9, 101, 121
armed forces, standing army, 28–9, 32–8, 45, 55, 165, 171, 180, 197; see also mercenary, militia
The Armie's Dutie, 10, 20
army, agitators, 179; refuge for tyranny, 231
Arnus (the Arno), 98
Asia, 88, 99, 108
Asia Minor, 93
Assembly of the People, 88, 99, 224, 243–4; see also Comitia
Association of 1696, 32
Assyrians and Persians, 108
Athens and Athenians, 95–6, 98, 101, 102, 173, 198, 250
Atinian Law, 257
Attica, 84, 95
Atwood, William, 18, 120
augurs, 217, 220, 224–5, 237
Augustus, C. Octavius, 63 B.C.–A.D. 14, emperor, 109
Aurelius, Marcus, A.D. 121–80, emperor, 36, 91
Austria, house of, the Hapsburgs, ruled 1447–1807, Holy Roman Empire, 136
authority, built upon opinion, 217; upon dominion, 218

Bacchanalia, 213
Bacon, Francis, 1561–1626, first baron Verulam, and viscount St Albans, 53, 54
Bake, Cornwall, seat of the Moyle family, 21–2
balance, among European powers, 181, 200; in government, interest and property, 10,

balance (*cont.*)
30, 33, 46–7, 58, 226, 228, 230, 231–4, 237–9, 241, 243–4, 252
ballot, 6, 33, 106, 237, 240–1
Barebone's Parliament, named for Praise God Barbon or Barebone, 1596–1679, anabaptist and politician, 137, 177
Barère, Bertrand, 1755–1841, Girondist and revolutionary, 38, 39, 56, 205
Barnardiston, Sir Samuel, 1620–1707, 8
barons' Wars of the thirteenth century, 121, 129, 135
Baxter, Richard, 17, 40, 49
Bentham, Jeremy, 4
Bentivoglio, Guidi, cardinal and author, 5
Bergamo, 92
Bernardino da Udine, 175–6
Bible, 9, 51, 118
Bideford, Devon, 33
Billingbear, 5, 12, 13
Blackmore, Sir Richard, d. 1729, 23
Blois, 179
Blount, Sir Thomas Pope, 1649–97, 26
Boccalini, Trajano, 1556–1613, 65
Bosworth Field, 55, 81, 171
Boult, John of Warfield, 8, 12
Brennus, 97
Brescia, Venetian, 1426–1797, 92
Britons, 132
Brouselles, Pierre, 1576–1654, 138
Brutus, L. Junius, founder of the Republic and consul, 509 B.C., 212, 232, 235
Buchanan, George, 52
Buckingham, George Villiers, second duke of, 1628–88, 16
Buondelmontius, Zanobius, 15
Burgundy, Charles the Bold of, 1433–77, 168
Burma or Pegu, 108
Burton, Thomas, *Diary*, 8

Caesar, C. Julius, 102–44 B.C., 212, 255
Cain, 86
Cairo, 111
Callias, Athenian nobleman whose house is the setting of one of Plato's dialogues, 69
Calvin, John, 1509–64, 54, 112
Cambridge University, 25
Camillus, M. Furius, took city of Veii, *c.* 396 B.C., defeated the Gauls, 387 B.C., 222
Canaan, 103, 185
Cannae (Apulia), battle of, 216 B.C., 259
Canuleian Law, 445 B.C., permitting marriages of patricians and plebeians, 238

Capponi, Ferrante, 6
Capua, 98
Carthage, 217, 249, 250, 259
Castile and Leon, 140–1
catholic, disabilities, 14, 156–7; *see also* religion, anti-clericalism
Catiline (L. Sergius Catilina), died in battle, 62 B.C., 256
Cato, M. Porcius, *c.* 234–149 B.C., 'the censor', 255
Cato's Letters, 43
Caudium, the Straits of, Rome defeated there by the Samnites, 321 B.C., 259
Cebes, pupil of Philolaus and Socrates, 69
censor, 192, 235, 240, 254, 257, 258
Chancery, court of equity already known for its delays, 131–3, 166
change and dissolution in governments, 47, 56, 81, 87, 91, 100; change dependent on 'hinge of property', 110, 145; by insurrection, 158, 172, 225–6; derived by imitation, 229; on circle of change and corruption of states, and lack of balance, 231, 235, 239, 241, 242–57; on Roman decline, summarized, 253
Charles I, 1625–49, 6, 41, 144, 147, 163; attack on five members—Pym, Hampden, Holles, Haselrigg, Strode—149
Charles II, restored 1660, 9, 13, 80, 125; negative, 129, 147, 157, 159, 165, 171–3
Charles VII, king of France, 1422–61, 137
Chile, 27
China, 108
Christ, 10, 19, 76, 115, 154, 176
Christendom, 106, 140
Cicero, M. Tullius ('Tully'), 106–43 B.C., 9, 51, 83, 214, 217, 220–1, 223, 253, 256
Cincian Law, 204 B.C., 238
Civil wars, English, 1642–9, 6, 30, 80, 129, 148–50, 179, 197
Clarendon, Edward Hyde, first earl of, 1609–74, 197
Claudian Law, 218 B.C. (Moyle wrongly refers to as Flaminian), 239
Claudius Nero, C., censor, 204 B.C., 258
Claudius (Clodius) Pulcher, P., tribune 58 B.C., 214
Cleomenes, king of Sparta, 100
clergy, 115–19; Roman clergy guards of monarchy, 226; *see also* anti-clericalism
Cobham, Lord Henry Brooke, d. 1619, 162

coffee houses, Miles', 11; the Grecian, 15, 22, 25, 28, 33; Maynwaring's, 22; Will's, 22–5; the Tun and the Rose, 25
Coffin, Anne, 24
College of Heralds, 225
Collier, Jeremy, 1650–1726, 24
Cologne, 104
colonies or plantations, 26–7, 36, 42–3, 51, 94, 108, 111, 244–5, 249, 251–2
Colt, Sir Henry, M.P., 27
Columbus, Christopher, 1451–1506, 55
Comitia, Roman voting assemblies, 99; — Centuriata, major law making assembly, elected magistrates, voted for war and peace, 224, 236; — Curiata, confirmed appointment of magistrates, 236; — Tributa, of the plebs, elected their magistrates, 237
Commines, Philip de, 1445–1509, 66
common law, 120, 122, 124, 126, 128
Commons, see parliament, plebs
Commonwealth, 9, 11, 41, 58, 173; seeds of dissolution, 225–6
Concordia, goddess of concord, 219
Congreve, William, 1670–1729, 22–3
Constantinople, 55
'Consul's sons', sons of Brutus, 232
consuls, supreme military and civil magistrate of the Roman Republic, 92, 233, 235, 237, 247, 255
Copenhagen, 44
Coriolanus, led the Volscians against Rome, persuaded by wife and mother to turn back, 491 B.C., 212, 237
Cornwall, 3, 21, 24, 34
coronation oath, 128
corruption, 27–8, 81, 131, 191, 199, 239
cortes, the Spanish estates or parliaments, 52, 141–2
Cortiza, Sebastian, a Portuguese contractor, 140
Cosmo III of Tuscany, 1670–1723, 13, 14, 19
Council, Privy, 183; of State (Interregnum), 1651–2, 7; 1659–60, 11, 58–9; to take over policymaking on war and peace, armed forces, appointments and expenditure, 187–90, 195
Covent Garden, 15, 22
Crassus, L. Licinius, orator, consul 95 B.C.; censor 92 B.C., 247 (did not defend Norbanus), 258
Crassus, M. Licinius (Dives), killed at Carrhae, 53 B.C., 222

Cremona, 92, 110
Croft, Sir James (knighted 1603), 146–7
Cromwell, Henry, 1628–74, 8; Oliver, 1599–1658, Protector 1654–8, 3, 7, 9, 41, 57, 58–9, 177, 180, 186, 197; Richard, 1626–1712, Protector 1658–9, 9, 10
Curtii, Roman family of public servants, 212
Cybele, mother goddess of Anatolia, brought to Rome 205–204 B.C., 220
Cymbri, or Cimbri, celts, 97
Cyrus the Great, king of the Medes, 559–529 B.C., 94, 222

Damascus, annexed by Rome, 62 B.C., 111
Danby, Thomas Osborne, first earl of, 1631–1712, Lord Treasurer 1673, impeached 1678, resigned 1679, great manager of Parliament, 16, 181
Darius I, king of Persia 521–486 B.C., 98
Davenant, Charles, 23, 26
David, king of the Jews, 109
Davis, Henrietta Maria, 1677–1762, married Moyle, 33
dead-lift, the pull of a horse against a weight, 224
debt and debtors, 25, 94–6, 234, 236, 248
Decemviri, 101, 179
Decii, Roman family of public servants, 212
De Fresnoy, Charles, 1611–65, 23
De la Hay, author, 66
democracy, 42, 69, 92, 95–6, 100–1, 106–7, 173
Denmark, 9, 44, 55, 56, 136
Dennis, John, 23, 37
Devonshire, 33
dictator, a temporary Roman magistrate appointed in a time of crisis and possessing extraordinary power; dictatorial power, 234, 236, 238, 240, 254
Dionysius of Halicarnassus, d. 7 B.C., historian of Rome, 218, 219, 220, 223
Dionysius I, tyrant of Syracuse, 430–367 B.C., son, Dionysius II, ruled, expelled by Timoleon, 345 B.C., 179
divine right (jus divinum), 30, 50
diviners or clergy, 49–50, 212–13, 224–5, 237; see also augurs
doge, or duke of Venice, 27, 45, 124, 128
dominion founded on property, 68, 89, 218
Domitian Law, 104 B.C., made priestly offices elective, 219

Domitius Ahenobarbus, Cn., tribune of the plebs 104 B.C., consul 96 B.C., censor 92 B.C., 219, 258
Dort, scene of dispute between Remonstrants and strict Calvinists, 1619, 53
Downing, Sir George, 1623–84, English resident at the Hague, 8
'The Dry Club', 18
Dryden, John, 1631–1700, 22–3

Edward the Confessor, or St Edward, d. 1066, legislator, 131
Edward I, 1272–1307, famous for his laws, de Tallagio non concedendo here cited, 122, and for help to parliament, 123, 178, 184
Edward II, 1307–27, 178, 184
Edward III, 1372–7, 123, 178, 184
Edward VI, 1547–53, 161
Egypt, 84, 89, 111–12, 135, 181, 226
elective monarchy, see monarchy
Eliot, Sir John, 1592–1632, 21, 163
Elizabeth I, 1558–1603, 14, 147, 156, 158, 161; Treason Act, 13 Eliz. I, c.l., 161
empire of laws, 30, 42
England, Neville discusses the turbulence and diseases of the once prosperous England throughout Dialogue II and offers his remedies in Dialogue III; on government, especially 112–14, 119–31, 132–5, 144–5, 152, 160–1; on proposed reforms, 152, 187–90
England's Confusion, 9
ephors of Sparta, instituted traditionally by Lycurgus, ending A.D. 200, five men elected annually by citizens with authority to decide, when the kings were at variance with each other, 31, 46, 58, 178, 187, 190, 243
Epirus, 88
equality, 208, 228, 236, 247, 248, 252, 258; see also liberty
Etherege, Sir George, 22
Europe, 79, 83, 114, 216
Evander, son of Hermes or Mercury, led a colony to Italy, 222
Ewen, Mrs Susan, 16
Exchequer Chamber, appelate court, 8
Exclusion controversy of 1679–81 over the succession of James of York, a Catholic prince, 14, 15, 41, 57; see also Monmouth, and succession
Exeter, 34; academy, 36; college at Oxford, 22

faction, see party
Fawkener, John, 19
Fawkes, Guy, 156
Ferdinand II of Tuscany, 13
feuds or fiefs, 112–14; feudal system, 29, 55
fifteen tyrants of Thebes, 101
Fifteen, unnatural rebellion of 1715, 35
Filmer, Sir Robert, 41, 85
Finch, Sir John, 1626–82, 14
Flamines, priests, 216
Flanders, 71
Fletcher, Andrew, 29, 32, 40, 55
Florence, 74, 101–2
Florus, fl. A.D. 122, wrote epitome of military history much read in seventeenth century, 230
Fortescue, Sir John, 1394–1476, 42
France, 14, 52, 56, 57, 87–8, 106, 112, 114, 123, 136–40, 143, 168, 182, 199
Franco Gallia (1574), 52, 55
Frascati, 13
French disease, venereal disease, 158
French states or estates general, 179
Friuli, 92

Gailhard, J., fl. 1666, 66
Gascoigne, Sir Bernard (Bernardino Guasconi), 1614–87, 6, 12, 13
Gaul, 97, 255, 259
Gengis Khan, c. 1162–1227, Tartar warrior, 87
Gentz, Fred. von, 1764–1832, 56
'German woods', 54
Germany, 52, 71, 104, 135–6
Gianotti, Donato, 1494–1563, Florentine writer on Venice, 106
Gibbon, Edward, 1737–94, 33, 37
Gildon, Charles, 1665–1724, 23
Glanvill, John, 1664–1735, 23
Goddard, Thomas, 17
Godfrey, Denis, translator of Commines, 66
Godolphin, Sidney, first earl, 1645–1712, 33
Goldsmiths' Hall committee, 6
Gordon, Thomas, 29, 264
Goths, Godos, Scandinavians raiding Rome c. A.D. 238, 92–3, 97, 108, 112, 114, 140
government, all are born under, 84–5; any differences from interest, 193; best, 91; England's, 81, 132, 152; Europe, 114; free, 215; Gothic, 114; hinge of property for, 100; military, 226; mixed, 47, 243–4; natural part of its power, 113; ordained for happiness, 182; origin, 83–5; parch-

government (*cont.*)
ment, 133–4; paternal, 85–6; 'eternized' by property, 87; reformation of, 101; senate essential to, 103; violent constraint not, 111; well ordered, 9; *see also under* England, France, Spain, Holland, etc.
Gracchus, Ti. Sempronius, initiated land reform while tribune 133 B.C., assassinated within a year, 248, 252; C. Sempronius Gracchus, brother of above and also a reformer, assassinated 121 B.C.; Gracchi, 99, 133
The Grandeur and Declension of Rome (1734), by Montesquieu (*Decadence* in later translations), 38, 205–6
Greece, 88, 96, 173; seven wise men of (Thales, Solon, Periander, Cleobulus, Chilon, Bias, Pittacus), 76
Gregory, Francis, 36
Grotius, Hugo, 1583–1645, 53, 149
Guise, house of, dukes of Lorraine in later middle ages, 159
Gwynn, Sir Rowland, 27

Hague, 8
Halévy, E., 57
Halifax, George Saville, marquis of, 48, 59
Hammond, Anthony, 1668–1738, 22–32 *passim*
Hampden, John, 1594–1643, parliamentary hero, resisted the levy of ship money and tried, 1637; his case, 125–6
Hampton Court, 149
Hannibal, *c.* 247–182 B.C., 97
Hanover, John Frederick of Calenburg, 1667–79, 164
Harleian Miscellany, 15
Harley, Thomas, *c.* 1584–1631, sheriff of Hereford, M.P., 147
Harold, *c.* 1022–66, d. at Battle of Hastings, 121
Harrington, James, 1611–77, author of *Oceana*, 7, 10, 11, 12, 40, 51, 53, 247, 252
Haselrigg, Sir Arthur, d. 1661, 8
Hearne, Thomas, 37
Heathley Hall, Berks., 5
Hebrews, 51; *see also* Israel
Henry III, 1216–72, 174; — IV, 1399–1413, 123; — V, 1413–22, 123; — VI, 1422–61, 123; — Tudor, VII, 1485–1509, 171; — VIII, 1509–47, passed an act, 35 Hen. VIII. c. 1, devising the crown, 161
Heracles (Hercules), the hero, 218, 222–3

Heraclides, kings of Sparta, descendants of Heracles, 89
Hereford, Herbert Croft, bishop of, 146
Hippocrates, *fl.* 400 B.C., Greek physician, 71
history, 54–6, 68, 84, 225
Hoadley, Bishop Benjamin, 1676–1761, 56
Holland, 71, 182, 229; *see also* Low Countries
Hollis, Thomas, 1720–74, 67
Hortensius, Q., dictator 287 B.C., carried a law making plebiscites binding on the whole community, 248
Hottoman or Hotman, Francis, 1524–94, author of *Franco Gallia*, 52, 55
Hull, Kingston upon, in Yorks., 9
'The Humble Petition', 6 July 1659, 10–11
Hume, David, 1711–76, 27
Hundred Years War, 55
Huns, invaders of Roman Empire from A.D. 372 to 453, when Attila died, 92
Hunt, Thomas, 17
Hutcheson, Francis, 1694–1745, 49, 57
Hutchinson, Colonel John, 1615–64, 12

Interregnum, in England after the execution of Charles I, 1649–60, 16, 40
Ireland, 94
Isaac, 86
Isis, Egyptian divinity whose cult was celebrated in Greece and Rome, 220
The Isle of Pines, 3, 6, 13, 20
Israel, government of Sanhedrim or senate, 53, 86–7, 102, 103
Italian right (*jus italicum*), 253
Italy, 5, 7; the happiest land, 13–14; 75, 84, 93, 246, 250

Jacob, 86
Jago, George, *fl.* 1719, vicar of Looe near Bake, naturalist, 34
James I, 1603–25, 3, 146–7, 162
James II, 1685–8, as duke of York, heir to Charles II, and object of attempts to exclude from the succession, 9, 15, 16, 67, 80, 159, 165, 172
Janiculus, mount on west bank of Tiber, mobs fled to it 287 B.C., 248
janizaries, Turkish infantry, 109
Jefferson, Thomas, 1743–1826, 42, 58
Jethro, 103
Jewish ceremonies, 19; law, 76
Jews or Israelites, 102–3, 229

John, 1199–1216, ceded Magna Charta to barons, 174
Joseph, Jacob's favourite son sold into Egypt, 88, 135
Jupiter, 97
juries, 131
Justiciar of Aragon, 46, 142

King, Peter, first baron Ockham in Surrey, 1669–1734, 36
King, Richard, possibly 'Mr K.', 36

Laconia, 91, 94
land, usually equated with property, the centre of dominion, 232–5
Latin, language, 77; people, Moyle's *Essay* passim
law, empire or rule of, 42
lawgiver, see Lycurgus, Numa, Solon
laws, English, 130–1, 185, 188–9, passim;
— Roman, 224, 236–40; see also under names of laws
The League of the Public Weal, 168
Legge, Colonel William, 1609–70, 12
Leicester, Simon de Montford, earl of, 1208–65, Minister then enemy of Henry III, called an important parliament, 135
Leipzig, 36
L'Estrange, Sir Roger, 1616–1704, 18
A Letter Ballancing, 29
A Letter from an Officer, 7, 68
Levi, tribe of, 117
Leviathan, 41, 85 n.
Lewis or Louis, kings of France: Lewis the dauphin, afterwards Lewis VIII, 1223–6, 121; Lewis XI, 1461–83, 174; Lewis XIV, 1643–1715, 88, 112, 182, 199
lex posthumia, see Posthumous Law
liberty, 238, 250; protection of, 190, 243; factious, 247, 248
liberty of conscience, 213–14
Licinian Laws of fourth century B.C. to limit land holding (agrarian), to relieve debtors, to open consulship to plebeians, 96–7, 99, 238, 249, 254
Licinius Stolo, C., tribune of the plebs, 376–367 B.C., author of above laws, 96
limited monarchy, 44; see also monarchy
Liskeard, 22
Livius Salinator, M., censor 204 B.C., 258
Livy (Titus Livius), 59 B.C.–A.D. 17, historian, 51, 68, 208, 220, 238–9, 240
Locke, John, 18, 36, 41, 46, 50

Lombards, Teutonic invaders of Italy, settled *c.* A.D. 568, 92
Lombardy, 110
London, 3, 13, 71; Common Hall, 117; lord mayor, 129; Silver Street near Covent Garden, 15
Looe, Cornwall, 34
Lords, House of, see parliament; 'old lords', 10, 49; see also aristocracy, nobility, peers
Low Countries, 104–6
Lower, Dr Richard, 1631–91, 71, 119
Lübeck, 104
Lucan (M. Annaeus Lucanus), A.D. 39–65, author of *Pharsalia*, quoted, 239
Lucian of Samos, *c.* A.D. 120–80, Greek author and philosopher, 37
Lucifer, 177
Lucretia, wife of L. Tarquinius Collatinus, raped by Sextus, son of Tarquinius Superbus, 231
Lucullus, L. Licinius, *c.* 117–56 B.C., Roman general conquered Mithridates, 222–3
Ludlow, Edmund, 7, 11, 18, 40, 44, 45
lustration, purification by ceremonial propitiary offerings, 217
Luttrell, Narcissus, 18
Lycurgus, traditional lawgiver of Sparta, 43, 91, 94, 100, 169
Lysander, Spartan admiral, d. 395 B.C., ended the Peloponnesian War by victory at Aegospotami, 405 B.C., 100

Macedonia, 88, 143
Machiavelli (Machiavel), Nicholas, 1469–1527, 14, 15, 51, 52, 54, 65, 81, 97, 168, 190, 247, 253, 254, 259; 'Letter', 15, 155, 168
Macrobius, Ambrosius Theodosius, *fl.* A.D. 400, author, 223
Madrid, 142
Magna Charta, 1215, the great charter of liberties, 54, 123, 124, 131, 153, 163, 175, 185, 189
Mahomet, see Mohamet
Mamelukes, Moslem rulers of Egypt, 1252–1517, defeated by another Moslem, Selim, 111, 181
Mantua, 110
Marathon, battle 490 B.C., Greek victory over Persia, 98
Marcomanni, tribe in Bohemia, warred with Rome A.D. 166–80, 36

Margaret Tuder, sister of Henry VIII, married James IV of Scotland, 161
Mariana, Juan, jesuit, 44, 52, 156
Marius, Gaius, 157–86 B.C., held seven consulships; 101 B.C. defeated Cimbri; leader of the popular party against Sulla, 255
Mars, field of, public area near the Tiber, 221
Marten, Henry, 1602–80, 7
Marvell, Andrew, 8, 9, 12, 13, 199
Mary, queen of England, 1553–8, 161
Match me These Two (1647), 6
Mazarin, Jules, cardinal and ruler of France, 1643–61, 186
Medes, fl. 675–550 B.C., 173
Menheniot, 34
mercenary army, mercenaries, 43, 92, 109, 171, 180–1, 223
Messene, 31, 190
Michael, 177
Middle Temple, 22, 25
Milan, ruled by Visconti 1277–1447, then by Sforca until 1500, 181
militia, or citizen army, 28–9, 124–5, 129, 134, 189, 223, 228, 244
Militia Acts, 125
Miltiades, c. 550–489 B.C., 98
Milton, John, 1608–74, 40, 41, 46, 47, 177
miracles, 36
mixed monarchy, see monarchy
A Modest Plea (1659), 40
Mogul, important person, a Mongolian conqueror of India in the sixteenth century, 108
Mohamet, A.D. 570–632, 87, 154; life of by Dean Prideaux (Mahomet, 1697), 35
monarchy, absolute, 44, 86–7, 90, 108, 110, 124; impossible without alteration of property, 178; impossible if elective, 226; clergy and nobility, guards of monarchy, 226; divinely supported, 86–7, 207; elective, 52, 226–8; hereditary, 227; limited, 19, 109, 113, 228; limitations proposed 1679, 162–3; mixed, 87–108, 111; philosopher kings, 90
Monastero, in Spain, 140
Monmouth, James Scott, duke of, 1649–85, bastard son of Charles II, much supported by the Shaftesbury gang 1678–82 as heir to his father, 9, 16, 153, 164–72
Montesquieu, Charles Secondat de, 1689–1755, 38, 205–6

Monticello, the Sage of, 42
Moors, Moslem conquerors of Spain, 711–1031, 140
Morley, Colonel Herbert, 1616–67, 7
Moses, 84, 86, 102, 103, 211
Mosheim, J. L., 36
The Moyles of Bake, John, Joseph, Walter, father and grandfather, 21–2; Walter, author, 3–4, 21–39, passim
Mummius, Achaicus Lucius, consul 146 B.C., censor 142 B.C., 258
Musgrave, Dr William, 1655–1721, 34

Naples, 98
Nassau, territory pertaining to the princes of Orange, 105
naturalization, Rome allowed conquered Latins for example to obtain citizen rights by degrees; in England foreign protestants were often naturalized, 27, 226, 228–9, 237
Nedham, Marchamont, 40, 41, 46
Nero Claudius Caesar, emperor, A.D. 54–68, 154
Neville, Edward, M.P. E. Retford, 6; Henry of Holt, Leicester, 16; Henry, grandfather to author, ambassador, 5, 147; Henry, father to author, 5; Henry, author, 5–20, 40, 41, passim; Richard, brother, 6, 13, 15; Richard, nephew, 5, 18
New Testament, 116
Newes from the New Exchange (1650), 6, 20
Niebuhr, B. G., 1776–1831, 56
Nimrod, 87
Noah, 86
nobility, 88, 106–7, 114, 233, 236, 238, 247; see also aristocracy
Norbanus, Gaius, consul 83 B.C., 247
Normans, 121
Northampton, Henry Howard, first earl of, 1540–1614, 147
Numa Pompilius, second king of Rome, c. 715–673 B.C., 103, 154–5, 210–13, 219, 224–5; religion, 229, 244
Numitor, 228

Oceana (1656), by James Harrington, 4, 7, 10, 41, 46, 68, 232
Oedipus of Thebes, 79
Ogilvie, William, 1736–1819, 48
Old Testament, 117
Orange, prince of, later William III, 1650–1702, 171

INDEX

Orestes, son of Agamemnon and Clytemnestra, 223
Orleans, 179
Ottomans, Turks who conquered Asia Minor, Egypt, and parts of Europe in fifteenth and sixteenth centuries, 108
Overton, Colonel Robert, 9
Oxford, 5, 22, 34, 107
Oxford, Robert Harley, first earl of, 1661–1724, 28, 32, 62

Padua, 92, 107
palatines, Polish officials and nobles, 144
Paris, 138
parliament (for other than England's, see cortes, states and by country), annual, 144, 191; composition, 9, 47, 92, 114, 119; elections, 191; equated with ephors, 31, 46; Houses of: the Commons, 9, 10, 11, 31, 81, 134, 145, 193, 199; the Lords, 10, 31, 49, 88, 96, 129, 130, 134, 190, 192–5; origin, 119–20; powers, 112, 132; relations with king, 120, 128, with Lords, 130, 134–5; speaker, 127–8; specific parliaments: Edward I and III, 122–3; Richard II, 123–4; James I (1614), 146–7; Charles I (1628), 163; Long (1640), 6, 12, 149, 197, 199; Barebone's or Saints, 57, 137, 177; Rump of the Long, 6, 10, 11, 59; Richard Cromwell's, 8–11, 47; Long or Pensionary Parliament of Charles II (1661–78), 81, 191, 199; Westminster or second Exclusion (1680), 16, 184; Triennial of William III (1695–8), 3, 24–32; turbulence, 145–50; see also acts under ruler or title, Dialogues II and III passim
party, faction, 32, 44, 80, 155–6, 185, 208, 216, 234
patricians (patricii), 91, 96, 133, 192, 230, 234–5, 244–5
patronage, 208
Paul the apostle, 76
peers, lords, nobles, 45, 49, 129–30, 133–4, 192, 208
Pegu, Burma, 108
Peloponnesus, 100
Penn, William, 131
the people, 16, 49, 102, 120, 133, 232–3, 236
Perez, Antonio, d. 1611, 46, 142
Periander of Corinth, c. 625–585 B.C., tyrant, patron of the arts, 169
Persia and Persians, 143
Peru, 27

Peterborough, Charles Mordaunt, earl of, 25
Petition of Right, 1628, 44, 131, 163, 189
Petyt, William, 18, 120
Phaedon of Elis, freed slave, pupil of Socrates, 69
Pharaoh, 89
Philip II, king of Spain, 1527–98, 46, 142, 159
Philip V, king of Macedon, 238–179 B.C., 249
'Philopatris', a discourse by Moyle, 37
Pierrepont (Pierrepoint), William, 48, 196–7
Pine, George, hero of The Isle of Pines, 13
Plataea, in Boeotia, scene of Greek victory over Persians, 479 B.C., 98
Plato, c. 429–347 B.C., 69, 83
plebs, main body of Roman citizens, referred to as plebeians, commons, etc. Moyle, passim
Pliny the Elder, c. A.D. 23–79, writer, 224
Plutarch, c. A.D. 46–120, biographer, 51, 68, 84, 100, 229
Poland, commonwealth of king and nobles, 45, 52, 114, 136, 144
politics, a difficult science, 111, and history, 68
Polybius, c. 203–120 B.C., Greek historian of Rome, 51, 68, 231
polytheism, 211
Pompey (Gnaeus Pompeius), 106–48 B.C., soldier and statesman, 255
pontifex maximus, head of college of priests, 217
the poor, 26
Pope, 16, 153, 176
popery, growth of, 153–9
population, 26–7, 43, 237, 251; guard of liberty, 229
Posthumous Law (lex posthumia), law from the time of Numa concerning burial rights, 224
Potitii, family devoted to the cult of Hercules, 218
Poussin, the French agent, 32
poverty, 97
praemunire, to be served the writ was to be threatened with severe penalties imposed during reign of Richard II on supporters of papal supremacy, 161
praetorians, 99, 110
praetors, officials concerned with administration of justice, 214

272

Prance, Miles, informer, 16
prerogative, 33, 43, 126, 185–6
Prester John, legendary Christian hero, *fl.* 1316, 108
Prideaux, Humphrey, 24, 35–6
Pride's Purge, 1648, 12
Priestley, Joseph, 36
Priolo, Benjamine, 1602–67, 66
Procopius, Byzantine historian, d. A.D. 565, 66, 112
property, 49, 85, 87, 90, 92, 95–6, 100–1, 110, 131–9, 144–6, 152, 230–1; *see also* land, government
Prynne, William, 1600–69, 12
Pyrrhus of Epirus, 319–272 B.C., fought Rome, defeated, 275 B.C., 249
Pythagoras, sixth century B.C., philosopher, 212

Quarantia, 132, 187
Quinctius Flamininus, Lucius, consul 192 B.C., expelled from the senate by Cato for oppression in Gaul, 184 B.C., 192

Rawleigh (Ralegh, etc.), Sir Walter, 1552–1618, 162
Ray, John, 24, 34
Reading, election at, 7
rebellion, 17, 35, 167
recision, rescinding or cancelling of debts, 236; *Seisactheia*, 96
the Redentore, 176
registry, 196
Regulus, M. Atilius, consul 267 and 256 B.C., defeated Carthaginian fleet, later taken prisoner by Xanthippus, 255 B.C., frugal, simple Roman martyr, 217
religion, agreement on, 210; ceremonies, creed, etc., unnecessary to true, 115–19; conformity of Roman and catholic religions, 155; not essential to state, 153–4; immortality, 211–12; miracles and, 206–11; purity, 9, 11, 19, 155, 158; reconciliation, 196; Roman religion, 210–16
religious liberty, 11, 49, 57, 157, 213
renewal or return to first principles, 48, 52, 253–4, 257–8, 258–9
republicans, 40–59
resistance rights, 43
Restoration of Charles II, 1660, 3, 12, 129, 171, 173
Reuben, 86

revolution, American, 4; English, 15, 18, 30, 41, 229; French, 4; Roman revolution of kingly government to aristocracy, 229, 229–34, 233
Rhee, French island, 182
Richard II, 1377–1400, 123, 126, 184
Robinson Crusoe, 13
Robinson, Dr Tancred, d. 1746, 34
Roderigo, last Visigothic king of Spain, A.D. 710–11, 140
Roman emperors, 90, 109; — empire, 232
Roman Republic (509–31 B.C.), 17, 47, 50–1, 54; Moyle's *Essay, passim*
Rome, 5, 17, 38, 89, 100, 170, 259
Romulus, first king of Rome, 735–715 B.C., 84, 89, 94, 96, 102–3, 207–8, 228, 245
Rota Club, 11
rotation, 11, 33, 45, 187, 239–40
Rycaut, Sir Paul, 1628–1700, 65–6
Rye House Plot, 1683, reputedly to overthrow the Stuarts, 18

Sa, Emanuel, jesuit author, 43, 52, 156
Sacheverell, Dr Henry, 35
St Germans (Bake in parish of), 21, 37
St Stephen's, 7, 35
Salamis, Xerxes defeated there 480 B.C., 98
Salii, priests attached to the cult of Mars, 216
Sallust, *c.* 86–34 B.C., historian, 51
Saltash, Cornwall, 24, 35
Salway, Richard, 1615–85, 12
Samnites, inhabited Samnium in s. Appenines, 98, 249
Samuel, Hebrew judge and prophet, 86
Saracens, Moslem people who fought Christians in crusades, 87, 93, 96, 121
satraps, governors of Persian provinces, 108
Saturninus, L. Appuleius, tribune 103 and 100 B.C., law giving land for veterans, 256
Saxons, invaders of Britain, 116, 121
Scipio, P. Cornelius (Aemilianus), 185–129 B.C., defeated Carthage, 146 B.C., and Numantia 133 B.C., 255, 258
Scot, Thomas, d. 1660, 8
Scots and Scotland, 123, 142–3, 161
seditions, insurrections, broils, etc., found in decaying governments, 158, 190, 242, 246
Selden, John, lawyer and author, 53, 86
Selim, sultan of Ottoman Turks, 1512–20, 111
senate, 53, 103, 109, 130, 133, 192, 213–14, 234, 257

separation of powers, 11, 46, 58
Septenniel Act, 1716, L. Geo. I, stat. 2 C. 38, 28
Servius Tullius, sixth king of Rome, 578–535 B.C., 224, 230, 233, 235, 243, 245
Seth, ancestor of Noah, 86
Settlement, Act of, 1701, 12, 13 W. III, c. 2, 32
Sforza, Fr., 1401–60, established family at Milan, 181
Shadwell, Thomas, 22
Shaftesbury, Anthony Ashley Cooper, first earl of, 6, 16–17
Sherard, William, 34
sheriff, vice-comes, English shire or county official, 125
Shufling, Cutting, and Dealing in a game of Pickquet (1659), 7, 20
Sicily, 102
Sidney, Algernon, 6, 7, 12, 17, 30, 32, 40, 43, 44, 46–8, 52, 54
Sigonius, c. 1520–84, humanist from Modena, 253
silence of great men on policy, 48, 196
Simmias of Thebes, friend of Socrates, 69
Skepen, Dutch officials, 105
Smith, Sir John, 1558–1608, 5
Smyrna, 34, 65, 66
Socrates, 469–399 B.C., philosopher, 69
Solomon, 72
Solon, sixth century B.C. Athenian legislator, 96, 100, 169, 200
Somers, Lord John, 1651–1716, 29
spahis, Turkish cavalry, 109
Spain, 9, 52, 114, 136, 140–2
Sparta (Lacedaemonia), 35, 54, 89, 91, 95, 100, 126, 178, 190, 195, 243, 246
Spence, Thomas, 1750–1814, 48, 57
Sprigge, William, fl. 1657, 40
Stanneries, 35
Starkey, John, publisher of Neville's Machiavelli, 14
states, estates, diets, 87, 105, 114, 137–8, 179
Staverton, family of, 5
Stephens, Lewis, 34
Stolo, see under Licinius Stolo
Strangford, Thomas Smith, first viscount, 5
Strode, or Stroode, William, sheriff, 8
Stubbe, Dr Henry, 1632–76, 40, 47
succession, 153, 161–72
Suffolk, Charles Brandon, first duke of, d. 1545, 161

Suffolk, 8
Sulla, L. Cornelius, c. 138–78 B.C., dictator, 222–3
Sweden, 9, 136
Swift, Jonathan, 31
Switzerland, government, 42, 104
sword in hands of subjects, 226, 229, 243

tabellariae leges 240
Tacitus, Cornelius, c. A.D. 55–134, 51
de Tallagio non concedendo, 25 Ed. I, 122
Tankerville, Ford Grey, earl of, 1655–1701, 18
Tarquin family, 179, 232
Tarquinius Priscus, fifth king of Rome, 616–579 B.C., 230
Tarquinius Superbus, last king of Rome, 534–510 B.C., 221, 230, 232–3, 243, 244
Taylor, John, 1754–1824, 4, 42, 58
Temple, Inns of Court, 22
Teutons, Germans defeated at Aquae Sextiae by Marius, 102 B.C., 97
Thales, Ionic philosopher of sixth century B.C., 96
Thebes, 101
Thelwall, John, 201, 207, 212, 230, 231, 251, 252, 256
Themistocles, c. 528–462 B.C., Athenian statesman, 108, 173
Theodosius I, emperor of the east, A.D. 379–95, 215
Theopompus, king of Sparta, eighth century B.C., 178
Theseus, son of Aegeus, founder of Athens, 84, 94–5, 102
Thucydides, historian of the Peloponnesian War, 68, 102
Tiberius Julius Caesar Augustus, 42 B.C.–A.D. 37, 220
Tierrisi, Francesco, 14
timars, land for soldiers, timariots in Turkey, 108–11
Tory, 32–3
Tower of London, 12
trade, 26, 93, 188
transubstantiation, 118
Tredenham, John, 32
Trenchard, John, 25, 32, 40, 50
Treviso, in Po Valley, 92
tribunes, magistrates of the plebs, 91, 214, 218, 236, 240, 246, 247, 254, 257
Triennial Acts, 144
A True and Perfect Relation, 8

A True Picture, 32–3
Trumbull, 7
Tullus Hostilius, third king of Rome, 673–642 B.C., 229
Turkey and Turks, 65–6, 107–12, 136, 232
Tuscans and Tuscany, 13, 93, 98, 220, 249
twelve Caesars (from Julius to Domitian), 247
tyrannicide, 156; tyranny, tyrants, 16, 43, 52, 87–9, 109, 136, 179, 180, 215–16, 232, 247

Union with Scotland, 1707, 33
United Provinces (Low Countries), 42, 104–6
United States, 6, 56, 58
Urnuscaperie, or *Herne, Vroedschappen*, council of Amsterdam, 105
usury laws (*leges usurariae*), 357 B.C., 239, 254
Utrecht, Union of, 105

Valerian Law, 509 B.C., 219, 234
Vandals, German tribes moving southwards, A.D. 170–439, 97, 103
Vane, Sir Henry, the younger, 6, 7, 8, 9, 40, 49
Varro, M. Terentius, 116–27 B.C., writer, 223
Vaughan, John, judge, 8
Veii, Etrurian city fought Rome until destroyed, 396 B.C., 222, 250
Venice, 5, 17, 42, 43, 71, 93, 107, 114, 124, 158, 175, 195, 246
Verona, 92
Vestal Virgins, six, serving the cult of Vesta for thirty years, 223
veto, 10, 128–30, 188, 193
Veturia, mother of Coriolanus, 212
Vevey, Switzerland, 12

Vicenza, Venetian city, 92
Victor, Aurelius, *fl.* A.D. 360, historian, 222
villeinage, 133
Vindiciae contra tyrannos, 1579, 52
Visconti, dukes of, ruled Milan 1277–1447, 181
Volturnus, 98

Warfield, Berks., 5, 12, 19
Wase, Christopher, 1625–90, vicar of Preston, 66
Weaver, John, d. 1685, 8
Webster, Noah, 1756–1843, 38, 56
Westminster, 124, 149
Weston, Sir R., 1577–1635, treasurer, later earl of Portland, 147
Wharton, Thomas, 1648–1715, 15
Whig, 32–3
Whitehall, palace of, 149
Whitelocke, Bulstrode, lawyer and author of *Memorials* (London, 1682), 148
Wildman, Sir John, 16, 18
William III, 3, 28, 59; William of Orange, *see* Orange
William the Conqueror, 1066–87, 121
Windsor Castle, 149
Wycherley, William, 22
Wymondsolde, Walter, 32

Xenophon, *c.* 430–354 B.C., historian, 56
Xerxes, king of Persia, 485–465 B.C., 98, 108, 173

yeomanry, 133
Yonge, Sir Walter, 26
York, James Stuart, duke of, 1633–1701, *see* James II

Zaleucus of Locri, 211

CAMBRIDGE STUDIES IN THE
HISTORY AND THEORY OF POLITICS

TEXTS

LIBERTY, EQUALITY, FRATERNITY, *by James Fitzjames Stephen.*
Edited, with an introduction and notes, by *R. J. White*

VLADIMIR AKIMOV ON THE DILEMMAS OF RUSSIAN MARXISM
1895–1903. An English edition of 'A Short History of the Social
Democratic Movement in Russia' and 'The Second Congress of the
Russian Social Democratic Labour Party', with an introduction and
notes by *Jonathan Frankel*

STUDIES

1867: DISRAELI, GLADSTONE AND REVOLUTION. THE PASSING
OF THE SECOND REFORM BILL, *by Maurice Cowling*

THE CONSCIENCE OF THE STATE IN NORTH AMERICA, *by*
E. R. Norman

THE SOCIAL AND POLITICAL THOUGHT OF KARL MARX, *by*
Shlomo Avineri